Harry Pollitt

LIVES of the LEFT is a new series of original biographies of leading figures in the European and North American socialist and labour movements. Short, lively and accessible, they will be welcomed by students of history and politics and by anyone interested in the development of the Left.

general editor David Howell

J. Ramsay MacDonald Austen Morgan
R. H. Tawney Anthony Wright
Thomas Johnston Graham Walker
Arthur Henderson Fred Leventhal
William Lovett Joel Wiener
John Maclean Brian Ripley and John McHugh
John Strachey Mike Newman
Daniel De Leon Stephen Coleman
John Wheatley Ian Wood
John Reed Eric Homberger
George Lansbury Jonathan Schneer
J. A. Hobson Jules Townshend
Walter Reuther Anthony Carew
George Orwell Stephen Ingle
Ernest Bevin Peter Weiler

Harry Pollitt

Kevin Morgan

MANCHESTER UNIVERSITY PRESS
Manchester and New York

Distributed exclusively in the USA and Canada by St. Martin's Press, New York

Copyright © Kevin Morgan 1993

Published by Manchester University Press,
Oxford Road, Manchester, M13 9PL, UK
and Room 400, 175 Fifth Avenue, New York, NY 10010, USA

Distributed exclusively in the USA and Canada
by St. Martin's Press, Inc., 175 Fifth Avenue, New York, NY 10010, USA

British Library Cataloguing-in-Publication Data
A catalogue record for this book is available from the British Library

Library of Congress Cataloging-in-Publication Data
Morgan. Kevin, 1961-
    Harry Pollitt / Kevin Morgan.
        p.   cm. — (Lives of the left)
    Includes bibliographical references.
    ISBN 0-7190-3243-1 (hardback)
    1. Pollitt, Harry. 2. Communists—Great Britain—Biography.
3. Communism—Great Britain—History—20th century. I. Title.
II. Series.
HX244.7.P65M67 1993
324.241'0975'092—dc20
[B]   92-35132

ISBN 0 7190 3243 1 *hardback*

Set in Perpetua
by Koinonia Ltd, Manchester

Printed in Great Britain
by Bookcraft (Bath) Limited

Contents

Acknowledgements

Probably this is the first study in which an outside historian of the British Communist Party has been able to draw so extensively on internal Party sources. For this I must first of all thank Francis King and George Matthews, who unlocked for me the treasures of Communist Party archive and helped me with many incidental queries.

The second major primary source I used was the Dutt material now deposited in the Working Class Movement Library. This battered suitcase of correspondence was judged by Dutt too sensitive for the Party archive and the reasons will be seen especially in the second chapter. To Edmund and Ruth Frow I am as ever indebted not only for access to this material but for their constant support and advice.

Among the librarians and archivists who assisted me I should particularly mention those at the Working Class Movement Library, the Marx Memorial Library, Birmingham and Coventry reference libraries and the university libraries of Warwick and Hull. I am also grateful to Elizabeth Al-Qadhi for allowing me to see the papers of her father John Strachey.

I should also like to thank those contemporaries of Pollitt who gave me interviews, some for the second or more time: Noreen Branson, Gabriel Carritt, Gladys Easton, Michael Foot, the late Margot Heinemann, Rose Kerrigan, Frank Lesser, George Matthews, Olive Parsons, Bert Ramelson, Betty Reid, Sam Russell and Harold Smith. In particular I must thank Brian Pollitt who offered no interference as I wrote his father's life but only help and encouragement.

A number of historians of the CP shared their thoughts on Pollitt with me and among those who let me see unpublished writings and manuscripts were Noreen Branson, David Fernbach, Nina Fishman, Monty Johnstone and Stuart Macintyre.

Shaun Spiers and Alan Robinson offered helpful comments on several of the chapters. By its experiment with job-sharing, the Historical Manuscripts Commission enabled me to write history and eat at the same time. Colleagues in the office there helped me with many tasks and Peter Wodjtyczka and Anne Breheny were particularly concerned that these receive acknowledgement. To Julie Johnson I again owe a special debt.

With the prospect of further official archives soon to be opened, it is more than usually necessary to state that all errors and misconceptions are my own responsibility.

List of abbreviations

ASE   Amalgamated Society of Engineers
BSP   British Socialist Party
CI   Communist International or Comintern
CP   British Communist Party
CPSU   Soviet Communist Party
EC   Communist Party executive
ECCI   Executive Committee of the Comintern
ILP   Independent Labour Party
KPD   German Communist Party
LBC   Left Book Club
LWC   London Workers' Committee
MM   Minority Movement
PB   Communist Party Political Bureau
PCF   French Communist Party
RILU   Red International of Labour Unions or Profintern
TGWU   Transport and General Workers' Union
TUC   Trades Union Congress
WSF   Workers' Socialist Federation

Note on terminology: from the early 1920s the CP's leading bodies were the Central (Executive) Committee and the Political Bureau. During the Second World War these were renamed the Executive Committee and Political Committee respectively.

Harry Pollitt

Courtesy of the Communist Party Picture Library and Archive.

1 Before the Communist Party

A century after his birth, Harry Pollitt strikes us very much as a man of his time and place. Those who see in the Communism he espoused only an alien intrusion into our temperate affairs will find much in his life to confirm their preconceptions. The Comintern agents and Moscow gold, the political somersaults and conclaves with Stalin, are all there, and documented in a way impossible even a few years ago. However, for those seeking a more balanced insight into the character of British Communism, the biographical approach adopted here compels us also to chart the indigenous formation of arguably its outstanding leader. For the first three decades of Pollitt's life there was no such thing as a British Communist Party and he was to bear the marks of this secular upbringing for the rest of his life. Born in the heart of industrial Britain, his passionate sense of identity with his own working class would underpin and occasionally clash with his allegiance to international Communism. An aristocrat of labour, he combined pride in the skills and traditions of his craft with bitter memories of earlier family poverty. Consigned to factory life at the age of twelve, his was almost the last generation of those gifted autodidacts whose rich and defiant culture was so largely of their own making. He was, too, one of the last of those consummate platform orators whose skills were developed in the equal cut and thrust of the street-corner meeting. Most of all, perhaps, he was a product of that open, generous socialist culture that predated the First World War and which, in view of later developments, it is difficult not to sentimentalise. This legacy in particular Pollitt would always cherish. How in later years he came to project the ideals of his youth onto a dictatorship more brutal than anything experienced in Edwardian Britain is the tragedy, had only Pollitt himself come to realise it, of the study that follows.

Harry Pollitt was born on 22 November 1890 in the textile village of Droylsden, on the road from Manchester to Ashton-under-

Lyne. Already half a century earlier Engels had described this as the 'classic soil' of manufacturing capitalism, and by the turn of the century the industrial civilisation of South Lancashire had reached its grim apogee. 'Under smoky skies are dirty huddled towns, linked together by clanking chains of hideous railway', wrote a *Clarion* journalist in the 1890s. 'Everywhere you will find steam hissing and smoke scowling: factories, forges, furnaces, chimneys, coalpit heads, streams fouled by chemical works...'[1] Pollitt's early years were as typical of the region as the mean little red-brick terrace in which he spent them,[2] and it was not solely for political effect that he later described their outstanding characteristics as 'poverty, sickness and death'. Of the six children his mother bore in perfunctory breaks from her work as a weaver, three died in infancy. Those that survived, of whom Harry was the eldest, were straight away entrusted to friends and relatives while his mother returned to the mill. It was thus that Harry and his sister Ella, closest to him in age and temperament, became 'little mothers and fathers long before our time', precociously acquainted with the early deaths of the twins their mother bore in 1901. Pollitt's father, a blacksmith's striker with a fondness for drink, was not always the support to his family that he might have been. If they did not experience the very depths of poverty, they knew well enough the constant, numbing pressure to make ends meet. It was under this compulsion that at the age of twelve, after what then passed for an education in the basement of a local church, young Harry joined his mother as a half-timer at nearby Benson's Mill. When before very long the buxom girls in the cardroom daubed his private parts with oil and packed him up with cotton waste, their high-spirited victim could regard himself as properly initiated into the world of labour.[3]

In all this there was little to distinguish Pollitt from tens of thousands of his contemporaries, not a fraction of whom came to share his commitment to revolutionary socialism. The real clue to his political identity lay not so much in his early experience of deprivation, though that was fundamental to it, but in the profound and enduring influence on his outlook that his parents had. A helper in a local Congregational church, one of a succession of religious bodies from which the irreverent and mischievous youngster was excluded, was quite emphatic as to the harm caused him by the 'rabid atheists' who spawned him. 'There was a definite religious streak in Harry's nature', she recalled with regret, 'but his mother crushed this and taught him to become a rebel.'[4] Certainly it was through his parents that Pollitt first became acquainted with socialism, in a household with no family Bible but a Chambers' Dictionary in its place, and the *Clarion* and *Freethinker* delivered weekly. However, he owed to his family background far more than an exposure to radical ideas. It was through his regard for his mother and father that Pollitt acquired a sense of injustice, a standard of conduct and a feeling of pride in his own class which would give to his socialism its passionate, impatient, emotional edge.

Pollitt's earliest and deepest attachment was to his mother, Mary Louisa Pollitt. It was on her shoulders that the main burden of family poverty fell and Pollitt's bitter memories of his early years were very much bound up with his feelings of affection and obligation towards her. 'Every time she put her shawl round me before going to the mill on wet or very cold mornings', he wrote in his memoirs, 'I swore that when I grew up I would pay the bosses out for the hardships she suffered. I hope I shall live to do it, and there will be no nonsense about it... not that at that time I knew anything about systems, but I felt instinctively that something was wrong.' One must beware of any tendencies here to self-dramatisation, for Pollitt and the Communist Party were never to undervalue the legitimacy which its leader's proletarian authenticity conferred upon it. Nevertheless, none could read the dozens of letters that Pollitt received on his mother's death in 1939 and doubt the 'bonds of love and comradeship' between them, or the genuineness of the artless dedication to her with which he prefaced his autobiography *Serving My Time*. Moreover, it was not the mere fact of endurance that drew him towards her, but the dignity of her bearing in the face of affliction: the tired smile for her children after long hours at the mill, the readiness always to help out a neighbour, the fortitude with which she, like so many Lancashire women, combined the roles of wage worker and housekeeper and still kept an impeccable home. This in particular would be central to Pollitt's notions of working-class self-respect. 'Oh, that Lancashire cleanliness!', he recalled. 'That cleaning of the front steps and flags! That scrubbing down of the backyard! Those steel fenders and fire-irons! Those brass candlesticks that had to be polished till you could see your face in them!'[5] It was with the ruffled pride of his Lancashire origins, and

3

not simply through Stalinist intolerance, that Pollitt would many years later take Orwell to task for his tendentious portrait of the more squalid aspects of nearby Wigan. 'Most Lancashire women who read this book would like to dust Orwell's pants for his insults and delicate nose', he wrote of *The Road to Wigan Pier*. It might well have been his own mother that he had in mind.[6]

It was as Pollitt entered his teens that the mother and son seem to have become especially close. One factor may have been the death from pneumonia of two-year-old Winifred in 1903. She had been the darling of the family and the loss was felt terribly by all. 'I would pay God out', Pollitt recalled of his own unfocused sense of grievance. 'I would pay everybody out for making my sister suffer.' For his mother, coming so soon after the death of Winifred's twin brother this must have been the worst of the blows she had to bear and she was for a time inconsolable. She would not, in these circumstances, have been the first woman to have turned from her slightly bibulous and irresponsible husband to the bright, sensitive youngster before whom all was still possible. She began to involve him in her own activities, and it was thus that Pollitt made his first real acquaintance with socialism. Tagging along to meetings, he recalled particularly seeing Philip Snowden and Conrad Noel, while it was after the weekly class his mother attended that he would 'listen spellbound to her first explanations of economics and industrial history'. When a couple of years later she became involved in a local Socialist Sunday School, young Harry was onto it 'like a shot'; and appropriately it was she who in 1906 proposed him as a member of the Openshaw branch of the ILP. Moreover, the habit he acquired at this time of confiding in his mother his every hope and setback persisted with him till her death. Possibly indeed the weekly letter he strove always to send her provided the link he needed with his origins as he began to move in circles far removed from the scenes and expectations of his youth. 'My mother was my pal', he wrote on her death, and the intensity of his political commitments can only be understood in the light of this, his closest friendship.[7]

Samuel Pollitt, his father, was a very different sort of character, a prey it would seem to all the stock vices of the working man. He was always getting into debt, always out to beat the bookies and 'he thought he was robbing the publican if he sat in the Crossley Arms

4

without a full glass'. If he thus made his own contribution to the family's hardships, it is notable that his frailties did not produce in his son the degree of revulsion one might have expected. Other socialists from similar backgrounds would pledge themselves to a lifelong sobriety, which could sometimes be so easily mistaken for a dour self-righteousness. Pollitt himself, indeed, felt fitfully the impulses that moved a Hardie or a Lansbury, a Murphy or a Gallacher. A gifted reciter of dialect ballads and tales of redemption, his favourite theme, and his father's too, was that of the drunkard spurning the bottle for the purer pleasures of domesticity. Whatever Pollitt's disappointment as his appreciative listener sauntered out to the pub, enchanted but unreformed, it seems that he, like his mother, was seduced by his father's wit, his great fund of popular song and his very incorrigibility. In his memoirs he described the occasion on which his long-suffering mother packed her bags and set off with the children for her mother's, only to be greeted with the gravest formality as they passed in the street her wayward and tipsy husband. 'What could you do with a man like that?', Pollitt commented, which had not quite the note of prim disapproval that it might have had. While old Sam never really took to his son's politics – 'Harry, get thy feet under t'table like J. H. Thomas and that crowd', he used to tell him – his influence can nevertheless be detected in Pollitt's innocence of the slightest taint of puritanism. He liked his pint as much as the next man, and thus mixed on freer terms than he might have with his Labour movement peers. He had a great fondness for music hall and minstrelsy, he and the unemployed workers' leader Wally Hannington being known to drive from Mansfield to London without ever exhausting their boisterous repertoire. Then in 1930, when it seemed that nobody wanted to read the newly launched *Daily Worker*, it was Pollitt who put most forcefully the case for racing tips. It was this easy familiarity with the ways of Britain's easy-going working-class majority that saved Pollitt from some of the delusions to which a strident revolutionary minority was inevitably prone. The mixture of a fervent political commitment with his disarming unaffectedness goes some way towards explaining the extraordinary charisma he would exert over the faithful.[8]

Whatever his domestic shortcomings, Samuel Pollitt had as a worker a standard of conduct for which his son had nothing but respect. It was thus already with inherited notions of strict timekeeping, pride in one's work and loyalty to one's mates that in October 1905 young Harry embarked upon his chosen trade of boilermaker. Entry to the trade was generally through family connections and it was an uncle of Pollitt's who 'spoke for him' at Gorton Tank, the vast and teeming locomotive works where he served his time as a plater. The reward in the end was admission to one of the most exclusive castes in the engineering industry, but this first of all required a long and taxing apprenticeship bringing home only a few shillings wages.[9] Quite apart from his fifty-three hour week at the Tank, Pollitt had now to make good the inadequacies of his formal education. 'Until I was twenty-one I never missed attending night school four nights a week and doing all the homework that was given', he recalled. 'I took up mathematics, machine-drawing, construction and designing, tin-plate development, shorthand and economics, and by 1912 had finished serving my time.' He had by this time obtained an ordinary pass in the City and Guilds examination, and may well have done better but for the unstated distractions of the socialist movement.

The ceremony according to which Pollitt was now admitted to the Boilermakers' Society was hallowed by a half-century's usage, but even as he spoke his solemn oath the craft traditions to which it gave such dignified expression were fast succumbing to changing work practices and new technologies. There is some evidence that already Pollitt had embraced the broader conception of industrial activity that these changes demanded, and certainly his subsequent political development took him far beyond a narrow craft exclusiveness. Nevertheless, there would remain even in his Communism the unmistakable imprint of the skilled worker. Asked in 1939 to contribute to the symposium *Why I am a Democrat*, it was significant that Pollitt should have dwelt at such length on the traditions of his craft. 'The occasion of my initiation into my trade union will always be fixed in my memory', he wrote:

> The youngster, feeling rather awed and overcome, being taken in and introduced by one of the older skilled men, who had 'fathered' him in the factory, and hearing the official welcome of the trade union branch read out to him by the Chairman, and feeling that he was now one with all the men who were strong and skilled, and that in future he would stand side by side with them in their life at the bench. This is a guarantee that becomes part of the traditions of our country.

In a similar vein, he deplored the demoralising effects of replacing these 'skilled craftsmen' with mere 'girls and boys' and urged that 'the demand we make to do the job in a free way in a hierarchy of skill is the only way in which the job can be done, and the only way in which the people can call themselves free'.[10] It was because they were thus implanted within him that Pollitt would remain so sensitive to deep-seated trade union loyalties even when most actively seeking to transcend them. Moreover, already at Gorton Tank he had noticed that it was precisely amongst the skilled workers that the very few adherents to socialism were to be found. Perhaps it is to these early proselytising boilermakers that we owe the constant invocations in his propaganda of the 'serious-minded socialist and trade unionist'. He argued later that it was due to creative instincts frustrated by capitalism that these groups of workers dreamt of a better society in which their talents would be used to the full for the good of all. Historians have of course discerned other, less disinterested motivations in this process of radicalisation, but there can be no doubt that Pollitt's was indeed a craftsman's vision of socialism, one that would release the 'generations of craftsmanship, intelligence, initiative and organising ability' which he felt to be his inheritance.[11]

Important as Pollitt's early workshop experiences were, they are overshadowed in his autobiography by his vibrant account of the pre-war socialist movement. 'Glorious salad days' is how he described this period, and in advancing years his wistful thoughts would increasingly turn to this golden age unblemished by cynicism or compromise. These were the days when the corruptions and disillusionments of power had yet to be felt, when there was little in the movement to attract or nurture the careerist, a period of local assertiveness and organisational fluidity when overlapping allegiances blunted the edge of an exuberant sectarianism. The Openshaw Socialist Society, to which Pollitt's best efforts were devoted, was very much a case in point. Established on the initiative of the local ILP in 1906, it subsequently seceded from both the ILP and the local trades council before reconstituting itself a branch of the newly-founded British Socialist Party, a forerunner of the CP, in 1912. Whatever their national affiliations, when they had any, the Openshaw socialists remained very much a law unto themselves. Amongst Manchester socialists generally there was, associated with the so-called Fourth Clause policy, a strong aversion towards having any truck with the Liberals. Noting the apparent congruence between Liberalism and Labour in their unequal progressive alliance, the Openshaw socialists took this a degree further and at successive municipal elections opposed to the official Labour candidate their own red-blooded nominee. In thus flouting official BSP policy, the contests brought the branch into sharp conflict with head office in London and drew from Hyndman himself the damning epithet of 'impossible anarchists'. Pollitt, the branch secretary, was an enthusiastic supporter of the policy, and for the first of the three contests, in 1911, he penned his first leaflet, *Socialism or Social Reform?* Reading now the ponderous didacticism with which he enlightened the toilers of Openshaw with Marxist axioms learnt by heart, the repeated failure of the society's candidates is not altogether surprising. 'The result augurs ill for Labour misrepresent-atives in future', Pollitt insisted in 1912, after the ardent revolutionary scorning palliatives had obtained a mere 260 votes. The expression of defiant optimism in the wake of defeat was something he was going to have get used to.[12]

The contesting of elections was, however, the very least of the society's concerns. Based at the splendid Socialist Hall in Margaret Street, built so largely through voluntary efforts and opened with grand ceremony by Robert Blatchford in 1908, Openshaw's young visionaries kept up a constant stream of varied activities. 'Every night in the week, something or other was going on', Pollitt recalled; 'classes in industrial history and economics, socials to raise money, choir practice, lectures, the whole round of local Labour life and work'. Pollitt himself was for some years a regular attender of the Sunday morning classes and Sunday evening lectures, but even these did not satisfy his insatiable appetite for drama and enlightenment. On Sunday afternoons he would make his way to the Secular Hall in Rusholme Road to hear exposed the miserable fallacies of religion, while his Saturday evenings were enlivened by the weekly debates of the Manchester County Forum. This was not a specifically socialist venture, but provided a stage for local characters of the most disparate views and disputatious temperaments to pit their wits in public. Amongst those figuring in Pollitt's fond recollections were the legendary socialist and Wagnerian, Moses Baritz, and the stentorian bearded radical, Mr

Whittle. 'When Mr Whittle started, he could be heard a mile off', Pollitt recalled, 'and invariably when he had got to his loudest, some wag in the audience would cry, "Speak up, Whittle!" and he never failed to fall for it.' Further happy memories were provided by the Clarion Cycling Club, also based at Margaret Street. Off the youngsters would set on a Sunday morning to escape the dreary city streets and fire the indifferent villagers of North Cheshire with the anthems and rhetoric of socialism. 'I have heard a lot of scoffing at fellowship', Pollitt reflected in his memoirs, 'but in this Club it was a reality which made hard, poverty-stricken lives much brighter.' For this rare Communist who even at the height of Stalinism would admit that he had 'never been enamoured of salutes, slogans and badges', the innocence and even sentimentalism of these early escapades would remain all his life a source not of shame or embarrassment but of inspiration.[13]

On these cycling expeditions it was generally Pollitt himself who supplied the socialist rhetoric, and it was as a public speaker that he first began to attract attention in northern socialist circles. Of his earliest efforts as a street-corner evangelist, the crowd puller of future years was fondly dismissive. Hardly anybody ever stopped to listen, he confessed, nor indeed could they reasonably have been expected to, as he discoursed interminably on the themes of primitive communism and chattel slavery, feudalism and mercantilism, even getting round to capitalism and socialism. Anything more lively and immediate had, of course, the taint of reformism and was therefore anathema to him.

Despite these inauspicious beginnings, Pollitt had a natural talent for public speaking and he learnt quickly from the peripatetic socialist missionaries of the day, whose meetings he often chaired. Amongst those who particularly helped him were Bill Gee, the 'Socialist Dreadnought', and F. G. Jones, the 'Silver-tongued Orator' whose inspiriting depictions of the socialist future led Pollitt to describe him as 'the greatest orator I have ever heard'. As he observed in such company how to win and sustain the interest of an audience, his own reputation as a speaker grew. One instructive anecdote has him employed by a local picture house to drum up interest in a film then showing of Zola's searing novel of a coal strike, *Germinal*. On another occasion during the Dublin lockout of 1913, Pollitt was paid the singular honour of being asked to deputise for the Irish transport workers' leader, Jim Larkin, at a solidarity meeting at Grimsby's Tivoli Theatre. Indeed, although he claimed to have been until this, his first big meeting, 'still only a "street-corner boy"', he was by this time in regular demand for open-air meetings right across Lancashire and Yorkshire.[14]

To judge from what we know of his reading habits, the ideas expressed in Pollitt's speeches must have been fairly representative of that generation of proletarian rebels so splendidly evoked for us by Stuart Macintyre.[15] Like so many others, he devoured the pamphlets that came pouring off the socialist printing presses and studied with the autodidact's eager thirst for knowledge the Marxist texts and commentaries emanating from Charles H. Kerr & Co of Chicago. His feelings of pride when his mother presented him with a copy of *Capital* on his twenty-first birthday were characteristic not only of the man himself but of the distinctive sub-culture to which he belonged. There were one or two influences, however, which though widely shared had a special resonance for Pollitt. One was Robert Blatchford and the weekly paper he edited, the *Clarion*. 'Appealing primarily to the young thinking men and women in the clerk and artisan classes of Lancashire and the West Riding', a historian of the period has written, 'its files mirror admirably their hobbies and ideals – cycling, literature, arts-and-crafts, "rational" dress, feminism, vegetarianism, and back-to-the-land – all gaily jostling one another in a generous and Utopian atmosphere of socialist enthusiasm.'[16] It thus provided something of an antidote to the earnest dogmatism of the Marxist sects, and with their simple eloquence Blatchford's best-selling expositions of the socialist case, *Merrie England* (1893) and *Britain for the British* (1902), would in due course provide Pollitt with a model for his own writings.

By Pollitt's own account, however, there was something missing in Blatchford's books. They lacked, he felt, 'that bitterness against Capitalism and the Capitalists that is so essential in steeling one to do battle against the capitalist system'. This 'class feeling', this 'hatred and contempt of the rich', he found most memorably in Jack London's novel-cum-political tract *The Iron Heel*. So inspired was he on first reading it in 1912 that he 'went round the street corners of Openshaw, Ashton-under-Lyne, Oldham, Salford, Manchester, Leeds and Liverpool, speaking on The Iron Heel and then getting down from the Mineral Water box and going round selling the book'. The theme that had so taken hold of him was that of the remorseless struggle between a flint-faced capitalist oligarchy, moved only by its brutal lust for power, and the selfless fraternity of revolutionists 'who were clean, noble, and alive, and all that the capitalists were not'. It was an antithesis somewhat facile even then and increasingly to be belied by history itself, but it was this antithesis that drove Pollitt on in politics and which explained the fascination that *The Iron Heel* had for him.

In his favourite chapter the novel's hero, a proletarian superman figure with the Bolshevik-sounding name of Ernest Everhard, enters the very heart of the oligarchy and by pure force of intellect reduces the cool captains of industry to 'snarling, growling savages in evening clothes'. 'He was the spirit of regnant labour as he stood there, his hands outstretching to rend and crush his audience', London wrote. 'He had an encyclopaedic command of the field of knowledge, and by a word or a phrase, by delicate rapier thrusts, he punctured them.' In his fascination with Everhard one detects the need for intellectual and moral certainty in his cause that was to be Pollitt's greatest strength as well as his greatest weakness. It explains perhaps the hero-worship he would feel for Lenin, like Everhard a man of thought and man of action, invincible in the rightness of his cause. Possibly too it helps explain the regard that Pollitt had for so many years for Raji Palme Dutt, whose encyclopaedic knowledge and coruscating analyses offered Pollitt himself the chance to emulate his fictional hero. In the fusion through their unique relationship of worker and intellectual, perhaps Pollitt caught a glimpse of himself from time to time as the spirit of regnant labour.[17]

A further influence that has to be mentioned is Tom Mann. Born in 1856, Mann was an extraordinary, mercurial character whose career seemed over a period of more than five decades to have taken in practically all the main developments in British labour history: the ASE, the SDF, the New Unionism, the ILP, syndicalism and finally the Communist Party. It was during this last period that his life intersected closely with Pollitt's, but already during the pre-war industrial unrest his pamphlets and flamboyant oratory had captivated the young boilermaker. 'That's how I want to be', Pollitt whispered to his father as Mann strode about the stage of Manchester's Gaiety Theatre in 1911. What inspired him in the man he idolised and thought to emulate was the very simplicity of his

11

expression as he roused his audiences to 'wrath and indignation' and warmed them with his 'comradeship and revolutionary fire'. 'To have robbed life of a little of its greyness and to have given a glimpse of what life under Socialism could be like', wrote Pollitt. 'That was always Tom Mann's aim.' It would be Pollitt's aim too, and, in Manchester at least, among those responsive to their message there would be no greater attraction than a double bill featuring the two of them.[18]

Mann was an exemplar for Pollitt in other ways too. A skilled engineer and eventually secretary of the ASE, he nevertheless embraced the cause of all sections of labour and aimed through his manifold activities at the broadest mobilisation of an entire class. A lifelong rebel, he refused to trim his sails with advancing years and by his allegiance to Communism gave some credence to the tendentious socialist version of apostolic succession with which the CP sought to legitimise itself. Then there was the fact, noted by H. M. Hyndman, that among Labour leaders none put on less 'side' than Mann. 'After a speech which has roused his audience to the highest pitch of almost hysterical enthusiasm, down Tom will step from the chair in the open air, or from the platform in the hall, and take names for the branch or organisation, and sell literature to all and sundry as if he were the least-considered person at the gathering.'[19]

The words might almost have been written of Pollitt himself, and it is no doubt these shared characteristics that help explain the deep attachment between the two men. Amongst the somewhat austere fraternity of Britain's home-grown apparatchiks, Mann provided Pollitt with a precious personal friendship rooted in a shared culture free of all sanctimoniousness. It is evident in the very few letters of theirs that survive, as for example when, during his brief and bitter removal from the Party leadership in 1939-40, Pollitt described for Mann's enjoyment the homely pleasures of an engineers' smoking concert in his native Manchester. The 'tankards flowed freely', wrote the unreconstructed boilermaker, 'and what do you think... when a comrade broke down singing that hoary old engineers favourite called "Thora" I stepped into the breach and helped him out'. One savours too Pollitt's indulgent account of how, as a 'sort of secretary' to the older Communist, he used to escort Mann and his contemporary in struggle Ben Tillett as they staggered arm-in-arm from their drinking sessions in the Strand, distributing largesse to every flower girl and match seller in sight.

It was a warm and genuine attachment, but it reveals something of Pollitt's character that it was also quite without sentimentality insofar as politics entered into it. It is fascinating to discover that it was not Pollitt but the more calculating Dutt who in the 1930s proposed Mann's elevation to the Party leadership. It was not that the octogenarian was likely to have much of a contribution to make, as Dutt himself admitted, but even as 'our only ornament... history requires that his biography should reach completion as member of CC of CP...' Pollitt, his affection for Mann notwithstanding, would have none of it. 'The old gentleman you suggest', he wrote back to Dutt, '"no a thousand times no"... big liability already, worse if actual part of leadership'. No doubt it was Mann's stubborn individualism that he had in mind, and particularly the reluctance to have a speech or statement prepared for him that had already caused so many 'bitter and heated scenes' between the two. It was nevertheless Dutt whose view prevailed.[20]

While Mann provided a unique link between first-generation British Marxism and Communism, the First World War is commonly seen as a watershed for the British left. Radicalised by the war and galvanised by Bolshevism, the most ardent spirits of a younger generation were in the post-war excitement sucked into a new and allegedly alien political formation. For better or worse, few ever disputed that the foundation of the Communist Party in 1920 marked a sharp break with a good deal of its indigenous heritage. Pollitt's own development was in many ways representative of this first generation of British Communists. The Openshaw branch of the BSP was from the start amongst that party's restive anti-war faction and we have it on Pollitt's own testimony, confirmed by at least one other source, that he lagged behind nobody in giving expression to these views. On the very first Sunday of the war, as Britain's preachers and their flocks wished death on the Hun, Pollitt was due to speak at Ashton market with its nearby barracks. Throwing caution to the winds, he tore into the warmongers and their lying jingo propaganda until at last he drew from his audience, dotted with swaggering scarlet tunics, the tumultuous response he must surely have expected. Dragged around the market place in a cart with a protective chair held aloft, it finally took two policemen to escort him to the Openshaw tram and safety. This seemed only to produce in him a taste for further such escapades, one of which was

13

staged with all its attendant disorders directly outside the Yeomanry Barracks at Brook's Bar, Manchester.[21]

At this stage it can hardly have been the carnage and destruction of war that moved him to such performances. His opposition to the war would indeed remain simply an extension of his opposition to the bloated plutocrats who perpetrated such evils, without any detectable qualitatively new dimension to his radicalism. In his memoirs he does mention the feelings of revulsion that the incessant troop movements and returning casualties produced in him while he lived for a time in Southampton. It is nevertheless significant that there is nowhere in his writings any mention of the loss or maiming of a friend or relative that might have brought home to him in more personal terms the real cost of war; significant, that is, because Pollitt's opposition to war was of course to take the least pacifist of forms. All that the war taught him was the hypocrisy of those who, having fought their own bloody struggles to the bitter end, would then seek to confine the working class to peaceful means of change. Like Orwell's Auden in *Inside the Whale*, Pollitt's blithe acceptance of political violence was that of the man for whom, until the Moscow trials and Spanish war at least, these things were always at one step removed. His was an engineer's, not a soldier's war; and it was in his broadening experience of workplace exploitation and the daily struggle against it that the main impact of the war on him was felt.

Affected perhaps by the general restlessness of wartime, Pollitt made in these years his first real break with his Mancunian roots. In June 1915, after a succession of jobs in local engineering factories, he left Manchester to seek shipbuilding work in Southampton; and then in January 1918, after a further spell back in Lancashire, he made the more fateful move to a London stirring with thoughts of revolution and Bolshevik intrigue. Already by this time he had earned something of a reputation as an industrial militant. Discovering on his arrival in Southampton that the local BSP branch had folded, he joined instead the ILP, but found at its meetings that he 'could not stomach the pacifist character of the propaganda'. Much more congenial to him was the well-organised Boilermakers' Society: he soon found digs with its district delegate and, having started work at Thornycroft's shipyard, became active in the society's affairs there. It was thus that in September 1915 he became involved in what proved to be something of a test case under the anti-strike provisions of the recent Munitions of War Act.

The occasion for the dispute was the first instalment of dilution at Thornycroft's, and indeed the first apparently in the South of England. As so often the strike that immediately ensued combined a legitimate stand against the high-handedness of employer and state with what was essentially the defence of a craft privilege. 'The boilermakers particularly objected to men who were non-unionists working with men who, according to the rules of the Boilermakers' Society, must be unionists', wrote the government's chief industrial commissioner, not altogether unfairly, 'but at the same time were very loth to admit new men to their ranks.' Pollitt was prominent on the strike committee and in future years would treasure the inscribed watch he received for his services during the dispute. If the men were eventually defeated, with fifty of them having been fined under the provisions of the recent act, the dispute was nevertheless full of lessons for the aspiring militant. It was, for example, a first experience for him of unofficial industrial action, as state, employer and union officialdom combined to bring the strike to an end. In particular Pollitt recalled the appeal to the men of the ASE's chairman J. T. Brownlie, whose sonorous platitudes as to the danger to the ship of state were met with the ribald retort that he shouldn't in that case 'send piss-pot jugglers into the engine-room'. The impetuous young agitator learnt also that his fellow boilermakers did not always take kindly to the introduction of politics into their society's affairs and that it was sometimes necessary in a cannier way to 'try to kill the two birds with one stone'. He also encountered again the problem of sectionalism, as the strikers sought the solidarity only of their fellow boilermakers, while he ended the dispute with the sober realisation that 'popularity at the climax of an exciting strike and popularity after that strike has been lost are two very different things'. How much of this he appreciated straight away and how much only sunk in with time is not clear; but certainly he gained more from the experience than just a silver watch.[22]

Politically, on the other hand, the city was somewhat quiescent and for a while Pollitt's main activity seems, out of necessity as much as inclination, to have been that of reading and private study. How much more at home he must have felt when in 1918 he encountered in London a socialist culture as vigorous and kaleidoscopic as that he

15

had known in Manchester. During his first year or so in the capital he addressed meetings for the BSP, joined the *Herald* League, applied for a job as an ILP organiser, gave lectures on industrial history for the London Labour Educational League, frequented the bookshop of the anarchist James Tochatti and, as a confirmed opponent of affiliation to the Labour Party, campaigned for Arthur Henderson in the post-war Khaki Election. It was, however, the tangle of organisations centred on the personalities of Sylvia Pankhurst and W. F. Watson that provided his main sphere of activity. Pankhurst's Workers' Socialist Federation had its only real presence in London's East End, where Pollitt now lived and worked, and in its propaganda he discovered something resembling his own fervent identification with triumphant Bolshevism and the notion of Soviet power. Sunday evenings would find him at the dock gates in Poplar, where with Pankhurst herself or the tireless Mrs Walker he preached the cause of the Russian workers. It is not entirely clear whether it was through the WSF that Pollitt became involved in the London Workers' Committee or vice versa. The latter organisation had been re-established after an earlier false start by the engineer and industrial unionist W. F. Watson in March 1918. Affiliated to the Shop Stewards' and Workers' Committee Movement and sharing the national movement's basic aims, the London committee nevertheless lacked the organisational pull of its counterparts in Glasgow and elsewhere. Indeed, like the Amalgamation Committee with which Watson had previously been associated, it was essentially 'a propagandist body without direct contact with the London engineering workshops'. The committee had very close links with the WSF, sharing premises with it at various times and using as its mouthpiece Pankhurst's weekly paper the *Workers' Dreadnought*. Apparently Pollitt was involved in the production of both the *Dreadnought* and Watson's own short-lived *Masses* and it is in these papers that some of his earliest journalistic efforts can be found. It was moreover through the combined exertions of the two organisations that there arose in 1919 the movement through which Pollitt first acquired a certain wider prominence and a set of experiences that would profoundly affect the rest of his political life. How often in future years did he invoke that memory encrusted with myth of British Labour's solidarity with the infant Soviet republic! The defiant slogan *Hands Off Russia*, with

16

which he was now to be associated, was one to which he would remain faithful long after Russia had found all sorts of ways of its own to see to these matters.

It was as an industrial militant of proven capabilities that Pollitt came to the fore of the Russian solidarity movement. On arriving in the capital he had transferred to his union's London No 11 branch and as its delegate to the district committee he was on 1 January 1919 appointed to the honorary post of its London district secretary. This not only gave him a grounding in the conduct of union negotiations but also, which mattered more to him in those turbulent times, provided him with 'many opportunities for developing contacts and increasing the influence of the revolutionary movement'. He was moreover a key figure in the River Thames Shop Stewards' Movement, set up in the latter part of 1918. Within its more limited scope this body had a far greater workplace presence than the Workers' Committee and succeeded, as Pollitt put it, in organising shipyard committees 'from Chiswick to Tilbury'. Electricians' and Woodworkers' union activists had apparently initiated the movement, but it was with Pollitt's influence amongst the Boilermakers and Watson's amongst the ASE stewards that the committee felt strong enough in January 1919 to call an all-out unofficial strike for a 15s wage increase. Similar actions were developing elsewhere, and on the Sunday that Pollitt secured a mandate for the strike from eight thousand cheering workers packed into Poplar Hippodrome, the rising tide of militancy must have seemed irresistible. 'The example of the workers in the Port of London would inspire others to follow', he declaimed in the euphoria of the moment, 'and so they would go on together building the city of the future'.

In reality, however, that winter's fragmented strike movement only underlined the shop stewards' lack of any effective national co-ordinating body, while in London as elsewhere the want of official support would prove a greater problem than ever heady rhetoric would admit. For three weeks the strike was solid and Pollitt, as the committee's paid organiser, was indefatigable in his efforts to secure victory. In due course the strike began to crumble, however, and as its main spokesman Pollitt 'the Bolshie', as some now called him, encountered a very different mood amongst the workers involved. Indeed, at the same Poplar Hippodrome just four weeks later it was

17

as much as the Bolshie could do to get himself a hearing. The 'roar of hostility', he wrote later, after much experience of these things, was such as he had never heard before or since. As the strike collapsed, so in effect did the Thames-side shop stewards' movement. Nevertheless, with his well-honed agitational skills, his links with both the official movement and rank-and-file initiatives, and above all with his unequivocal commitment to Bolshevik Russia, it meant that Pollitt was a natural choice to help run the emerging Hands Off Russia movement.[23]

In the development of this movement, the names of Pankhurst and Watson again loom large. The People's Russian Information Bureau, with which the movement originated, was set up through their agency and Russian subventions in July 1918 and operated first from Watson's LWC offices in Holborn and later from the Fleet Street premises of the *Workers' Dreadnought*. It was likewise through their initiative that a broader-based solidarity committee was established at a 'Hands Off Russia' conference under the LWC's auspices the following January. The BSP and the Socialist Labour Party were among the bodies represented as the conference agreed to promote the idea of a general strike against Allied intervention. Pollitt moved the resolution and was included on the committee of fifteen syndicalists and revolutionists elected to carry the agitation forward. As concern about the government's Russian policy spread throughout the Labour movement, however, this body in its turn gave way in the summer to one very much more representative. Among those who became involved in the new Hands Off Russia committee were such prominent trade union figures as C. T. Cramp of the Railwaymen, John Bromley of ASLEF, John Hill of the Boilermakers and Alf Purcell of the Furnishing Trades and the TUC Parliamentary Committee.[24]

That such influential names promised more in the way of a general strike than ever Pollitt and his immediate circle could did not mean that the latter's role in the movement was thereby diminished. On the contrary, he was in September appointed its full-time national organiser and, having been asked to base himself in the industrial North, proceeded to conduct his affairs once more from the Margaret Street Socialist Hall in Openshaw. Pollitt was thus for the second time that year in receipt of a full-time wage for his activities, and he can have been in no doubt as to whom he had to thank for that. We know that Pankhurst amongst others had for some time maintained contact with Bolshevik emissaries bearing gifts designed to safeguard the first workers' revolution and hasten the ones that were to follow. By those most closely involved, this seems to have been regarded as a perfectly natural expression of fraternal solidarity. Possibly at that early stage they were even right, though one can hardly be so indulgent about Watson's decision to accept for a while a weekly handout from the Special Branch for what he later claimed to be regular instalments of disinformation. Pollitt drew a veil over this brief cause celebre in his memoirs, but there is no evidence that he felt the slightest compunction about the Russian subventions that paid his wages. He did, on the other hand, claim to have felt restless in his functionary's office, removed in these stirring times from his fellow workers. After a short while he therefore returned to London and took up his tools again, the more effectively to foment sedition in the docks and shipyards.[25]

It was thus that Pollitt could, and did all his life, claim some of the credit for the legendary Russian solidarity actions of the summer of 1920. His own attitude to the revolution that had for the first time toppled the hated capitalists was, from the start, one of almost instinctive support. 'I did not then fully understand the significance of the polemics between one section of social democracy and another', he later wrote. 'All I was concerned about was that power was in the hands of lads like me, and whatever conception of politics had made that possible was the correct one for me.' It was thus inspired that through the early months of 1920 he kept up a constant stream of meetings and leafletings, armed with well-learnt notions of direct action and armfuls of Lenin's *Appeal to the Toiling Masses*, with which Pankhurst kept him plentifully supplied. With the Polish attack on Soviet territory towards the end of April the sense of urgency was heightened, and throughout the Port of London eyes were now peeled for any sign of British assistance to the aggressor. It was consequently a proud day for Pollitt and his comrades when on 10 May 1920, three days after the fall of Kiev, London dockers refused to coal the S.S. *Jolly George*, loaded with munitions marked for Poland. Possibly this was not quite the 'action which completely changed the international situation', as Pollitt claimed, but it certainly acted as a stimulus to the indignant battalions of British Labour. As fears of direct British involvement in the war mounted,

19

the whole movement, from Lansbury to Thomas, was swept along by the clamour for direct action. The campaigns of the left had their fine and all-too-rare culmination in August when an officially constituted Council of Action, speaking for the Labour Party, the TUC and 350 local such councils, threatened the government with a general strike in the event of war. Stepping back from the brink, the Prime Minister Lloyd George insisted that Labour was in any case pushing at an open door, and here the historian is inclined to agree with him. There can be no doubt, however, that it was due in no small measure to the preceding two years' agitation that the door was open in the first place. There was, therefore, some substance at least to the cherished left-wing myth according to which British Labour had by its actions on this occasion 'stopped a war'.[26]

Britain's Communists were in due course to become familiar with a rather more extravagant gloss on the same events, for with his usual eye for national particularities Lenin described the councils of action as soviets; noted how the 'English Mensheviks, who are even more despicable than the Russian Mensheviks' were compelled to trail behind the English Bolsheviks; and concluded that Britain had reached a stage of dual power analogous to that in Russia after the February Revolution. One doubts whether Pollitt, so much closer to the pulse of things, was ever much deceived by this. The Hands Off Russia campaign did, however, leave him the enduring message that, with the right tactics and the right issue, the militant element could get the whole of British Labour moving and commit even despicable English Mensheviks to the advanced positions of the class war.[27]

Contributing in a rather small way to the crescendo of protest that August were the first pronouncements of the newly formed British Communist Party. They were not as yet of very much concern to Pollitt, however. Apparently he did turn up as a visitor at the Party's founding 'Unity Convention' and counted himself as one of its foundation members by virtue of his continuing membership of the Openshaw branch of the BSP. However, he played no role in the negotiations leading up to the convention and may not even have been very sympathetic to their outcome. He was by now most closely identified not with the BSP but with the Workers' Socialist Federation, which took no part in the Unity Convention and saw in the new grouping's leanings towards parliamentarism and Labour Party affiliation the stigma of reformism. These were misgivings fully shared by Pollitt, who may have felt with syndicalist associates like Jack Tanner a degree of scepticism as to the value of the new organisation or indeed of political parties as such. Walton Newbold knew Pollitt well through Hands Off Russia, and later he grouped him with the Gallachers and Pankhursts whose leftism was challenged by Lenin himself. 'Men and women may be persuaded to abandon their rooted preconceptions... with the honest determination that characterised the change-over from anti-parliamentarianism of Willie Gallacher and Harry Pollitt', wrote Newbold, 'but they do not become able thereby to adapt their methods of thinking and acting to a course from which they had deliberately swung away and to which they swung back without spontaneity.'[28]

Newbold's is an apt assessment of Pollitt's formal conversion to the new Communist orthodoxy. In March 1919 he had been quite happy to accept nomination for the Boilermakers' parliamentary panel and described the election of their own MPs as 'more than ever necessary for the trade unions'. The following year, however, as he followed the debate over the uses of Parliament in the revolutionary press, he declined a second such nomination on the grounds that more could be achieved by the industrial movement than ever through 'the use of the present parliamentary machine'. In a piece for the *Workers' Dreadnought* in September 1919 he saw in the formation not of a revolutionary party but of a National Shipbuilding Workers' Council the first step on the road to workers' power. 'Mere aims of higher wages and so on, lose their interest, as larger issues come into view by means of your new organisation', he wrote. 'So you gradually build up the structures whereby you will one day take your stand with workers similarly organised in other industries. Thus you will finally be able to take over the ownership and control of all the productive forces.' As to the role in all this of any political party, he had nothing to say. For some time to come, indeed, his own preoccupations would remain very much with the problems and potentialities of the workplace. 'In fact, I am afraid I was looked upon more as a militant trade unionist than as a Communist', he recalled. 'There was a great deal of truth in this. All my activity had necessarily been in the workshops and trade unions, and naturally had influenced my outlook and way of looking at things.' Now, however, that very outlook was to bring him within the ambit of the Comintern, as it sought through its agencies

21

to perpetuate or perhaps appropriate the organisational legacy of Britain's bitter industrial struggles. It was thus that during the fourth decade of his life Pollitt came to make the transition from 'militant trade unionism to Communism', so effectively indeed that he was to end the decade as the general secretary of the Communist Party.[29]

2 Organising the revolution

It would be quite wrong to follow Pollitt's memoirs and official biography in portraying his adhesion to Communism as a natural, almost an inevitable, progression from the lower forms of socialism he had previously espoused. After all, the greater number of his left-wing contemporaries either steered clear of the CP or quickly withdrew from it. Amongst them were major figures like A. J. Cook and John Maclean and close associates of Pollitt's like Sylvia Pankhurst and Jack Tanner. For Pollitt, however, the combination of the millenarian fervour of the world revolution with the successful exercise of workers' power was to prove irresistible. What Communism offered him, far grander than the rival inducements of MacDonald's backbenches or some comfortable union office, was a sense of involvement in the extraordinary adventure of doing away with capitalism the world over. From this exhilarating perspective even the seamier aspects of Comintern politics, with which Pollitt was quickly to be acquainted, had their apparent justification. Indeed, for one reared on the romances of Jack London, the movement's very conspiratorialism, the forged papers, the coded letters, the stowing away in ships, must have seemed a guarantee of its seriousness and sense of purpose.

To add to its attractions, Pollitt had dangled before him almost from the start the prospect of himself leading the British section of this great world army and of contributing to its counsels at the highest level. That he was an ambitious man there can be no question, but it speaks for a certain stubborn integrity on his part that he should have come so completely to identify his ambitions with those of the party he served. Certainly, in the impact he made on the wider Labour movement in the 1920s there lay before him a much surer route to political advancement, and we can well believe Pollitt that insidiously moderating influences did not fail to remind him of the fact. In this sense he was indeed incorruptible. What

23

moved him primarily was not some tawdry concern with self-advancement but a fierce desire to end the rule of class; and as in this period capitalism reduced great industrial regions like his native Lancashire to an abject semi-activity; as it drove towards a new war, even as those crippled by the last littered the streets of Europe's cities; and as in country after country it turned to armed thugs to beat down the working-class movement that threatened it, Pollitt never doubted that his place was with those sworn to bring this wretched system crashing down. Many years later, after he had broken with Communism, John Strachey acknowledged his acute sense of loss at the vision it had represented between the wars, the 'noble dream of perfected brotherhood, security and well-being, abruptly to be realised, here and now, out of the successful revolt of the miserable and the exploited'.[1] It is a vision to bear in mind as we trace with Pollitt the early years of Communism and wonder perhaps whether it was ever by these methods that this dream would be realised.

It was as an industrial agitator and organiser that Pollitt became embroiled in the early intricacies of Communist Party politics. The reports of the previously sceptical Gallacher on his return from the Comintern's Second Congress at the end of September 1920 convinced Pollitt too that the new party was, after all, correct to seek Labour Party affiliation. He had in any case begun by this time to address the odd CP branch meeting.[2] Direct and continuous involvement, however, began only after the return at the end of the year of another of the delegates to the Second Congress, J. T. Murphy. With him Murphy brought instructions and the necessary funds to set up what would shortly become the British Bureau of the Red International of Labour Unions. The role of the new international, also known as the Profintern, was to provide an opposite pole of attraction to the 'yellow' or 'Amsterdam' International of reformist unions, utilising whatever existing organisational resources were available. In Britain it drew its leading personnel from the workers' committees and various vigilance and reform committees, and it was therefore quite natural that in February 1921 Pollitt should have been appointed its London district organiser. Using old connections and developing new ones, he soon got together a committee representing most of London's main industries: not only the Engineers, a predictably strong presence, but the Workers' Union,

24

the Clerks, the Garment Workers, Printers, Electricians, Woodworkers and Dockers. Over the next month or two Pollitt was very much to the fore in attempting to muster local union support for the new body. His efforts were capped with success when in May some two hundred branches were represented at a London conference demanding the widest support for the Profintern's forthcoming founding congress in Moscow. It was as part of the British delegation to this congress that in June 1921 Pollitt set off with its chairman, Tom Mann, on the first of his many visits to the Soviet Union. It was, he recalled later, like a visit to the Promised Land.[3]

Running concurrently with the RILU congress was the Third Congress of the Comintern itself. Possibly because its British contingent had been somewhat depleted by arrests and harassment back in London, Pollitt was instructed at short notice to attend several sessions of this, the very forum of the world revolution. He made no contribution to either congress and we can be sure that he felt overawed by the occasion: the thrusting, confident figures who bestrode the congress platform as they bestrode the revolution itself; the moving renditions of revolutionary songs, uniting the world's exploited even in their separate languages; and the incongruous opulence of the great Kremlin hall, which fascinated and repulsed the worker from Openshaw, confirming and intensifying his sense of class hatred. 'Money must have poured like water to tickle the degenerate palates of those pre-revolutionary parasites', he recalled, more certain than ever of the simple justice of expropriation. 'I realise now... that these impressions of the contrast between a country where the good things of life belong to the people and a country where a tiny class use them to enslave the masses affected me more... than the speeches and resolutions.' This indeed was hardly surprising, given that the main speeches were delivered in German and translated only into Russian. Soon Pollitt would discover, however, that what went on behind the scenes at the Comintern was quite as important as its public performances. Indeed, he may already have attracted the notice of those who discreetly wielded its considerable powers of patronage. Despite generous disbursements, the British Party amounted by this time to something less even than the sum of its constituent parts and its leaders seemed stuck in the rut of their own sectarian traditions. With his apparent innocence of such vices and his evident capacity for effective mass work, Pollitt must have seemed much closer to the ideal type of Communist Party leader. Later in the year Michael Borodin, the Russian-American now supervising British Party affairs, praised his performance at the Cardiff TUC in an article for the *Communist International* generally critical of the CP. 'Let this lesson not pass unnoticed for those Communists who are still cherishing the idea of "their own circle"', he wrote. 'Only those comrades who have carried [their] banner at Cardiff... are genuine militant Communists. It is to such Communists that the future belongs.'[4]

Borodin's articles were but one indication of the serious concern felt in Moscow at the CP's rather shambolic beginnings. Another was the visit to Britain in the latter part of 1921 of a Comintern commission to conduct an exhaustive enquiry into all aspects of Party activity. Again Pollitt must have made something of an impression, for he was asked in February 1922 to accompany the CP's chairman, Arthur MacManus, to discuss the commission's report in Moscow and attend the first plenary session of the Comintern Executive (ECCI). The upshot of it all was that at the CP's Fourth Congress that spring a three-man commission was appointed to survey and overhaul the Party's entire organisation in line with official Comintern thinking. Drawn from outside the existing leadership, it comprised the rather anonymous brother of the Party secretary, Harry Inkpin; the youthful editor of the *Labour Monthly*, R. Palme Dutt; and Pollitt himself. By this time Pollitt had, as national organiser for the RILU British Bureau, won the trust and respect of the sturdy proletarian figures who predominated in the Party's leading circles. Dutt, on the other hand, was already perceived as a threatening and possibly disruptive element, having recently issued the EC with a sharply critical memorandum on the Party organ the *Communist*. It was thus that in the backstage negotiations that decided the commission's personnel, Pollitt, like Inkpin, was put forward by the executive majority as a counterweight to the middle-class schemer with his Russian connections. In this they were to be gravely disappointed, for within a matter of weeks Pollitt was already falling out with his RILU colleagues and getting along splendidly with Dutt. Between them they marginalised Inkpin, marginalised their official Comintern adviser and struck up a partnership that they would all of them have to come to terms with.[5]

Between Pollitt and his new political mentor there could hardly have been a greater contrast. A tall, shy man whose clear-cut features betrayed his mixed Indo-Swedish parentage, Dutt had both the Oxford manner of one who had studied classics at Balliol and the intellectual agility of one who had excelled at it. 'Any tendency to excessive verbalism or logic chopping', he wrote to Bernard Shaw many years later, 'I must attribute to the pernicious effects of the traditional Western mandarin education of the pre-1914 Balliol scholarship type, where we spent our time composing Greek verse and philosophising and received no practical training whatever.' The taunts of logic-chopping and a certain remoteness from reality would haunt Dutt all his life, and he was not himself oblivious to his political limitations. It was in the 'Boilermaker from the East End', as Pollitt described himself with a touch of mocking self-deprecation, that Dutt found the contact that he lacked with the British working class in its daily struggle; and he found too the vehicle he needed, not for his personal ambitions, for these were indeed negligible, but for his political aspirations. Pollitt in turn found in Dutt, and in the shadowy presence of his wife Salme, the secret of the workers' triumph in backward Russia: the secret, that is, of the revolutionary party. It was to establish such a party in Britain, with Pollitt at its head and the Dutts his closest counsellors, that they worked so assiduously in the 1920s. When in later years they clashed politically, it was with the special intensity of their conflicting temperaments and a fractured intimacy. All this lay a long way in the future, however. For the time being they were swept along by the excitement of their shared aims, each learning from the other's strengths as he provided for the other's failings. Certainly, when in 1939 Pollitt claimed to have learned more from Dutt than from any other Communist, this was no empty platitude for public consumption but a simple statement of fact.[6]

The task into which Pollitt was drawn by the Dutts was that of transforming the organisational shambles of the early British Communist Party into a machine for revolution, wrenching it from the bankrupt traditions and leadership it had inherited from its predecessors. It was a perspective that came easily to Dutt, for whom these traditions and personalities had in any case meant very little. He had, it is true, held grudging memberships of both the ILP and the BSP, but even the latter he had resigned in 1918 with the

27

portentous declaration that he would 'henceforth regard myself as waiting for the formation of a Communist Party'. His frustrations were apparently shared on her arrival in Britain in 1920 by his future wife, the Comintern representative Salme Pekkala. The main responsibility for that year's Communist Unity negotiations rested with Theodore Rothstein, a Russian émigré long active in British socialist politics. According to Dutt's later reconstruction, Pekkala urged on Rothstein that he bypass Britain's tiny Marxist sects with their interminable sticking points and catch on the flood tide the 'enormously wider mass wave of enthusiasm' generated by the new Third International. Provisional local committees should be established to elect delegates to the party's foundation congress, she argued, 'after which the old organisations could dissolve to give place to the new, in place of continuing like fossils inside the new party to carry forward old antagonisms and traditional separate loyalties and interests'.[7]

The scheme had the utter disregard for practicalities that one tends to associate with the Dutts, and it is not surprising that Rothstein, so much more experienced in the ways of the British left, chose to ignore it. Undeterred, the Dutts remained convinced that Rothstein's makeshift contraption would have to be overhauled. They had a powerful ally in Willie Gallacher, who on his appointment as Party vice-chairman in mid-1921 was appalled at the chaos and profligacy he uncovered. Already Gallacher was acquainted with the Dutts, whom he had introduced to each other in 1920, and the relationship was marked at this time by the highest respect on either side. Theirs in fact was the co-ordinated manoeuvre against the old Party leadership that secured the appointment of the organisation commission in March 1922. It was Gallacher, it should be noted, who carried the Party congress with him in resolving against the platform that the commission be drawn from outside the existing leadership. It was again at Gallacher's insistence, with what influential backing we can only conjecture, that Dutt was then appointed the commission's chairman. After two years' wait, the Dutts had at last their chance to design as if from scratch the revolutionary party of their desires. Happy in their joint work, that same month the couple were married at a clandestine ceremony that foreshadowed the troubled, semi-legal existence they would lead for the next two years.

Meeting in almost continuous session over the next six months, the commission drew up first a detailed indictment of the Party's current administration and then its own dense and ambitious proposals for its restructuring. It had as its guide the theses on organisation adopted by the Comintern's Third Congress, and in following these to the letter it introduced into Britain a method and vocabulary that were largely unfamiliar. In place of the federal structures adopted at first even by the Communist Party, it advocated a strong central executive, 'leading and directing and concentrating the members' activities the whole time'. This it would achieve through the 'cardinal principles' of reports and instructions: the reports flowing continuously upwards through the Party's several layers of organisation, while the instructions flowed continually downwards. Such methods demanded not the old-style party branch, as an occasional meeting place and talking shop, but a tight network of working groups, based directly in the factories and localities and embracing the entire Party membership. The objective was to exert a continuous organised influence over the workers in their daily struggles; and to achieve this required, in comparison with the loose, lazy propagandist traditions of the British left, as 'great a break in methods of organisation as the break in theory from democracy to dictatorship'.

There is little that one can positively identify with Pollitt in the report, which in certain passages seemed not only to reject but to belittle the traditions in which he had been reared. It had, for example, a note almost of contempt for the 'barren ritual' of the street-corner meeting, for the 'so-called "local speaker" who could be "turned on" with the same flow at any time for any audience'; and indeed for all those social activities in which the young Pollitt had discovered the meaning of fellowship and which he now, with his new collaborators, dismissed as a 'demoralising tradition'. While it was the Dutts who drafted the report and to whom these rather patrician sentiments should doubtless be attributed, Pollitt's involvement in the commission and ready identification with its outcome nevertheless represented a fundamental shift in his political thinking. At the centre of his concerns henceforth would be the revolutionary party, bringing its disciplined leadership to the myriad struggles of the working class and imbuing them with its own sense of revolutionary purpose. In this grandiose conception there was little room apparently for some of the basic tenets of his earlier socialism: the distrust of officialdom, for example, the traditions of local autonomy, or even the barest concern with the control of any organisation, let alone the leading party of the working class, by its own members. In his intoxication with Bolshevism, and perhaps also his disappointment at the ebbing of revolutionary hopes in Britain, Pollitt was evidently persuaded of the comparative poverty of his native revolutionary traditions and of the need to adopt the methods that history itself had shown to be successful. It was to the Dutts more than anybody that he owed this conviction, and it provided the basis for their close political understanding over the coming years. Only with time, as he acquired a greater confidence in his own instincts and a certain scepticism as to Dutt's fancies and blueprints, did it become clear that Pollitt's early influences were more deeply rooted than even he perhaps suspected.[8]

The adoption of the commission's report at the CP's Fifth Congress in October 1922 was virtually a formality. As its authors pointed out, it represented 'not the ingenious scheme of a few individuals, but... the deliberately chosen policy of the whole International', and was thus endorsed with the unanimity that this had already begun to imply. Moreover, a groundswell of support for the reformers was revealed when the congress put Dutt and Pollitt at the head of the poll for the new streamlined executive. Amongst the existing leadership, however, formal acquiescence in the reforms masked a continuing scepticism as to their feasibility. The resistance that Dutt and Pollitt had already encountered in preparing their report now manifested itself in what one of the older leaders himself described later as 'a certain passivity and bureaucratic formalism in operating the decisions'. There was in fact every reason for proceeding slowly, and Pollitt himself afterwards acknowledged that they had taken on too much at once. Indeed, there was a quite absurd disproportion between the struggling British Party and the attempt to impose on its two thousand scattered members the bureaucratic structures of successful Russian Communism. There were, for example, to be fifteen departments attached to the central organisation and political bureaux, with the same structure duplicated in each of the districts and a further nine committees at local level. Party nuclei, moreover, were to be organised in 'any trade union branch where' – a modest restriction, this – 'we have one or more members'. No wonder that J. T. Murphy, the most forceful and articulate of the sceptics, felt that many of the objectives were 'literally impossible'. Moreover, those of this viewpoint found they had a kindred spirit in the most unexpected quarter, for at the Comintern's Fourth Congress in November 1922 Lenin himself described the organisational theses as 'too Russian' and therefore 'quite unintelligible to foreigners'. Even the founder of Communism, it now transpired, accepted that the Bolshevisation of the European left could not be carried out overnight.[9]

The Comintern provided the doubters in the Party with further ammunition in the shape of the united front policy, originally propounded towards the end of 1921. In theory there was nothing in this approach that contradicted the prior commitment to build up separate communist parties on Bolshevik organisational principles: the new conception of the vanguard party, after all, was not held to imply any aloof and sectarian attitude on the part of Communists, but only that they should bring to all their wider activities an organised and co-ordinated presence. Indeed, neither Pollitt nor even Dutt could have been accused of any narrow preoccupation with internal Party affairs. Pollitt, of course, was already well known in industrial circles, while Dutt's journal the *Labour Monthly* expressed in its range of contributors and avoidance of 'stereotyped party formulas' the objective of reaching a broader readership communicated to him by couriers from Lenin himself.[10] Even so, given the Party's limited membership and resources, the far-reaching reforms they proposed seemed to cut across any immediate priority of mobilising general resistance to the post-war capitalist offensive. Recoiling from the sheer bureaucratic weight of their innumerable committees and relentless reports, some saw in the initiation of broader movements a quicker route 'To the Masses' – the Comintern's exhortation – than in the hypothetical Party nuclei, with their onerous duties and long months of probationary membership.

In Britain the controversy came to centre on the question of building up left-wing 'minority movements' in the trade unions. It was an objective that addressed the post-war reality of working-class retreat and the need for consolidation more soberly, perhaps, than the reformers' dreams of proliferating factory committees. The earliest proponent of the scheme was Michael Borodin, the Comintern agent sent illegally to Britain to assist in the Party's reorganisation in

31

1922. Under the innocuous nom de guerre of George Brown, he devoted a good deal of effort in South Wales and elsewhere to encouraging Communists and sympathisers to organise just such a movement in the mining unions. By these activities and by his consistent alignment with the old Party leadership, especially his acting secretary J. T. Murphy, Borodin quickly incurred the hostility of Dutt and Pollitt. Shortly before his arrest in Glasgow in August 1922, they broke off all relations with him; and on his involuntary return to Moscow after a six-month prison sentence, Borodin would remain for a time their principal antagonist.[11]

His personal indisposal notwithstanding, Borodin's approach had powerful supporters within the Comintern. Not the least of them was the secretary of the RILU, Alexei Losovsky. 'As far as Britain is concerned', Losovsky explained to the Fourth Comintern Congress in November 1922, 'we see clearly that it would be disastrous if the party were content to organise its forces only within its little Party nuclei. The aim here must be to create a more numerous opposition trade union movement.... The aim must be to create, to marshall, to integrate the opposition forces, and the Communist Party will itself grow concurrently with the growth of the opposition.' There could hardly have been a more direct challenge to the whole tenor of the Party's recently adopted reforms; and when the following summer Losovsky formally proposed the establishment in Britain of a 'trade union educational league' akin to that in the USA, Dutt did his best to thwart him. By this time, moreover, he and Pollitt had begun to organise more carefully to force through their own rather different ideas, and thus precipitated what the CP's earliest historian remembered as the Party's 'first serious crisis'.[12]

Given the interdiction by the Comintern's organisational theses of 'any rivalry for power or any contest for supremacy within the party', there was something rather ironical about the tactics adopted by those sworn to implement the theses in Britain. Dismayed by the continued foot-dragging of the old guard, the Young Turks organised themselves into what they themselves described as 'the nucleus', having as its object the overturning of the conservative executive majority and the instalment of one of their own number, namely Pollitt, as Party secretary. These aims they did not pursue through polemics in the Party press or an open campaign for a congress majority; that, after all, would not only have breached too blatantly the ban on factions, but have left undisturbed the emerging arbiter of all Communist affairs. For what the Dutt-Pollitt report left unsaid, but was made explicit elsewhere, was that the omnicompetent executive at the centre of their conception was itself beholden to the still higher authority of the International. It was thus behind closed doors in Moscow in the summer of 1923 that the first struggle for the British Communist Party reached its climax. So discreet were the manoeuvres of all concerned that the details have ever since remained obscure. It is only through the unexpected survival of an extraordinary cache of correspondence between the main conspirators that a fuller picture of the 'nucleus' and its intentions can at last be presented.

With the exception of Pollitt, who served as its proletarian figurehead, the nucleus was primarily a grouping of youthful intellectuals. Many, like Dutt, were associated with the CP's takeover of the Labour Research Department. Among them were Tom Wintringham and Esmond Higgins, both, like Dutt, Balliol-educated and both early visitors to Soviet Russia; Robin Page Arnot, the LRD's secretary; and a number of spirited young women of bourgeois antecedents who performed as secretaries, organisers and couriers. These included Mary Moorhouse, Lydia Packman, Rose Cohen and Eva Reckitt.

At the heart of the nucleus was what Pollitt described as 'the "Holy or Unholy Trinity"' comprising himself and the Dutts.[13] Already the grouping wielded considerable influence, not only through its representation on the Party executive but through its control of the main Party organ. The *Workers' Weekly* was set up under Dutt's editorship in February 1923 and conceived by him as 'an organ of working class life and struggle' directly rooted in the factories. Back in the shipyards after his work for the RILU and now bearing an increasing responsibility for the Party's industrial work, Pollitt's contribution was in this respect indispensable. He more than anybody, Dutt acknowledged later, built up the *Weekly*'s network of worker-correspondents and organised its own independent lines of distribution. The venture was a resounding success, doubling overnight the circulation of the paper's predecessor the *Communist*, which had been losing Comintern money hand over fist. The achievement did not pass unnoticed in the higher reaches of the International and Dutt's reputation there was enhanced accordingly.[14]

The least visible of the triumvirate, but evidently its moving force, was Salme Dutt, whose appreciable contribution to the CP's early history has hitherto gone unrecorded. Born in Estonia in 1888, Salme had already by the 1920s some considerable experience of revolutionary politics: first as a Moscow student who marched in the 1905 revolution, and later through her involvement with pro-Bolshevik elements of the Finnish left. Her first husband, Eino Pekkala, was a prominent Finnish left-wing social democrat who later became a Communist, while Salme herself maintained with her sister a recognised transit point for visitors to the early Soviet republic. She had by this time made contact with leading Bolshevik circles, and when she arrived in Britain on Comintern business in 1920 it was with Lenin's personal good wishes.[15] There can be no doubt that Salme derived some of her authority over her younger British comrades from this association with the grander achievements of Bolshevism. 'And now has come the hardest blow of all... leaving the world so sad and empty and the International somehow not meaning the same', Dutt wrote to her on Lenin's death. 'I felt through you Sa we understood so much all he meant, and therefore every word people say makes me angry.' On Pollitt too, who on his first visit to Moscow had felt a boyish impatience to see the revolution's leaders in the flesh and who regarded the day of his fleeting handshake with Lenin as the greatest of his life, her exalted background must have made a strong impression.[16]

Salme's authority rested on more than just the reflected prestige of the October Revolution, however. She had, as far as we can tell, for she did little work under her own name, a powerful and uncompromising intellect to which her associates evidently deferred. Already in 1922 she was involved in drafting the seminal report on Party organisation. Indeed, given that with their many other duties Pollitt and Dutt had only their evenings to spare for the work, it is more than likely that hers was the main contribution. During the period that followed it was only with considerable difficulty that she maintained regular contact with the rest of the nucleus. Living in Britain without papers and unknown even to most leading Communists, she was also afflicted by serious health problems which the lack of air, medical help and ordinary human contact only exacerbated. It was thus that she spent much of 1923 either recuperating far from London or else confined to her room near

Regent's Park, emerging, if at all, only after dark. In the wake of Borodin's arrest, security was understandably tight and for long periods even Dutt could communicate with her only by personal courier. 'Ever since your last letter I have so dreamt of just taking it on myself some long way round by early morning or night and simply appearing', he wrote wistfully in January 1924. 'But it would be madness and destruction.' In the meantime, their correspondence bore all the hallmarks of thwarted love and political subterfuge. 'I have been through all points with M, & all is clear', ran a typical letter. 'She should leave for P to-morrow, & return Tu evg or Wed morn. I should receive from her Wed aft document plus any new points if any, and we must again use emerg 1/1 3/2 7/2 2/3 1/4.' This may not be all that clear to us, but it does at least give something of the flavour of their correspondence.[17]

Though dependent on such awkward contrivances, Salme was consulted on all matters concerning the nucleus, while Pollitt at least felt it his duty to report to her on virtually his every doing. His was the role of the willing disciple, acutely aware of his own shortcomings and anxious to overcome them. 'Even if you did again have me placed against the wall and shot', he wrote to Salme after a rare personal audience, 'I don't mind, at least as long as you only talk about it. But I do just want to ask you, not to think you hurt my feelings when you criticise and tell me off, please go on doing it because it is what I need, and because I value your criticisms and help more than I can convey.' The note of humility was not Pollitt's alone but shared by their other collaborators. 'Get well quick', Dutt's assistant, Tom Wintringham, wrote to Salme in the West Country. 'We need a governess. I expect we are making horrible mistakes.'[18] Even Dutt himself felt in relation to Salme a sense almost of inadequacy far removed from the 'air of pontifical infallibility' he exuded in his dealings with others. 'I want to write on Leninism for the Notes', ran one of his requests for advice, 'but do not know if I dare.' Probably Dutt's writings are best regarded as a collaborative effort between the two, and at this stage at least Pollitt owed Salme a similar debt. 'I know its not fair to ask all these things off you', he wrote to her on one occasion, requesting a Party training manual and trades councils conference speech, 'but if [the] other crowd don't appreciate your efforts, you have a loyal group of comrades round you who do, and above them all, you know that

35

Yours sincerely Harry Pollitt does.'[19]

If Salme was, if one might so put it, the brains behind the nucleus, the further question then arises of her precise position vis-a-vis the Comintern itself. Through Dutt's secretary Mary Moorhouse, an associate from his days in student politics who later married Salme's first husband, the group appears to have had at least occasional contact with unnamed parties on the Continent. All that we know for certain, however, is that Salme had excellent relations with Otto Kuusinen, the Finnish Communist who was already emerging as one of the Comintern's most influential figures. Kuusinen's special responsibility was for organisational matters. He it was who had drafted the Comintern's organisational theses, and it may have been through his influence that the Dutts were given the job of forcing the new methods through in Britain. Certainly, he had known Salme back in her Finnish days and on her visit to Britain in 1920 he had provided her with the tsarist jewels that were then carried about almost as Comintern credentials. Apparently Kuusinen was a party to her secret relationship with Dutt, with whom he was 'already familiar' even before the latter's visit to Moscow in 1923. Indeed, although unable at the British commission that summer to obtain a hearing with the other Bolshevik leaders, Dutt had 'several long talks' with Kuusinen and 'reached a thorough understanding with him on our work & aims'. The following February Pollitt was similarly granted a five-hour audience with him, discussing amongst other things the Comintern statement on the new Labour Government that Kuusinen was drafting.[20]

Unlike Borodin, however, Salme appears to have had no official standing in Britain. Indeed, to judge from the secrecy in which it was shrouded, hers must either have been a private mission or else one sponsored only by the Comintern's innermost organs. It is certainly remarkable that her name crops up hardly at all even in confidential or unofficial memoirs of the period. The one exception is tantalising. In his book *Blowing Up India*, Philip Spratt recalled questioning the Indian Communist M. N. Roy as to the paradox of Dutt's 'dog-like loyalty' to Moscow. Roy had until 1929 been at the very centre of Comintern affairs and saw the 'key to the puzzle' in Dutt's beautiful and gifted wife. 'Dutt is completely dependent on her', Spratt wrote; 'Roy assured me that when he knew them, Dutt never published an article of importance unless she had certified its orthodoxy. Roy did not say so directly, but he led me to infer that she is a member of the highly secret inner organisation of the Comintern...'[21]

Presumably the reference is to the OMS or 'International Communications Section' of the Comintern, though if Spratt's inference was correct then it must also be stated that the CI's secret activities were in that case most inadequately subsidised. In later years in Brussels Dutt was reduced to haggling with the *Communist International* over unremunerated articles, while Salme herself was forced into 'irregular earning work' and later relied on the generosity of the Stracheys for help with medical treatment. Indeed, Celia Strachey recalled of visits to the Dutts that their intense and prolonged political discussions were rounded off, late into the night and to her epicurean disgust, by a frugal tin of sardines. The anecdote says as much about the Stracheys as the Dutts, but it does underline the disinterestedness of the latter's motives.[22]

If the overall picture is a confused one, what is certain is that in presenting their case in 1923 Salme's co-conspirators did their best to conceal the fact of her involvement. 'It is now pretty well known', wrote Pollitt, 'that Raji & I stood at the Bar of Justice and pleaded that we were the only two lads in the show...'[23] What one has to remember is that the Comintern was not yet the cumbersome monolith of later years, but like its British section was confused in its priorities and lines of command. It was, according to Kuusinen himself, a 'real bureaucratic muddle',[24] and it seems at least conceivable that, without the sanction or even perhaps the knowledge of sections of the Comintern apparatus, Kuusinen was backing the nucleus in its efforts to reconstruct the British Party in line with the theses for which he was responsible. Pending access to the official Comintern archives, that must remain a conjecture. What is certain is that through a series of mishaps and mis-judgements the nucleus botched its bid for the Party leadership and was fortunate to make even the limited political advances it did.

In their formal submissions on the British question, Pollitt and Dutt requested nothing less than the Comintern's direct intervention to replace virtually the entire existing Party leadership. The case they presented did little more than bring up to date that which Salme had put to Theodore Rothstein on the Party's formation three years earlier. Once again the CP's continuing

37

ineffectiveness was put down to the sectarian baggage it had to carry, as inherited leaders with inherited defects purported to lead the revolutionary struggle by 'the mere issue of manifestoes and statements in the air'. Even the formal adoption of Bolshevik organisational principles they had effectively stymied by their 'innumerable obstacles, conscious or unconscious'. 'The present conflict within the party', the rebels argued, 'is simply the fight with the old traditions and conservatism, which are still largely dominant and have the experience, while the new forces are young and inexperienced.' The struggle was no doubt inevitable and even salutary, but the intervention of the International was now necessary if the Party were not to waste itself on prolonged internal conflicts. 'This is only possible if the confusion, incomprehension and obstruction of the old forces are removed from the leading positions', as the rebels bluntly put it; and this they wanted settled once and for all by the higher authority to which old and new alike deferred.[25]

Even in the most favourable circumstances such drastic proposals would have met with strong resistance; and for reasons largely of the rebels' own making the circumstances were anything but favourable. Their first, and in Pollitt's estimation 'absolutely fatal', mistake was in not attending the sessions together. Immediately preceding the British commission was the Third ECCI Plenum, and yet for some unknown reason Dutt decided not to attend this, the first opportunity to discuss his proposals. How Pollitt wished afterwards that he had dragged him with him onto the boat train! Left to his own devices, he was forced to depart from their carefully contrived plans and put forward Dutt's name for Party secretary, simply because, as he privately confessed, he felt it improper to put forward his own. Such a proposal must have seemed almost as if designed to raise the hackles of the old guard. In any case, Pollitt seems by his own account to have adopted a fairly truculent approach to the proceedings. In particular he gave full vent to his old animus against Borodin, 'a RILU man first & foremost' who on the basis of reports from its British Bureau accused Pollitt of having sabotaged that movement in Britain. 'Borodin is hopeless', Pollitt fumed:

> Sneers at 'attempts to build a Party according to a diagram'. I waded like hell into him for this…. Everyone of the old school will hate me now. I shall be an Ishmael amongst them all. But we must go on now to the bitter end.

Possibly, in fact, the situation was less bleak than it seemed, for Pollitt had still at this point the support of Gallacher, of J. R. Campbell and of the sole Communist MP, Walton Newbold. He now had to return to Britain for the Labour Party conference, however; and with the appearance on the scene of Dutt, leaving Pollitt just an hour to 'play hell' with him for his late arrival, the rebels' baton passed to new and less competent hands.[26]

The proceedings that followed combined high drama and farce, with the latter predominating. The full plenum having broken up in haste with Dutt's propositions still to be discussed, it was then left to Borodin to organise the commission that would decide the British Party's future. The result Dutt described as a 'notorious absurdity'. 'It held only 4 sittings', he explained, 'none of which had any relation to the other, at each of which the personnel attending was largely different, at each of which the agenda was completely changed on the spur of the moment, and at none of which was any serious agenda taken.' Those intermittently present included Zinoviev, Radek and Bukharin, but none found time to discuss its business with Dutt. Only Radek seemed at all sympathetic to his case and the leanings of the others may perhaps be deduced from their invitation to the Party chairman, Arthur MacManus, to join them later for a holiday and further discussions in the Caucasus. No doubt they had in any case more absorbing matters to tear them from these rather desultory proceedings, and in due course the commission's business was passed to a sub-commission consisting to all intents and purposes of just Borodin and Dutt.[27]

By this time, moreover, the entire British delegation had been scandalised by an extraordinary provocation on the latter's part. For some time previously he had been running in the *Workers' Weekly* a fictional serial featuring a Manchester metalworker, passionately committed to socialism, who had moved down to London ready to give his all for the revolution. There was nothing at all subtle about the allusions, least of all when, in the issue that coincided with the rebels' bid for the Party leadership, the young hero came to terms in his own mind with the utter worthlessness of the 'old revolutionary chiefs'. Quite apart from their 'deep-lying petty sectionalism', their personal characteristics were subjected to the most outrageous slurs. One of them – apparently Tom Bell, formerly of the Socialist Labour Party – was dismissed as 'an old stubborn ass in everything

39

that runs counter to his old ingrained M.N.F. conceptions'. Another, 'not even sincere' but interested mainly in his salary, was branded as 'definitely demoralising, with all his old habits, including drinking'. That he even bore the same initials as MacManus, notorious in Moscow at least for his 'gargantuan boozing', betrayed if nothing else a certain heavy-handedness on Dutt's part. 'That started a real storm', Gallacher recalled of the episode. 'Dutt's proposition never had a chance but for a time it looked as tho this fictional effort would sink him and Harry Pollitt.'[28] Indeed, Gallacher was none too pleased about his own portrayal as an honest proletarian, but one easily led and over-indulgent towards his old cronies. 'You are talking like an old woman to-day, Jim', Gallacher's fictional alter ego was upbraided by the straight-talking hero; and it is not altogether surprising that the rebels' most influential ally should after that have supported them only in 'his characteristic idiosyncratic fashion, by absenting himself and keeping to his room'.[29] Dutt's awkward bourgeois manner only made things worse. Gallacher would long remember his inept proposal to replace the old chiefs with 'freshers', while Pollitt, on hearing of his comrade's blundering solo performance, immediately proposed to Salme 'a *united front* with me in an attack on Raji's shyness'. Whatever he had still to learn from his mentors, Pollitt had no doubt now to whom belonged the indispensable skills of political persuasion and leadership. When the 'prodigal son' returned, he wrote to Salme, it wouldn't be the fatted calf that got killed, 'but that damned old prodigal son stands a good chance any old how'.[30]

Pollitt's bantering recriminations apart, it was only against the rebels' own exaggerated expectations that the compromise reached by the commission could be construed as a defeat. True, there was no clean sweep and Pollitt was not installed as secretary. Even Radek, the most supportive of the Russians, felt the reformers wanted to go too fast, while Dutt recalled of the commission as a whole that 'it was as difficult to win their solid common sense for any new or startling proposition as to convince an average jury'.[31] Even so, the reformers were rewarded with a majority on the full-time Political Bureau, newly conceived as the CP's day-to-day executive authority, while Pollitt himself was given the key post of national organiser with responsibility for the Party's industrial work.[32]

40

On the main issue of principle, as to whether to launch a national opposition movement in the trade unions, the nucleus was less successful. In this proposal, pushed strongly by Borodin and by Losovsky of the RILU, Dutt discerned plans for the virtual dissolution of the Party and a reversion to the 'wide and shapeless movement' of local workers' committees long since found wanting. It would, he wrote, 'mean the replacement of the Party as an organisation with ramifications throughout the movement, and the establishment of a new system and outlook, corresponding more closely to the British temperament, national and "industrial" in character, and with weak links with the International'. His fears may not have been all that exaggerated, for according to one participant the proposed body was not at first conceived as 'a purely trade union and industrial organization' but as a 'broad workers' movement that would unite all left elements'. Possibly, as we shall see, it was only under Pollitt's eventual stewardship of the movement that such ambitions were definitely put to one side.[33] In the meantime, however, Dutt's objections were overruled, and as the new joint secretary to the British Bureau Gallacher was given the job of getting the new movement off the ground. 'The mind of the International', as a chastened Dutt put it to Pollitt, 'seems to be travelling in a different direction from what we have been thinking of.' Even so, with Gallacher's presumed willingness to liaise with Pollitt and their day-to-day contact on the Political Bureau, the old rivalry between the Party and the RILU seemed at last to have been overcome. Dutt's initial verdict that the rebels were 'completely beaten' was therefore somewhat melodramatic, and he at least was soon reconciled to taking the long view. 'It is clear that the Party is now going to be a slow and in some ways disheartening business', he wrote to Pollitt. 'I believe that we must work the compromise with an eye to the future, and above all maintain & build up our nucleus of a future party.' Pollitt remained less optimistic. 'I have no confidence in the new arrangement working at all', he wrote to Salme, 'and think it is all a — mess.'[34]

Pollitt's suppressed expletive expressed not only his disappointed ambitions but a sense of weariness with the endless sapping intrigues that now seemed set to continue. He was not of course immune to the jealousies and resentments that such conflicts produced. From South Wales that September, for example, he wrote bitterly of

41

obstructive local officials that he would 'live long enough to see a hell of a lot of people eat dirt'.[35] On another occasion Murphy was rash enough to mock the simplicity of Dutt's 'sheepish' acolyte, and was lucky to escape a hoof in the jaw. 'P said if it was anywhere but an EC', Dutt reported, 'he would "bash in" M for his impertinence.' Despite his pugnacity and quick temper, however, Pollitt was not one to thrive on these antagonisms or harbour for long a senseless grudge. Off-setting the scheming habits to which the Dutts had introduced him, he had developed already a strong sense of personal loyalty and of solidarity in the common struggle. For older comrades like Tom Bell he had a deep respect, and he remained on good terms with them throughout. Even the so nearly bashed-in Murphy noted in his memoirs that Pollitt's 'laughing brown eyes and readiness to crack a joke in the midst of the most serious discussion makes it difficult to quarrel with him even when the differences may be profound'.[36] In this natural charm and the good use to which he put it would lie one of the main clues to Pollitt's political effectiveness. His will to get on with people and achieve common ends was perfectly genuine, however, and that summer's internecine wranglings caused him real distress. It was, he wrote to Salme in tones of reluctant necessity, a 'bad job done' but 'one that had to be done sometime'. 'I have been downhearted many times these last three months, but your influence brought me back to my senses again', he went on. 'Its been a very hard and trying time, I suppose I can't make some of you understand how hard, just because there never existed the same feeling between you and the other people that there did between me and [them].... I do think that on occasions we are not pliable enough and we are apt to lose points because we try and push things too far.'[37]

From these traumas and collisions, Pollitt turned with alacrity to the bustle and purpose of the wider struggle. Even as he awaited Dutt's news from Moscow, he found in that summer's dock strike a more congenial focus for his activities. Day after day he was in the thick of it, organising the Party's supporters, stiffening the dockers' resistance and producing more or less through his own efforts four special editions of the *Workers' Weekly*. He thrived on the adrenalin of the class struggle, the speeches and processions, the banners and bands, the sense of engagement with the hated master class.[38] In his new role as CP national organiser he found at first a similar sense of involvement, as he travelled the country breathing what life he could into its flagging cadres. Despite his difficulties in South Wales and the 'depressing' state of the Party organisation, his overall impressions left him 'full of hope and confidence for the future'. It was a note he struck in a letter to the Wintringhams on their marriage at the end of August:

> Don't get downhearted in your work for the Party, because things appear to go slow, or because you meet with a certain amount of rebuffs from other people. I know this little Party inside out, and up and down this country are working some of the best comrades in the world, only their praises are not sung from the house tops, but they are steadily pegging away, unknown and unheard. These are the people who make the struggle worth the while, and the people to think of when things at King Street don't seem too pleasant, or when a lot of bloody fools are blathering about 'the intelligentsia', because none of you are any better than us poor *'workers'*, in fact the majority of you are a damn sight worse.

By this time he was acquiring too a growing confidence and indeed a sense of elation in his own burgeoning political talents. 'My political meetings have been simply wonderful', he wrote to Salme from Glasgow. 'I believe I can really tell the tale, the "MESSAGE" has been driven home, recruits won for the Party, the locals reinvigorated and its just been good to be alive.' In particular he described a meeting of some seventeen hundred workers in Greenock, addressed first of all by Campbell:

> Then the Chairman announced this lad, and in five minutes that audience was mine, and I had the time of my life. Made them laugh and made them cry, made them bitter and made them hopeful... and finally wound up amidst scenes of unparalleled enthusiasm by making 'The International' my peroration (Hurrah).

'Don't you wish you had been there?' he concluded. 'Of course you do.'[39]

Pollitt's uplifting national tour turned out to be something of an interlude, however. The excitement over, it was no doubt with a sinking feeling that he returned to King Street to encounter the same acrid atmosphere as before. That winter of 1923-24 there was indeed no shortage of issues to fuel the strife. One was Dutt's editorship of the *Workers' Weekly*. At the December EC Andrew

Rothstein, the son of Theodore, became 'venomously hostile' about the generous coverage the paper gave to Pollitt's activities. At the same blustery session Murphy indicted Dutt for his 'incapacity, bankruptcy and confusion' and spoke of replacing him as editor.[40] The formation of the first Labour Government in January 1924 provided another source of friction. Dutt had enormous problems making sense of the new phenomenon[41] and for his hesitancy and moderation was pilloried by Rothstein in the *Communist Review*. On this issue Zinoviev himself weighed in with a typically censorious communication in which the *Workers' Weekly* was again singled out for criticism.[42] It was a significant intervention, for on the decisions of the Comintern hung the outcome to the contest, and none of the jostling aspirants to its favours were so naive as to overlook the fact. In the pursuit of what Dutt described as a 'halo of authority' Pollitt himself made a further visit to Moscow in January 1924, and this despite his adversaries' best efforts to disrupt his plans. They were, Dutt reported, 'very contemptuous of running to consult the International', although they were not themselves above manoeuvring for the return of either Borodin or Rothstein's father Theodore as the CI's representative in Britain.[43] Even the organisation report reared its head again, as the reformers' 'organisational Fetishism' came under renewed attack in the *Communist Review*. Both Murphy and T. A. Jackson had their say, but the most trenchant contribution was that of the London district organiser, E. W. Cant. 'The truth is we have become so involved in organisational machinery that the essential spirit and life of the Party is being sapped', he wrote. 'Initiative is at a discount, and members are regarding themselves as mere Robots, creatures to obey the orders of the powers above, and not to think for themselves.'[44]

Pollitt's tart reply gave as little ground as ever to the so-called 'doubting comrades', and yet behind such displays of obduracy the nucleus was itself succumbing to all manner of doubts of its own. Indeed, so thoroughly did it rethink its strategy after its Moscow setback that by the time of the Sixth Party Congress in May 1924 it had conceded to its antagonists virtually every substantial point at issue. The change of heart was first signalled by Salme, who in her ill-health and enforced seclusion was no doubt particularly vulnerable to passing moods of despondency. To judge from Dutt's reply to a letter of hers that January, it would seem that on an assessment of the Party's size, influence and political competence, Salme had begun to wonder whether there might not be a case for actually dissolving the CP and establishing in its place a broader and looser body. It was precisely this alleged perspective of Losovsky's and Borodin's that Dutt had so fiercely resisted in Moscow, and he and Pollitt baulked at the audacity of the suggested volte-face. 'On all general theoretical grounds a case is made for dissolution', they conceded. 'But your "faint idea" that it would mean a step backwards is strongly echoed by us.' With his own recent experience of addressing crowds virtually the size of the Party's entire membership, Pollitt admitted that 'you would sweep in heaps to a "Workers Party", who are afraid of CP, that the thousands who attend C. meetings more numerously & enthusiastically than any others would come into some loose mass organisation'. After his recent tour of the Party districts, on the other hand, he felt with Dutt that the CP remained, with all its faults, 'perhaps... the best unifying crystallising factor in the movement'. With all the work they had put into the Party, they at least were prepared to give it another nine or twelve months or so, and their more cautious view prevailed.[45]

The very next month, however, a less drastic variant on the same theme presented itself, for on his visit to Moscow Pollitt was pressed by Losovsky to take charge of the broad industrial movement sketched out at the British commission. The intervening months had seen little progress in this direction, and for this dilatory performance Gallacher was held largely to blame. Having wanted Pollitt for the job in the first place, Losovsky now warned that a second refusal would mean the closing down of the British Bureau and the reallocation of its funds to the CP itself. Six months earlier the nucleus would have wished for nothing better. Now, however, Dutt favoured acceptance, if only as a means of subordinating the new movement to the Party as 'the inner and outer of the same thing'. Pollitt's position as national organiser was in any case becoming a severely circumscribed one, for like most of the notionally full-time Political Bureau he was by this time receiving no wages. In the organisation of the new movement he no doubt saw a more constructive outlet for his energies that kept him in step with the International and accorded with the new thinking of the Dutts. Moreover, in his desperation to secure his talents, Losovsky had promised him a comparatively free hand to shape the movement and thus minimise the dangers that he and Dutt had perceived at its inception. Devoting himself to industrial work, it was thus Pollitt who presented the resolution on the Minority Movement at the Sixth Party Congress that May and who was then elected the movement's secretary at its inaugural conference three months later.[46]

The decision meant a still more painful breach with Gallacher, who took the moves to replace him as a personal slight and swore to teach his detractors a lesson. It was, wrote Dutt of the 'long stupid wrangle' that ensued, a 'dismal scene like the murdering of a baby'.[47] With the loss of a further influential ally in Newbold, who was gradually detaching himself from the CP, the nucleus was gravely weakened; and this may explain the rebuff it received at the May Party Congress. In particular, the EC report put it quite bluntly that the 'over-concentration on the scheme of organisation' had 'resulted in the deterioration in the political quality of the party' and recommended a whole number of 'organisational adjustments' to remedy this. There was a breath almost of heresy as it went on to deplore the remoteness of the national and district leaderships, the neglect of old-style propaganda meetings, the indiscriminate profusion of directives, the overwork at local level and the lack of opportunities for social contact and political development. It is not at all clear, however, that on these questions the erstwhile rebels were any longer putting up much of a fight. Indeed, in advocating a qualified return to regional representation on the Party executive, Pollitt and Dutt retreated further even than the majority leadership found acceptable. It was indicative of their changing priorities that, having pressed so hard for the Party secretaryship a year previously, Pollitt did not even contest the last election to that post by the congress itself. It was not that he was incapable of winning, Dutt wrote, for Pollitt was indeed at the head of the poll for the EC, but 'he can't, it would disqualify all his Lab. movement work'.[48] The rebels had, it would seem, decided to work in the channels approved by the International, certain in the knowledge that their day would come.

Over the next three or four years Pollitt was concerned less with the CP's internal affairs than with the wider industrial movement of which it was to form the core. The Party was in any case relatively free from controversy in this period – as Pollitt wrote to one associate late in 1924, 'we are all becoming throroughly respectable and have forgotten the gentle art of fighting each other'.[49] Pollitt himself had neither the inclination nor the opportunity to renew old quarrels. Although nominally a member of ECCI, for example, it is not clear that he attended its meetings and he certainly did not attend another of its plenums until July 1929. Nor was he a delegate to the two world congresses held in the same period. On the one recorded occasion that he did visit Moscow on Party business, it was, characteristically, in connection with his industrial responsibilities. His pronouncements in the British Party press and at its congresses reflected the same concerns, and towards the end of the decade he was to find that amongst his 'dear comrades' there remained those who felt that 'Pollitt was a good trade unionist, but not a political man capable of becoming secretary of a Communist Party'.[50]

What such comments reveal among other things, perhaps, is that the shrewd and stubborn realism that Pollitt had acquired through his industrial activities was not a quality necessarily sought after in a Communist Party leader. His continued involvement in the wider Labour movement reinforced in him, not only the rhetorical and organisational skills valued by the Comintern, but a certain independence of outlook that the narrower confines of a King Street office might well have stifled. Like Horner among the South Wales miners and Hannington among the unemployed, Pollitt experienced at first hand the pressures and constraints under which Communist policies had actually to be carried out. To these insights he would owe much of his effectiveness as a working-class leader, outspoken sometimes in his impatience with the Tatlin-like constructions of Comintern ideologists. It was a trait that in due course would set him definitely apart from those abstracted functionaries, the Dutts and Rusts, who seemed to flourish only in their own rarefied surroundings.

The National Minority Movement, to which Pollitt's main energies were devoted, was the successor in many ways to the old workers'-committee type of movement, albeit more systematically organised over a whole range of industries.[51] At its peak in 1926 over five hundred organisations were represented at its annual conference and it had thriving mining, engineering and transport sections. In theory the movement was subjected to tight Communist discipline, exercised through structures analogous to the Party's own and reinforced by its financial dependence on the Profintern. In practice, however, what Pollitt and his colleagues managed to piece

47

together was an untidy patchwork of personal contacts, local committees and Labour movement affiliations, requiring of its organisers a good deal of supple pragmatism. Indeed, the movement's ambitions went much further than winning for its nostrums the Cooks, Tanners and Gossips publicly identified as its supporters. As its very name suggests, it was conceived not as the nucleus of an alternative trade union centre, but as a vehicle for the transformation of the Labour movement from within. Pollitt had thus among his many tasks to organise the minority's supporters at the majority's official gatherings. Every year from 1921 until his disqualification on political grounds in 1928, he was elected by handsome margins to represent the Boilermakers at the conferences of the Labour Party, TUC and General Federation of Trade Unions. Evidently his eloquence and straightforwardness made a wide impression and he soon learnt better than to squander this by snubbing well-wishers, as he had Ben Tillett at his first TUC. Even in the case of MacDonald he drew the line at the personal insults that were to give the Communists such a bad name. 'It is idle to deny this fact', he chided his associates in 1925, 'the English Movement is used to conducting its politics in a "gentlemanly" way and the acute personal criticisms that has [sic] been a rather marked feature during the last 12 months against MacDonald, has not strengthened us, but has certainly made it easy for Mr MacDonald to play upon it... [and] leave vital points of principle untouched...'[52]

Of course there was a strong element of calculation in this, although it is interesting that the TUC secretary Walter Citrine – as unyielding, though not as vain, an adversary as MacDonald himself – should have recalled Pollitt fondly in his memoirs. The Communists as a whole Citrine thought a very poor lot, with their 'hackneyed phrases and stereotyped vituperation'; but Pollitt and Arthur Horner he remembered as 'inherently decent fellows' with 'good reasoning faculties except when Communist dogma bemused them'. 'Neither of them', he went on, 'ever seemed to bear any resentment towards me personally.' Already Pollitt was demonstrating his priceless ability to win the confidence of those who abhorred his politics. It was testimony indeed to his personal magnetism that even an observer from the fiercely anti-Communist SPD paper *Vorwärts* should have described him in 1929 as 'a highly gifted man who towers head and shoulders above the average trade-union leader'.[53]

Pollitt's profound familiarity with the ways of British Labour derived not only from his insider's feel for the movement's basic institutions but from his daily contact with the class he aspired to lead. Strictly speaking, his post as Minority Movement secretary was an honorary one and until the end of 1927 he had still by and large to seek a living at his trade. This lived experience of post-war slump and underemployment were an antidote, no doubt, to romanticised notions of working-class heroism more easily sustained at a distance. In a letter to Salme in 1923, he described seeking work at the shipyard each morning, only to find that he was marked already as a Bolshevik and troublemaker. 'My youthful beauty goes unappreciated', he wrote, 'the Boss walks by & scorns me':

> I told the Boys this, and in my enthusiasm, expected them to down tools, because I was being victimised but did they? Did they blazes, instead they went on working harder than ever, and even went on overtime.
>
> Oh the Masses, oh the solidarity of the workers, I could sing their praises in ten different languages, and then reserve something for an encore.[54]

At this stage at least, it would appear, Pollitt had that first requirement of effective Communist leadership, a clear appreciation of the distinction between the rhetoric of the struggle and its daily realities.

During this period as Minority Movement secretary, the whole thrust of his public pronouncements was towards overcoming the sectional divisions of organised Labour. If a single event could have summed up the lessons the early 1920s had for militant trade unionists, it was Black Friday, 15 April 1921, when after a threatened general strike the miners were abandoned to fight and lose their cause alone; and if the Minority Movement had one aim above all others, it was that when next the lines of battle were drawn there would be neither wavering nor disunity in the workers' ranks. While the old objectives of industrial unionism were by no means discarded, the Communists sought a more immediate antidote to sectionalism in a strengthened TUC General Council. Pollitt himself spoke to this effect as early as the 1922 TUC and it was to be one of the guiding aims of the Minority Movement. 'The anarchy of separating competing unions... and an unreal powerless General Council is utterly unfit to lead a united and disciplined working-class army', he wrote in 1924. 'We stand for the creation of a real General Council that shall have the power to direct, unite and co-ordinate all the struggles and activities of the trade unions, and so make it possible to end the present chaos and go forward in a united attack...'

The conception of a general staff, empowered to call out its disciplined battalions, was certainly in keeping with the centralising imperatives of Communism; but the drive for unity had a local dimension too, in the mainly hypothetical factory committees and in the trades councils. The National Federation of Trades Councils was in fact set up largely on the Communists' initiative, and it was Pollitt who delivered the presidential address to its second annual conference in November 1923. The General Council, he wrote on that occasion, was like a 'head without a body' and it would more and more fall upon the trades councils to execute the 'plans and campaigns of a centrally directed trade union movement'. Even internationally the watchword was unity, as from its establishment in 1925 the Russians sought through the Anglo-Russian trade union committee to heal the breach between the 'red' and 'yellow' trade union internationals. It was on this issue that Pollitt had sought instructions in Moscow the previous November and over the next few months he took the lead in promoting 'international trade union unity' in Britain. It was indeed an issue that tied in perfectly with the call to strengthen the General Council, for by its tenderness towards the Russians that essentially timorous body managed to deceive even hard-nosed revolutionaries as to its real character. Was it not Pollitt himself, after all, who after the Scarborough TUC of 1925 declared that 'outside Russia, the British Movement is the real International leader'?[55]

Needless to say, Labour's parliamentary advances drew from Pollitt no such effusions. On the contrary, his underlying belief in the primacy of the industrial wing of the movement over its political manifestations betrayed rooted syndicalist instincts that not even his grooming by the Dutts had eradicated. Indeed, in their differing evaluations of economic struggles there was detectable from the start a certain tension between Pollitt and Dutt that would at a later time surface in their first open disagreement. Even as they put the finishing touches to their report on Party organisation in 1922, Dutt subjected the idea of a TUC general staff, empowered to lead the workers' struggle, to a scathing refutation in his 'Notes of the Month'. Given their daily contact at this time, his public criticisms must surely have echoed many a private argument with Pollitt, for he called into question not just a particular slogan but the very notion of a revolutionary trade unionism. 'The economic struggle', he asserted, 'is always separatist, it only directly affects different sections of the workers at different times, as the employers' campaign is skilfully turned, now on this section, now on that... and that is why the General Council, arising out of and for trade unionism and the economic struggle, can never unite the workers.' Only their political party could achieve this, he went on, for only the basic issue of political power affected every worker equally in a common interest. This emphasis of his helps explain, perhaps, what has so often seemed inexplicable, namely Dutt's initial warmth of feeling towards the first MacDonald Government. '[The] object is not... this or that sectional or limited aim', he wrote on its formation, 'the object is Power itself, the Power of Government and the State, Power to mould the world anew and bring in a workers' society.... Therefore the first need for all of us... whatever our differences, whatever our criticisms and distrusts, is to unite in support of a Workers' Government and its supremacy first and foremost and to exert all our forces one and all to fight on its behalf foursquare against the whole capitalist world.'[56]

Both his disparagement of the economic struggle and his intoxication with the Labour Government, Dutt had quickly to set to rights. In this respect it was rather Pollitt whose instincts accorded more closely with the priorities of the Comintern. Even as they scorned the Labour Party, the likes of Zinoviev nurtured fond hopes that the unions would at last provide the elusive opening through which Communism would arrive in Britain. Until the debacle of 1926, indeed, the fixation with the TUC took almost as firm a hold of the Kremlin as of King Street. In the meantime Polllitt continued to voice sentiments not so very far removed from his earlier anti-parliamentarism. In 1922, for example, he complained after the Southport TUC of 'the blighting hand of the Parliamentarians', 'afraid of a General Staff that might develop to the extent of overshadowing them' and resistant to 'any movement in the industrial world that is likely to challenge their power'. With Labour in office two years later, he put it that the government's obligations were to the TUC and not vice versa, and that the latter should issue MacDonald with a 'definite ultimatum' as to his future lines of policy. The CP's defeats at the same year's Labour conference he then put down to the 'middle-class politicians' bent on 'Liberalising the Party, and making it easier to appeal to the petty-bourgeoisie'. 'The conference is a machine', he went on:

> It does not represent the workers. It is dominated by Parliamentary candidates, Labour Party and Trade Union officials, and intellectuals, all of whom have forgotten the bitterness of the class struggle. Consequently, the air of unreality, intrigue and compromise is ever present.... The class struggle is suppressed because it isn't gentlemanly.

Pollitt's own alternative to the party charades of Westminster, inasmuch as he spelt one out, had a pronounced syndicalist flavour. The 'supreme revolutionary objective' of trade unionism he defined in 1924 as the control of industry 'by the workers engaged in production organised on the basis of production'. Certainly he acknowledged that this required the conquest of political power, but he nevertheless seemed to accord to the organs of economic struggle the pre-eminent role in achieving these aims. 'The Trade Union Movement', he wrote, 'can only realise itself when it enters unhesitatingly into the struggle for the dictatorship of the prole-tariat, and organises all its forces for the objective of capturing the control of production.' The absence in this as in most of his pronouncements of any explicit role for the revolutionary party, either in securing or administering the new society, should not perhaps be over-emphasised. After all, when a year or two later Pollitt had to choose between his trade union ambitions and the Communist Party, there was never any question but that he would opt for the latter. What is clear, however, is that Pollitt's Communism had by no means entirely displaced the syndicalism through which he had originally come to the Party. In the confusion of ideas and ideologies in the 1920s, probably not even Pollitt himself could have said whether the CP existed to provide the trade unions with effective revolutionary leadership, or whether it was rather the unions that were to provide the CP with the mass movement it needed to carry out its revolution.[57].

Such casuistries aside, the Minority Movement's basic perspective was nevertheless clear: one of mounting economic clashes, ever broader in scope and culminating at last in a gigantic head-on clash with the employers and their state. That was the meaning behind all the talk of general staffs and disciplined armies; and for just a moment in 1925, amidst the euphoria of Red Friday and the braggadocio of the Scarborough TUC, it seemed as if there might indeed be something in these well-worn military metaphors. Certainly Pollitt could not resist that conclusion. '…the trade unions have won a great victory this week', he wrote to a union colleague of Red Friday, 'not by democratic means, or talking about the will of the people at the ballot box, BUT, My Lad, By the threat of Direct Action. Which would have meant civil war had it been put into operation.'[58]

From this perspective, the General Strike of May 1926 was both a prophecy fulfilled and a vision shattered. In many respects, the Communists' analyses and prognoses were fully borne out by the event. On the one side was revealed the crude partiality of the state, to which Churchill's armoured cars added an appropriate note of visual drama. On the other, there was the massive solidarity of the strikers, a million and a half strong, and the resourcefulness displayed by the trades councils as the local organising centres of a class in struggle. There was more than enough here to construct a myth with, and by their own outstanding contributions up and down the country the Communists fully earned the right to promote their own version of it. Nevertheless, in the manner and basic fact of defeat, the strike dealt a heavy blow to their most cherished political scenarios. On the one hand, the CP's exaggerated hopes in its Labour movement allies were dashed by the TUC's pusillanimous retreat. What, after all, could have echoed more forlornly than the slogan *All Power to the General Council* as that body scurried to retrieve the gauntlet it had thrown down to the government? It was moreover clear that the Communists had little more idea than anybody else as to how so momentous a conflict could successfully be resolved. If they at least understood that this was no mere wage dispute but a challenge to the constitution, they could nevertheless envisage no bolder outcome to the crisis than that quintessence of constitutionalism, a Labour cabinet.

As Thomas plotted and MacDonald fretted, nothing perhaps could have summed up better the CP's impotence in the face of defeat and confusion as to what might have constituted a victory. If what they perceived as a shameless betrayal left the Communists with a bitter legacy of distrust, there was a profounder lesson too that they did not for a long time come to terms with. Just as Red Friday had succeeded Black Friday, so the Communists would look to a new wave of industrial strife to pose again the question of power and avenge the crushing of the miners. On this occasion, however, the setback was of a qualitatively different order. The years of overreaching militancy were at an end, and the vistas closed that had lured a whole generation of revolutionaries. It was a lesson that came most readily to those to whom it was most welcome. 'The failure of the General Strike of 1926 will be one of the most significant landmarks in the history of the British working class', wrote Beatrice Webb in her diary on the very day the strike began. 'Future historians will, I think, regard it as the death gasp of the pernicious doctrine of "workers' control" of public affairs through the trade unions, and by the method of direct action.... it was a proletarian distemper which had to run its course...'[59]

While the strike was thus an event of immense significance to Pollitt and the movements in which he played a part, his personal involvement was less even than that of Beatrice Webb in her Hampshire retreat. This, needless to say, was not a decision of his own making. In a single eventful week the previous October he had first married the Communist schoolteacher Marjorie Brewer and then, with eleven of his comrades, been arrested on charges of seditious libel and incitement to mutiny. It was the flimsiest of eighteenth-century pretexts, and in launching the prosecution the Tories betrayed a hint of the panic and paranoia of their forebears in an earlier age of revolution. It was, in C. L. Mowat's words, 'the chief instance of a purely political trial in the interwar years' and Pollitt was one among three of the accused who mounted the political defence the charges warranted. Neither his eloquent restatement of the case for Communism nor the objections of the lawyers were to sway ex-Tory MP Mr Justice Swift. Sentenced to twelve months as a previous offender, it was thus that to his immense frustration Pollitt spent the period of the General Strike in Wandsworth Prison, studying history and sewing mailbags. What affronted him most about the experience, he later recalled, were the egregious sentiments of the prison chaplain, the insanitary and disgusting shaving facilities and having to wash greasy plates in cold water. During the ten months he spent there he had ample time to reflect on the nature of British justice, and we can be sure that his thoughts brought him no closer to the acceptance of conventional liberal pieties.[60]

By the time he was released on 10 September, the miners, left once again to fight alone, had entered the final stage of their dogged, hopeless struggle. Already in the less militant coalfields the trickle back to work had begun, and in October Pollitt repaired to the East Midlands to impart to the wavering and half-starving his own sense of determination. 'Harry, go and tell them that before the men shall go back to longer hours, we'll eat grass!', he reported a miner's wife in Hucknall as saying, and these were indeed the only sentiments that he wished to hear. To the very end the Communists preached total intransigence and reserved their fiercest invective for the alleged treachery by which the union leaderships, and they alone, had forestalled victory. This miserable scurvy of reformism was the only proletarian distemper that Pollitt would have recognised, and so far from accepting that the tide of direct action had now receded, the Communists looked even in defeat to the resurgent militancy of the masses. 'The General Strike, given a new leadership, is still the most powerful weapon in the workers' armoury', Pollitt insisted in February 1927. 'The plain facts of the class struggle make future General Strikes inevitable.' That summer the CP went even further in pressing for the immediate organisation of such a strike to defeat the Trades Disputes Act and bring down the government.[61]

The unreality of such aspirations, at a time when mainstream union opinion was edging towards a closer accommodation with victorious capital, only served to widen the breach opened up already by the post mortems on the General Strike. The TUC itself and a number of individual unions were beginning to adopt measures designed to marginalise or exclude the Communists, and amongst them Pollitt's own union was one of the first. In 1927 his co-delegates to the TUC accused him in the society's *Monthly Report* of speaking chiefly 'in favour of the Russian point of view as against our own'; and in view of the membership's recalcitrance in repeatedly electing him to this position, the executive followed this up the following year by banning Communists from contesting all such elections.[62] The rift between Pollitt and the society's left-leaning secretary John Hill was but one expression of a more or less general divergence between Communists and the rest of the Labour movement. During 1928-29 this renunciation of reformism and everything tainted by it would take a hysterical and near-absolutist form, as the whole Communist International cavorted to the left. That Pollitt was one of the pioneers of this so-called 'new line' in Britain had less to do, perhaps, with any special intensity of feeling on his part than with the privileged access he apparently had to the mind of the International. This in itself was very much bound up with his continuing relationship with the Dutts, now domiciled a boat journey closer to Moscow in Brussels.

After the British commission of 1923 Dutt's immediate thought had been that the nucleus had somehow to 'proletarianise' itself if it were to acquire a greater credibility in Communist circles. He in particular had been derided as an 'intellectual' and 'phrasemonger', and to dispel the impression he made earnest efforts over the following few months to organise a Party fraction in his local branch of the General and Municipal Workers' Union. This period of 'rough and tumble' work, conscientiously reported to Salme, was to prove short-lived.[63] Evidently the couple were drawn by some swifter and more congenial route to their political goals, for late in 1924 they removed themselves to the foreign city whose physical remoteness rather conveyed something of their relationship with the British working class. Ostensibly the cause of the move was Dutt's ill-health, although it is not at all clear what Brussels had to offer in the way of treatment or climate that England had not. There is no doubt that, in the words of one of the all-night staff at the *Workers' Weekly*, Dutt 'ruined his health working day & night without stopping'. In his correspondence with Pollitt there are moreover numerous references to his infirmities, treatments, relapses and collapses. These were not however such as to confine him to Brussels, and by the time of his return to England in 1936 Dutt had paid visits to Paris, Moscow, Helsinki and Lausanne, amongst other cities. Salme's health problems, including asthma, arteriosclerosis and at one point semi-paralysis of both arms, were far more serious, but these required treatment not in Brussels but in Berlin and Wiesbaden.[64] Nor had the couple eloped to secure a more normal married life, for after weeks of careful plotting they had earlier in 1924 been legally married at the British Consulate in Stockholm and Salme thus accorded her rights of British citizenship.

One can only assume, therefore, that the Dutts had crossed the Channel to link up in some way with the Comintern's West European network, although how exactly and in what capacity is not entirely clear. From mid-1929 we know that Dutt received from the International a monthly stipend of ten pounds, presumably on account of his considerable contribution to British Party affairs.[65] From his flat in Brussels he drafted a great number of leading Party documents, maintained a close working contact with the Political Bureau and sent regular communications on Party policy to be read or circulated to the entire Central Committee. To judge from their pedagogic and occasionally officious tone, these carried more than just Dutt's personal authority, and of his claim in 1929 that he was 'shelved away in a corner... and only occasionally intervening at all with very humble expressions of opinion', one can only say that it was that of a veritable Uriah Heep.[66]

Before the big shake-up of the Party leadership that year, however, the picture is much more fragmentary. We know that Dutt's brother Clemens, heavily involved in the anti-imperialist activities organised by the Comintern from Paris, paid him a number of visits. We know too that on at least one occasion Dutt's secretary Mary Moorhouse had talks with Kuusinen in Moscow, while Salme's sister Hella also called to see him on her frequent visits to the Russian capital. Indeed, when Aino Kuusinen was interrogated in the Lubianka about her husband's alleged espionage activities in 1938, she felt certain that it was on the basis of his relations with these three women that the trumped-up charges had been concocted.[67] Beyond that, however, we are stumbling in the dark: like the Belgian police who first arrested Dutt and Moorhouse in 1925 and then let them go without charging them. It should however be noted that in the same year the British Party raised the question of Dutt's prolonged 'leave of absence' with the International and evidently received a satisfactory reply. The anomaly by which he served on the Party's leading bodies from a foreign country thus went without public challenge, even as during the late 1920s he posed once again the sharpest possible threat to the existing leadership. That, when one considers the moves to exclude two of Dutt's allies from the Central Committee on the grounds that, living in Moscow, they could not attend its sessions, was really rather extraordinary.[68] The same year there was some suggestion that Dutt be removed but, as

Pollitt put it to his colleagues, 'if this Central Committee strikes out R.P.D. the C.I. will rightly put him back'. He at least understood that in his self-imposed exile Dutt had powerful supporters within the Comintern apparatus.

Amongst the British Communists with whom the Dutts maintained contact in the 1920s, Pollitt remained the closest to their concerns. Only the odd letter between them survives, unfortunately, but this is enough to give a hint of their warm but zealous stewardship of his affairs. 'My Dear Ward', Pollitt addressed Salme, a reference to Kuusinen once having instructed him to take care of her during her English sojourn and a characteristic inversion of their actual relationship,

> My Dear Ward, My Dear Wards Husband, & My Dear Mary, the Protector of My Ward, My Wards Husband, and all the other members of the Flock.... I swear on my Beard that I will come over before November is out. I was going to the Plenum, but now I have to get back in the workshop again and that is impossible. I do want to see you, just as much as you want to see me.

That was written on the very day that Pollitt was arrested in 1925. Even before his release the following September, Dutt had set out for him seven pages of tightly packed guidelines for the forthcoming TUC. 'Of course', he added, 'as soon as you are through the TUC (hoping and praying you get there) I have quite separate a diary of political events in general for you so as to make up leeway for the twelve months.' No doubt it was in this connection that Pollitt attended the founding conference of the League Against Imperialism in Brussels the following February. In general, however, the workshop and all that that involved meant that he was unable to heed Dutt's repeated entreaties to visit him and suffered the latter's reproaches accordingly. 'I don't count those half hour snatches between trains', Dutt wrote after a rare difference of opinion, 'and I know if only we could have a proper visit from you, with time, we could clear up a lot, and it would make a whole world of difference.'[69]

That was in March 1928. By this time, however, the old sparring partners had already entered a new and productive phase of their relationship. In the Comintern's headlong plunge to the left, evident already by the end of 1927, they saw the chance at last of a renewed

58

assault on the Party old guard, this time with the support of the International. Just as in 1923, it was Pollitt they envisaged at the head of the Party, and the two of them therefore got together for a fateful tête-à-tête in Brussels. 'I said that the opportunity we had been waiting for had now arisen', Dutt recalled, 'and I would guarantee that he would be General Secretary of the Party in twelve months.' Only a few months later than Dutt had anticipated, that was indeed what came to pass in August 1929. In the long term it meant the fulfilment of Pollitt's most cherished ambition and a role that he would, over the next quarter of a century, make his own. In the short term, however, it meant another wearying internal struggle which, as Pollitt later recalled, reduced the Party to its 'lowest ebb in membership, organisation, morale and leadership', and left even Pollitt himself briefly disillusioned with the spoils of victory.[70]

3 New line, new leader

It was only at the end of the 1920s that the Comintern was reduced by Stalin to its final state of undifferentiated subservience. In his monumental history of the Russian Revolution up to that time, E. H. Carr rightly accorded the International a prominence in that country's early affairs that for the ensuing period would have seemed merely eccentric. Throughout that first decade there remained in this relationship a real element of friction and interaction, as Communist policy in Germany, China and even Britain sparked off debates within the Russian Party, while the latter's factional struggles had an echo in even the most parochial and far-flung of its offshoots. Even the final clearout of 1928-29 had something of this character. Its principal target, Bukharin, was not only a force within Russia but the head of the Comintern, and Stalin therefore pursued his vendetta against the right through every one of its national sections. If superficially this marked a shift to the left, the real significance of this last wave of exclusions and preferments was to annul all such factions and distinctions within Communist politics. Instead, there was installed at the head of each purified Central Committee some pliant figure for whom neither left nor right existed except in so far as Stalin defined them. In Germany, for example, it was in 1928 that through the Comintern's intervention Ernst Thaelmann survived a last challenge to his leadership, to see off the 'rights' and 'conciliators' as he previously had the 'lefts'. In the USA, the dominant Lovestone group was hounded out the following year, and the inconspicuous figure of Earl Browder added to the secretariat to take full control in 1930. In France, Poland, Sweden, Australia, in every country where Stalin's writ ran the pattern was essentially the same.

Britain was no exception, and Pollitt's elevation to the Party leadership in the summer of 1929 should thus be seen as but the native expression of a much broader phenomenon: the emergence of what we might call the Stalin generation of Communist Party leaders. The linkages with events elsewhere were graphically illustrated that March when Pollitt represented the Comintern at the defiant Sixth Convention of the CPUSA. Accompanying him was Thaelmann's lieutenant Philip Dengel, and together they budged not an inch as their bludgeoning orders from Moscow provoked the just indignation of the convention's recalcitrant majority. Possibly it was Pollitt's imperviousness to argument and mere force of numbers on this occasion that confirmed for those above him that here indeed was fit material to lead a Communist Party. Certainly, it was one of the few such disputes in which Stalin himself took an overt personal interest, and in his entrustment with this important business Pollitt was bestowed an unmistakable mark of favour.[1]

If in Britain Pollitt was thus 'the Comintern's man in charge', as Henry Pelling put it,[2] his position was nevertheless a good deal more ambivalent than that implies. Already as he was manoeuvred into the leadership, there was apparent in his motivations and behaviour much that distinguished him from such ultramontanes as Thorez and Thaelmann. It was not simply that he evinced significant reservations about the new line, even as it propelled him towards the leadership. Nor was it his identification in many respects with the discarded Party old guard, although that too entered into it. More fundamental than these temporary aberrations were the stubborn notions of collective responsibility, personal loyalty, common sense and plain speaking that made of Pollitt such an unlikely instrument of Stalin's dictatorship. He did not, of course, survive twenty-five years as CP general secretary without a very clear appreciation of the limits to this plain speaking and of the constraints upon all but his primary allegiance to Moscow. But if Pollitt was part of the bureaucratic web that Stalin threw round the Comintern, he also knew the feeling of being entrapped by the very structures that supported him. Even as he succeeded to the leadership, indeed, it was in such sour and divisive circumstances that he felt no gloating sense of triumph but rather 'despondency and disbelief in everything about the party'.[3] The paradox was that, just as in 1923, Pollitt himself had played no small part in instigating the very controversies that, as their full consequences were worked out, he then found so dispiriting.

At the heart of the new line of 'Class Against Class' was the Comintern's analysis of the so-called 'third period' of post-war

61

capitalism as one of economic catastrophe and revolutionary opportunity. The defining issue was thus the approaching struggle for power itself, setting Communists against all who abjured their insurrectionary aims and particularly against all forms of social democracy. Perceived anew as the last bulwark of class rule, the latter was eventually designated 'social fascism', as for a while there seemed to be almost no limit to the Communists' all-surpassing sectarianism. Its full development took time, however, and when first sketched out in relation to Britain the new line took only the comparatively modest and defensible form of a breach with the Labour Party.

Pollitt was associated with the new policy from the very beginning. When first British Party representatives were consulted on the matter in December 1927, they had the impression on arriving in Moscow that their business had already been discussed and definite conclusions reached. Amongst those privy to these earlier discussions, albeit in an unofficial capacity, was Pollitt. In October and November 1927 he had visited Moscow and there discussed the new approach with leading international figures including Stalin and Bukharin. Initially he resisted their line of argument and from one of the comrades 'got a hammering... which lasted 8 hours'. Even so, to the grudging convert from anti-parliamentarism who had never really overcome his suspicions of the Labour Party, the call for a sharper assertion of the CP's separate identity cannot have been entirely unwelcome. On other issues Pollitt would drag his heels, as his colleagues did on this, but in this instance he appears to have agreed there and then to pursue the same objectives from within the British Party. It was in this connection no doubt that he packed away his tools on his return, to devote himself henceforth to full-time political work. Already he must have stopped by in Brussels to co-ordinate his efforts with Dutt, for even before the January Central Committee debated the question the latter was writing to clarify for Pollitt what he called 'our line'. On the Central Committee itself the rebels were, as five years previously, in a minority, but this they now regarded as no more than a temporary inconvenience. 'Our duty is to strengthen the hands of the International in every possible way', Dutt wrote to Pollitt before the three-day long debate. 'We need not be troubled if we are defeated this time. The issue will arise again, and can only end one way.' It was thus that when the

Comintern's Ninth Plenum the following month held a special commission on the British situation, it was presented not only with the Party's majority viewpoint but with a minority statement in Pollitt's and Dutt's names that conveyed the essence of what the International wanted to hear.[4]

In this statement, drafted by Dutt, were present already many of the key elements of 'Class Against Class'. Its central theme was the growing disjunction between the ever-deepening class struggle and the pacific and coalitionist orientation of the Labour Party. The previous seven years of capitalist decline, it was argued, had seen the 'continuous *revolutionisation*' of the working class, taking the movement higher even than the 'temporary boom point' of 1920 and giving promise of still sharper struggles to come. None of this found expression in the Labour Party, however, which had in the same period abandoned its loose ecumenical structures for a 'limited opportunist basis' and 'openly reactionary programme'. The Communists themselves were being systematically excluded, leaving only a 'pseudo-left' indistinguishable in practice from the right. For these reasons, Lenin's advice to Communists in 1920, to work through the Labour Party and for a Labour government, no longer held good. Already the latter part of the miners' struggle, with 'three-quarters of a million miners... following the direct lead of the Communist Party', had marked out the clearer path of independent leadership. It was to further this approach that Pollitt and Dutt put forward their specific recommendations. The next general election, they argued, the CP should fight in direct opposition to the Labour Party, contesting as many seats as possible and targeting particularly those of prominent Labour leaders. In the meantime, the Party should drop its campaign for affiliation and work within those Labour Party channels still open to it exclusively for purposes of 'agitation and exposure (not collaboration)'. Only on the question of the National Left Wing Movement, which united Communists and their Labour Party sympathisers, did they take a more cautious line, and that was because Dutt overrode his more impetuous partner. Pollitt's own instincts had been to liquidate the movement straight away and thus oblige its supporters to make their choice between Communism and Labour.[5]

As neither Pollitt nor Dutt attended the Moscow plenum, their case was entrusted to a close associate of theirs since the days of the nucleus, R. Page Arnot. Superficially the commission's decisions, particularly that to continue the campaign for Labour Party affiliation, represented something of a compromise. The essential thrust of the resulting thesis, however, was that of the minority submission, and Dutt, who had in any case foreseen the need for some initial sop to the existing leadership, had no hesitation in describing it as a 'smashing vindication' of his and Pollitt's position. On the points that remained unresolved there followed many months of continually renewed debate until the Central Committee was eventually won for the full application of the international line. Always, whether the question was Communist affiliation to the Labour Party, urging the unions to disaffiliate or campaigning for by-election abstentions, Pollitt was to the fore in dragging his colleagues to the left.[6] Only on the question of withholding the political levy did he hold back, and this itself reflected no lingering attachment to the Labour Party but the centrality of the unions to his political designs. '... so long as... we pay the levy as a means of conducting an offensive fight against the Bureaucracy, and... of interesting the masses in revolutionary politics', he wrote after successfully defending this policy at the CP's Tenth Congress in January 1929, 'by winning more support for the local retention of all the levy in support of our Party policies... we place the whole question of trade unions and politics in an entirely new and revolutionary perspective'.[7]

As the earliest and most consistent protagonist of the new line, it was only appropriate that Pollitt should have been its main standard-bearer when it faced its first major electoral test. In the general election of May 1929 he took on MacDonald himself in the Durham mining constituency of Seaham, and his doomed, quixotic effort was like a microcosm of the period's follies. There was, for example, his initial adoption meeting at which not a soul turned up, the penalty no doubt for being drawn to Seaham by the Labour leader and not by any existing Communist organisation. Then there was Pollitt's address, drafted for him by Dutt and with not a word of it that could be called ingratiating. 'DOWN WITH CONSERVATISM, LIBERALISM AND LABOURISM – THE THREE ALLIES OF THE UNITED FRONT OF MONDISM AND EMPIRE!', it thundered. Down with their sham elections and parliamentary puppet show, and 'forward under the battle-cry of "Class Against Class"'. There was too, almost like a minor allegory, Pollitt's election-day cavalcade: a battered baby Austin, bravely fluttering with red bunting but pelted with mud and rotten fruit until at last, confronted with the glistening complacency of MacDonald's Rolls Royce, its wheel came off in despair. More ominous, of course, was the 'stony silence' in which the electors heard Pollitt's case, 'for no matter what I did in Seaham Harbour', he later recalled, 'it was impossible to raise any enthusiasm for our policy'. Evidently the workers did not take to hearing the Labour Party described as 'their most dangerous enemy', nor were they enticed by the prospect of a 'revolutionary workers' government'. It was thus that on polling day Pollitt's 'pathetic little bundle' of fourteen hundred votes was but a fleabite to the insufferable MacDonald and his thirty-five thousand supporters. It was a tale later to be recounted with good humour, but who knows what sober reflections this first test of strength must have prompted at the time?[8]

In purely selfish terms, however, the result meant little to Pollitt. Elections he enjoyed for the platform they offered and the thrill of the contest, but his parliamentary ambitions were nil. It was a matter very much closer to his heart when, at a Comintern meeting in Berlin the same month, his name was proposed as the next general secretary of the Communist Party. This, as Pollitt afterwards described it, meant 'the fulfilment of an ambition which I had cherished ever since I first came into the revolutionary movement'.[9] Confirmed and put into effect in August, his appointment was but the first of a series of changes which by the end of the year had swept aside many of the Party's established leaders. It also marked the emergence of a very different type of Party secretary, for to the quiet administrative skills of his predecessor, Albert Inkpin, Pollitt added the gifts of exposition and execution that political leadership required. If there were those among his colleagues who shared one or other of these qualities, there was none who combined them all with Pollitt's early adherence to the new line. Moreover, in his close relations with Dutt, and in his dependence on him for theoretical guidance, there lay the assurance, or so it seemed, of his future good conduct. That, at any rate, must have been amongst the Comintern's calculations, for if there was any one thing that might have disqualified Pollitt in its leaders' eyes, it was his evident knack of solid, independent reasoning. Indeed, even as he had bestowed upon him the Comintern's ultimate mark

65

of preferment, he evinced already unmistakable signs of deviant behaviour.

Pollitt's most basic and persistent difference of principle with the International concerned the application of the new line in industry. This had proved a much slower and messier business than in the field of politics, and neither the RILU nor Comintern congresses of the spring and summer of 1928 had posited any decisive change in trade union policy. Behind the scenes, however, the Profintern chief Losovsky was agitating for a showdown with the reformist unions, and by the latter part of the year he felt sure enough of his position to give an explicit lead to this effect. 'The masses must be organised and led, if necessary *without* the trade union apparatus and *against* it', he wrote, '[for]... the reformist organizations are tools in the hands of the bourgeois state... to crush the revolutionary wing of the Labour movement and to enslave the broad proletarian masses.'[10] This of course was anathema to Pollitt, whose main work since 1924 had been to build up the Minority Movement, 'not', as he put it, 'as outside, yelping, little unofficial bodies, but as a well-organised internal and integral part of the movement'.[11] According to his interpretation, the new line meant not the abandonment of the unions but their winning for revolutionary policies and eventual alignment with the Communist Party. This enduring commitment to trade unionism he restated in unequivocal terms in the run-up to the Tenth Party Congress in January 1929. Taking issue with those who, blindly following Losovsky, sought a wholesale reversal of the Party's industrial strategy, Pollitt disputed the need for any 'elaborate thesis' on the question and called instead for simply 'a short declaration stating the importance of work inside the existing unions'. While he paid lip-service to the 'fight against the fetish of constitutionalism', what was more remarkable in the context was his insistence that Communists fight for every available position, 'however nominal or apparently menial in character'. 'If we had twenty comrades holding branch secretaries' jobs in half a dozen of the more important unions', he wrote, 'we could wield a tremendous influence both in the workshops and the branches.' This, as he need hardly have pointed out, was a 'vastly different thing from much of the present indiscriminate talk about "new unions" on the one hand, or giving up trade union work on the other'.[12]

As the Minority Movement's secretary and still the Party's leading industrial figure, Pollitt was well placed to give practical effect to his views. He managed, for example, to fight with a degree of success the dual unionist tendencies inherent in Losovsky's alien formulas. In 1928 he helped forestall the creation of a red seamen's union, and might also have stifled the breakaway United Clothing Workers' Union had he not been out of the country at the time of its formation. He managed moreover to resist pressures from some Communists to treat this and Britain's only other red union, the United Mineworkers of Scotland, as a 'lesson and an example' to others.[13] Within his own union, Pollitt adopted a similar approach. Excluded by its leadership from most of the union's activities, he was no stranger to that most basic of arguments for Class Against Class: 'Let's have a go at the bastards.' He was not for this reason going to leave the 'bastards' in uncontested control of his society's affairs, however, and in the monthly paper the *Boilermaker* he produced between March 1928 and May 1929 he gave not the slightest sustenance to abstentionist impulses. Even this most traditional of craft oligarchies he proposed not to abandon to its pressing financial and administrative problems, but to rationalise and democratise on a sustainable, industry-wide basis.[14]

A particularly interesting episode, in which Pollitt was for the first time roundly attacked for his right deviations, was the Dawdon colliery dispute of March-June 1929. The strike was provoked by a threatened cut in piece rates and, as in three successive ballots the men rejected their leaders' advice to settle, it provided an ideal platform for 'independent leadership'. How this should be exercised, however, was the subject of some considerable disagreement. The Tyneside district organiser, Maurice Ferguson, was a fervent supporter of the new line, and in an initial strike leaflet the local CP preached the total rejection of officialdom. 'Away with the Defeatists and Cowards', it urged. 'Elect a Strike Committee, *excluding* those officials who advised you to accept Londonderry's terms.' The following week, however, as the colliery fell within his prospective Seaham constituency, Pollitt arrived at Dawdon to take charge of the Party's activities there. Immediately he struck a very different emphasis. Instead of a new strike committee, for example, he called merely for the extension of the old one and the formation of a 'vigilance committee' to exert rank-

and-file pressure on the strike's leaders. The latter he criticised only in comparatively modest terms for their lack of 'drive and punch'. It was this refrainment of his from 'the sharpest possible criticism of the local officials' that did most to cause the ensuing breach between Pollitt and the local Party leaders. As an example of his 'legalist fetish' the latter cited Pollitt's efforts to have the CP-sponsored feeding centre officially approved by the miners' lodge, while they were so affronted by two bulletins he put out for the Minority Movement that they promptly issued a scarcely concealed rejoinder of their own. To the Tyneside comrades, Pollitt's behaviour exemplified the 'contradiction between the formal acceptance of the new line and the operation of the old'; and when they gave wide publicity to their allegations later in the year, they included for good measure a sweeping attack on his Seaham election campaign, whose traditional methods of electioneering, they noted acidly, 'would have done credit to the ILP in its better days'.[15]

What the ultras on Tyneside expressed was no mere local discontentment. Some of their criticisms were afterwards taken up by the Party's Political Bureau, while in its communication to the CP's Eleventh Congress the Comintern itself identified the Minority Movement as a veritable hotbed of right deviations.[16] Until finally he bowed out as secretary at the movement's annual conference in August 1929, Pollitt did indeed persist with the old orientation towards the unions; and it took a brusque last-minute intervention by Losovsky to remove from the conference resolution all traces of the old line and insert instead a denunciation of the movement's past practices.[17] Only after this does one detect in Pollitt's utterances the obligatory slighting references to the unions, his compliance at last with the International being confirmed when he publicly condemned in himself the 'uncertainty, vacillation and criss-crossing' he had displayed at Dawdon. Indeed, in the same article, his first of any length as Party secretary, he gave the 'Right danger', as every other aspect of the new line, the full, derivative, *Inprecorr*-style treatment.[18]

Already there had arisen, however, another very different issue on which Pollitt again stood on what then passed for the right. Although nobody talked more about fetishes than the proponents of the new line, there was no greater fetish than the proposed daily paper they conceived as the very essence of independent leadership. There had begun already the arguments as to style and content that would bedevil the *Daily Worker* in its early years, but the main bone of contention in the latter part of 1929 was the date of the paper's launching. Money, thanks to the Comintern, was not initially a consideration. What concerned Pollitt, however, was that to rush into publication without adequate preparation would mean imposing on the workers an 'artificial production' inspiring none of the loyalty its long-term success would require. Advised by Tom Wintringham, now working full-time to get the new daily going, Pollitt therefore recommended to the Party's Eleventh Congress that the paper's launching date be postponed. Held in November-December 1929, this was Pollitt's first congress as Party secretary and his categorical defeat on this question provided him with a rather discouraging inauguration. As one of his many critics observed, his instincts of delay were 'the essence of the Right danger. (Hear, hear.)' Indeed, lest anybody think that he was received as general secretary by acclaim, it should be noted that his two-and-a-half-hour report was heard by the delegates in 'stony silence'. 'If it hadn't been you', Gallacher rather doubtfully reassured him afterwards, 'you would have got the bird. Awful, but stick it, Harry.'[19]

If there was any chance that Pollitt might not 'stick it', it was not because he failed sometimes to get his own way on such questions but because of the sheer mean-spiritedness of the polemics they generated. As comrade vied with so-called comrade to establish left credentials with the Comintern, the denunciations, alibis, recriminations and self-criticisms were such as the CP had never before really experienced. This, as was made abundantly clear at the Tenth ECCI Plenum of July 1929, was a situation on which the Comintern had quite definitely calculated. There Manuilsky extolled the daunting virtues of the German comrades who, weighing up every slightest word or gesture, 'attack the least deviation, respecting no persons'. The British Party, on the other hand, he chided for its insularity, its excessive politeness and for the special camaraderie he described with heavy irony as that of 'a society of great friends'. 'Not once', he complained, had 'the fundamental problems of Right and Left deviations been thrashed out'. Forgetting the Party's pleasant instincts of solidarity, it was time at last to make a start.[20]

All this ran very much counter to Pollitt's own conceptions of loyalty and responsibility, and the ensuing degeneration of Party life pushed him into repeated clashes with offending colleagues. A good illustration was provided by the plenum itself, where the Russians' manifold criticisms of the British Party were echoed from within by the YCL leader William Rust. Like his counterparts elsewhere, Rust was a vigilant observer of his elders' transgressions and commended as such by Manuilsky. Nevertheless, his 'prepared brief of all the shortcomings and deviations of our Party' received short shrift from Pollitt. In particular he resented the suggestion that the CP's rejected policies were its own exclusive responsibility and even worked out in defiance of the International. 'From the moment the Party was formed until January 1928, our policy was a policy of the Comintern', he retorted, 'and if we were only a revolutionary left in the Labour movement, that was as much the responsibility of the Comintern as it was of the British Party.'[21] What was implicit in so blunt and true a statement was that there should be no KPD-style hunting down of scapegoats for the discarded policies. It was not Pollitt, indeed, who had the Inkpins, Bells and Stewarts ousted at the subsequent Party congress, but the combined pressure of disaffected rank-and-file elements and the Comintern itself. In a confession of supposed weaknesses after the plenum, Pollitt admitted that he suffered from 'great subjectivity and instability' and had in the past 'not spoken out for the changes I knew were necessary because of the personal friendships that existed'. When the question of even more drastic leadership changes came up in the ensuing months, he was again amongst those who warned of the 'danger of a clean sweep'. What the CI required, however, was what Rust described as a collective act of abdication, and it sent the German Communist Walter Ulbricht to assist the Party in the task. Fully two-thirds of the Central Committee were removed as a result, and the Party apparatus overhauled.[22]

What was especially revealing was the concern Pollitt showed for the comrades thus displaced. Theirs was indeed a sorry plight. Wholly dependent on the Party through long years of service to it, they were now cast aside with as little thought as Stalin's worn-out socks. 'I would not complain if the attacks of capitalism enforced this', protested the former London district organiser, Ernie Cant, faced for the fourth time since 1920 with the break-up of his home, 'but I was sent into Nottinghamshire by the Party and am now stranded here without the remotest chance of obtaining any sort of employment.' With no trade, no references and twenty years as a 'professional revolutionist' behind him, Pollitt's predecessor as secretary, Albert Inkpin, faced a similar predicament. Pollitt had had his differences with both of them, and it was indeed another of those involved, J. R. Wilson, whom he had in 1923 vowed to see 'eat dirt'. Now, however, no thought could have been further from his mind. On the contrary, it was Pollitt who virtually alone argued that some provision be made in the districts or ancillary bodies for the Party's vanquished opportunists. His twelve months in prison he had spent working at the same table as Inkpin, and he regarded his case in particular as a 'dastardly piece of economic victimisation'. What especially incensed him were the malicious rumours that Inkpin actually kept a pub and was moreover holding the Party to ransom over assets held in his own name. In a characteristic outburst at the Political Bureau, Pollitt declared that he 'would no longer be associated with the comrades responsible for... such a policy', but he found himself in a minority of one. On the Central Committee the position was much the same, and it was only through an appeal to the CI that Pollitt secured for Inkpin at least a post in one of 'the Institutions'. Foremost amongst those who scorned his 'somewhat sentimental appeal' was again William Rust, who would have no let-up in the fight against the so-called 'foreign elements'. It is not surprising, perhaps, that at this time Pollitt himself came under renewed suspicion as a supposed 'right-winger in disguise'.[23]

Sadly there are accessible no letters of Pollitt's bearing witness to the frustrations he felt in this period. Much is revealed, however, by the other side of a fascinating correspondence he had with Dutt in the autumn of 1929, and particularly a sermon Dutt sent him in the second week of November. Already on Pollitt's appointment as secretary, Dutt had warned him not to take it amiss if the critics in the Party were not assuaged by an 'inner palace-change of which they hardly know. They are helping you in reality', he went on, 'because your energy and enthusiasm ought to be backed up by the best kind of PB.' Pollitt saw things differently. As his energy and enthusiasm were sapped by the ceaseless carping intrigues, and as he felt himself transformed 'from a Prince Rupert to a Social Fascist', he tended after the Tenth Plenum and his appointment as secretary to retreat into anodyne technical and administrative tasks. At the October Central Committee Rust, Stewart and Gallacher all commented on this, with Rust also proposing Pollitt's removal from the Party's leading bodies as a consequence. Dutt too, to whom Pollitt evidently unburdened himself after this session, had harsh words for him. It was not simply that he seemed impelled by the attacks on the leadership to put himself forward as its main defender, and thus largely confirm the original criticisms. What was more serious was that, overwhelmed by the Party's temporary troubles, he seemed in his surpassing cynicism to be 'losing political grip'. In Pollitt's own phrases, or near approximations of them, Dutt summarised the main points of his recent letters:

1) that all the politics in the party is jabber and cant
2) that the new forces are impossible fools and mechanical parrots and gramophones
3) that the differentiation in the leadership is an unprincipled fight for jobs
4) that the only clean place is away from the communist workers in the party with the non-communist workers in the workshops
5) that you wait for the party to cut the cackle and get on with the 'real work'
6) that you receive the criticism of yourself with contemptuous superiority as so much jargon, and wait for them to call you a 'social fascist'...

Ninety per cent of what he had to say was true, Dutt admitted, but it was precisely the other ten per cent that ultimately mattered:

You see all the mess, but you don't see clear enough or steadily and constantly enough the big thing that is happening through it all... the beginning of real politics, the new life and fight and kick, the spirit of revolt, the coming closer to the International, the fight against the Right that has poisoned the party since its inception and stultified all our efforts... All this should make you exultant & shout for joy, even though it hits you hard personally all over in the process. And instead – the effect of your letters is... like someone very tired, seeing only the seamy side of the whole thing.

What Pollitt had to do, Dutt concluded with a characteristic emphasis, was to clear his mind of all extraneous details and straighten things out *in relation to the international line*. After all, he wrote, 'have you ever known a revolutionary Marxist leader treat any situation in this type of way, or write in this way by so much as a single expression?' It was an unsparing letter, and it is not surprising that Dutt hesitated some days before sending it.[24]

In general terms Pollitt must have accepted the longer view that Dutt put to him, for 'stick it' he did. In the process, however, he had his first serious falling-out with his minder in Brussels. As early as March 1928 he had shown the first signs of divided loyalties, and of displeasure perhaps with Dutt's slightly underhand political methods. At that time Pollitt had approved a formal censure of an article of Dutt's which, while expressing their shared opinions, rather prejudged questions still before the leadership. It seemed, as Dutt wrote to him, 'that you feel as a burden your association with me and S, and that you want to be free... of the constant necessity of fighting in isolation, and glad of any opportunity to disclaim connection... and be in unanimously with the rest'.[25] The breach was swiftly healed, however, whereas that of 1929-30 lasted the best part of a year. Possibly Pollitt took umbrage at Dutt's appearing to side with his left-wing critics, although Dutt did in fact specifically exclude him from his strictures and for this was himself denounced as 'the representative of conciliationism in this country'.[26] Possibly too Pollitt simply wanted to find his own feet as leader, while Dutt's particularly severe ill-health in the first part of 1930 meant that his contacts with the Party as a whole were very much diminished. As early as the previous October, however, Gallacher had indicated that the two were no longer in touch,[27] and with the exception of that one acrid exchange they appear to have had no further contact until the end of July 1930. 'Hooray for your letter', Dutt wrote on the renewal of their correspondence. 'Of course we were convinced that you were angry with us and had cast us off.'[28]

Henceforth, almost as if nothing had happened, there resumed the constant toing and froing of letters, drafts and theses and, though never so regularly as his hosts would have wished, Pollitt called many times to take counsel with the Dutts. Nevertheless, there was something perceptibly changed in their relationship. If Dutt had his province in matters of theory and world affairs, so too had Pollitt his in the practical realities of British working-class politics. With his growing assuredness of the fact there developed a keener appreciation of the limits to his mentors' competence and a willingness sometimes to challenge it. In their close and troubled collaboration were personified the fractures and tensions in Communist politics over the subsequent decade, with Dutt tending to represent the basic Leninist world-view and Pollitt the adaptation

73

to contemporary realities that was insidiously undermining it. Usually their different emphases could be accommodated, but sometimes their *pas de deux* was more like a tug of war. 'Ward sends her best greetings', Dutt concluded his letter, 'and is happy to have her Warder back.' They would both of them find, however, that the Warder had returned a less malleable figure with some very definite ideas of his own.

The occasion for their resumption of relations was yet another of the Comintern's British commissions, for which Pollitt sought Dutt's written contribution. Possibly he felt the need again for Dutt's unrivalled insight into the underlying logic of events, for by its mundane appearances alone Pollitt's first year at the Party's helm could hardly have been more discouraging. There was by this time general agreement that the CP was in an absolutely parlous state, although stubbornly this was attributed not to the new line itself but to its narrow and mechanical application. '... the best policy in the world', as Dutt put it to Pollitt in his picturesque fashion, 'when handed out to our party in its present state, comes out as a dead rat at the other end.' Certainly, while world slump and the paralysis of reformism had apparently confirmed the Comintern's guiding prognoses, the CP had not only failed to thrive on soaring unemployment and a beleaguered Labour Government but was actually smaller and more isolated than ever before. It was this discrepancy that dominated the British commission and prompted Pollitt on his return to tackle the problem of the Party's sectarianism in a series of articles for the *Daily Worker*. In doing so, he had no shortage of easy targets. There was the crazy maximalism of the Party's demands, as when during that spring's Bradford woollen strike it advanced the slogan of 'the struggle for power'. There was the Communists' remoteness from ordinary concerns, as they droned on about 'Chinese Generals' and the social revolution and left more workaday questions to 'the hated Social Fascist bureaucracy'. Worst of all, perhaps, was the branding of all who did not swallow the full Party line as 'Social Fascists', 'sham "Lefts"' and 'all the other paraphernalia of our Communist phraseology', leaving Communists immured in their own self-righteousness.

The remedy that Pollitt proposed in the last of his articles was the Workers' Charter, a programme of immediate demands devised at the British commission and destined to play a central role in the

CP's subsequent activities. Superficially the campaign was not without effect. Pollitt's initial *Workers' Charter* pamphlet had a reported sale of 120,000 and at the 'National Charter Convention' held in April 1931 there were some eight hundred delegates, over a hundred of them representing local charter committees. The problem was that these somewhat incorporeal entities represented no genuine broadening of Communist influence. Around half the delegates present, indeed, had already attended Minority Movement conferences in the 1920s and simply brought along with them different credentials. It was 'no use having half a dozen bridges to the masses, if we find only the same faithful few going over them in every case', Pollitt had written in his *Daily Worker* articles. The Charter Campaign did not succeed in increasing the flow of traffic.[29]

Within the constraints of the new line there was almost inevitably something bogus about these 'united front' initiatives. It was noteworthy that, as practically the CP's only effective mass organisation, the unemployed workers' movement was constantly under fire for its legalism and opportunism and that in 1932 its able leader Wal Hannington was for this reason removed from the Central Committee.[30] It was as if by the mere fact of its having some forty thousand real members and concerning itself with their actual problems the NUWM was somehow failing in its duty. With this exception, it was largely through the projection of distorted images of itself that the Party contrived an appearance of unity without ever combining its forces with anybody else's. To the Minority Movement, as the broader channel through which the CP would approach the workers, were now added the charter committees to perform the same function for the Minority Movement; and if the latter was but 'a shadow of the party', with 'practically no members' and only a vestigial presence in any major industrial centre,[31] then the Charter Campaign was but a shadow of the Minority Movement. Pollitt was amongst the keenest to find a way out of the impasse, but it only added to the general air of unreality that his initial battles with Dutt and Rust centred on the respective roles and profiles of precisely these apparitions. Practically, it was a question of whether Comrade Bloggs of Clapham should march on rallies with a Charter placard or as a Minority Movement contingent. The seizure of power itself, however, could not have been discussed with greater solemnity. With its comic remoteness and rectitude even in error, one letter of Dutt's in particular conveys something of the period's otherworldliness. 'Dear Harry', he wrote,

> I am glad to learn... that the Profintern wire exactly confirms the line put forward in my previous letters... even to the extent of making the mistake that I did... of assuming that a London MM Council already exists, with which to bring the proposed London Charter Campaign into close association. As against the two views put forward (1) for a London Charter Ctee to exist instead of and replace a non-existent London MM Ctee; or (2) for a London MM Ctee to be elected at a Charter Conference and no Charter Ctee, the principle... that any District Charter Ctee must be in close association with and subordinate in practice to the governing District MM Ctee... may be regarded as confirmed. The only question remaining is the mechanics of the association.

No wonder that Pollitt described Dutt as 'sectarian through and through', although as yet his own more pragmatic impulses had in the charter committees a most inadequate form of expression.[32]

As practically unnoticed the campaign petered out, Pollitt was however impelled towards more radical conclusions that marked the beginning of a fundamental shift in the Party's industrial work. It was not this or that movement that had to be abandoned, he began to argue, but the extrinsic approach to the masses that was common to them all. 'Who launched the demands?', he asked of the now defunct Charter. 'Who formulated them? Half a dozen of us sitting and talking about them!' It was the same when it came to industrial disputes. 'One or two comrades', drafted in from who knows where, proclaimed themselves 'a Council of Action or General Strike Committee' and in a 'purely formal and superficial' fashion trumped the reformists' demands, the better to accuse them afterwards of betrayal. No wonder that, in Pollitt's rather harsh assessment, the Communists had with just one exception 'played no decisive role in a single struggle'. 'No committee should call itself a strike committee unless it speaks with the authority of the workers', he insisted, and it mattered less whether its demands were large or small than whether the workers were prepared to fight for them. What was required of Communists was not that they seek to impose on the workers' struggles their preconceived programmes and forms of organisation, but that they bring forth 'the actual demands of the

76

workers themselves' and on this basis provide them with revolutionary leadership. Only at a later stage, 'when the mass movement is an actual fact', should they seek to consolidate their advances organisationally.[33]

This virtual disavowal of the Communists' separate organisational ambitions had as its corollary a decisive reorientation towards the workers' existing institutions and particularly the trade unions. In theory there was nothing new in this. Following the British commission of August 1930 much had been said about the need to work within the 'reformist' unions and Pollitt had echoed this strongly in his propaganda for the Workers' Charter.[34] Nothing systematic was done, however, and though buttressed by formal resolutions, Pollitt's exhortations were negated by the stronger apprehensions about the snares of the bureaucracy. 'Our attitude... is surrounded with so many "ifs", "ands" and "buts"', he wrote in the latter part of 1932, 'that the only firm impression... is that in reality we are against trade unionism.' To put this right was amongst the principal objectives of the Party's 'January Resolution', unveiled with some ceremony in January 1932 and drafted during an exhaustive enquiry into its activities in Moscow the previous month. To give practical effect to its provisions, and because he had been instructed to save money, Pollitt announced at the same time a thoroughgoing revision of the Party's methods of work. Efforts were to be concentrated on four districts, to which the Political Bureau, henceforth meeting only fortnightly, was to be dispersed. The number of functionaries was to be reduced and all leading comrades attached to a local Party organisation and held personally responsible for their Labour movement work. The perspective was that of building the Party, like the mass movement around it, 'from the bottom upwards', and whether born of necessity or design it marked perhaps the real beginnings of an effective Communist presence in this country. 'If someone gave me to-night the money to be able to send 10 or 15 functionaries out... it would not be devoted to that objective', Pollitt insisted in March to one querulous colleague. 'If we can get every comrade who is in a factory to understand that in 10 minutes' conversation on what is the situation confronting the workers in that particular industry it is worth all the speeches of national speakers sent down from the Centre.' The days of Minority Movement 'flying squads', it seemed, were over.[35]

Always a grudging convert to the new line in industry, Pollitt was one of the first Communist leaders, in Britain or anywhere else, to seize the chance to bury it. Inevitably this meant conflict with those whose commitment to it was greater. Already his rejection of the Profintern's prevailing organisational forms had caused him to clash with Losovsky at the RILU Central Council of November 1931.[36] Encouraged no doubt by the appearance of Losovsky's criticisms in the *RILU Magazine* and *Inprecorr*, there were those in Britain too who found his suspicions confirmed by Pollitt's interpretation of the January Resolution. At the heart of the dispute was the Minority Movement, dismissed by Pollitt as 'a small organisation boxed up in itself' and neglected by him in favour of the rank-and-file movements emerging in several major unions.[37] There were others, however, who felt that these broad and amorphous movements, based on union branches and thus replicating their demarcations, provided no proper basis for what, after its German model, was called the Revolutionary Trade Union Opposition or RTUO. Amongst them was Pollitt's old adversary Maurice Ferguson, now Birmingham district organiser. During that winter's Lucas dispute Ferguson had not only desired against instructions to recruit whom he could into the Minority Movement but had objected to 'bringing the mass, now under our influence, into the influence of the reformist unions'. 'We need a M.M.', he wrote later in the year, 'because we stand as much chance of capturing the trade union machine and using it for our own ends as we do the capitalist State.'[38] The likes of Ferguson, Pollitt could cope with; but Ferguson was in correspondence on these matters with Dutt, and Dutt himself had by this time an understanding not only with Pollitt but with his colleague and rival Bill Rust, now editing the *Daily Worker*. On a visit in the summer Pollitt had lengthy discussions with Dutt on the trade union question, but their differences remained.[39] It was thus that in August, with the next Party congress looming, Pollitt decided to clear the air once and for all.

He did so by means of a calculated deviation and provocation. In articles for both the *Worker* and the *Communist Review*, he went far beyond existing commitments to work within lower union organisations to embrace the unions as a whole. Equating them with the most resolute and class-conscious sections of the workers, he postulated for the first time in several years their transformation by pressure from below. His perspective, quite explicitly, was '*to take the unions out of the hands of the existing leadership*' that they might thus 'again be made into effective instruments to strengthen the workers' resistance and build up their united action and power against capitalism'. Dutt can hardly be blamed if he saw in this a 'tendency to revise our whole trade union line', and Pollitt's *Worker* article drew from him a detailed correction and rebuttal. It was not the leaders alone that the Communists fought, Dutt insisted, 'but the great part of the existing opportunist reactionary constitutions, machinery, traditions, methods and general disorganisation of reformist trade unionism'. Whether it was the content of Dutt's reply or its pompous and didactic tone, Pollitt was stung to a still more powerful restatement of his case. 'I cannot write in the brilliant analytical manner that made readers say... "My word, Pollitt's got it in the neck"', he confessed. 'But I believe I am correctly interpreting the views of a large section of our Party who do realise what has to be done to win the trade unionists and their trade unions, but have been hesitant for fear of being accused of wanting to "reverse international decisions" or... "go back to the old line".'[40]

The ensuing debate, with several leading Communists weighing in on one side or the other, generated a good deal of ill feeling for which Pollitt was as culpable as anybody. No doubt he had aimed in his impatience with Party policy to bypass the usual preliminaries of thesis formulation, in which the hairsplitting drafting experts like Dutt were supreme. Even so, in signalling a major shift of stance on his own initiative he showed, as he often would when decided on a particular course of action, a certain contempt for the normal processes of collective decision making. Generally it would be the Party membership that was thus excluded, though on this occasion he pre-empted even Dutt and his secretariat colleague Rust. Indeed, if after some three weeks these two broke ranks in public it was because of Pollitt's persistent unavailability to discuss the issues he had raised. First of all attending a Moscow plenum without stopping off as promised in Brussels, he then went to assist in the Lancashire weavers' strike from which Rust could not entice him back to King Street. This was the more regrettable in that Willie Gallacher, as fierce and impetuous in his loyalties as ever, was putting it about that behind Dutt's intervention there lay a conspiracy with Rust to oust Pollitt as secretary. Dutt, we can be sure, was justified in dismissing this as 'childish personal nonsense': his commitment to Pollitt's leadership was one that survived their differences, and even when some years later he was the agent of Pollitt's temporary deposal, he made sure that neither Rust nor anybody else emerged to take his place. From his point of view, if Pollitt and Gallacher chose 'on the strength of a private exchange of opinions' to revise the Party's policy without prior discussion or decision, then it was 'only natural and reasonable' that he should step in 'solely to protect the PB line, the international line'. Pollitt himself, while surely aware of the waywardness of Gallacher's splenetic allegations, was scarcely less antagonised. It was 'not from the point of view of microscopes or letters from afar' that they had to decide these questions, he put it to the Politbureau with robust allusiveness, 'but from the point of view of... what we would do if we were our lads'. With Pollitt backed by 'old Bill' and Dutt by 'young Bill', it was, Dutt warned, turning into an 'old-style party stink'.[41]

The outcome of the dispute was a modus vivendi that said a great deal about the protagonists' divergent priorities. Formally, the resolution for the forthcoming congress was amended to exclude all references to strengthening the unions and highlight instead the role of the 'RTUO', a phrase that Pollitt detested. With Pollitt's eve-of-congress admission to 'certain unclear formulations', Dutt could thus congratulate himself on having rescued the international line.[42] To Pollitt, however, as he made clear in the same statement, these semantic points were of 'secondary importance' to his basic insistence on more positive and concerted work in the unions. He could concede to Dutt his formulas and hypotheses as long as they did not bring into question the immediate practical necessity of such work. He could allow too the future prospect of a 'Trade Union Militant League', as long as the primary emphasis was on the rank-and-file union movements that would form its basis.

The most enduring of the latter was the London Busmen's Rank and File Committee, set up at the height of the trade union controversy and cited by Pollitt as an exemplar of the approach he desired. In vain Dutt protested in the months to follow that, through an exclusive emphasis on 'immediate economic bus interests', the Communist contribution to this work was simply that of 'clerical-technical assistants'. 'We need all the time... to be making understood our most elementary revolutionary conceptions, the understanding of capitalism, of the class struggle, of the crisis, of revolution, of the proletarian dictatorship, of bourgeois democracy, of the state, of the role of the party, of the role of the trade unions, of revolutionary organisation, of revolutionary tactics, of what is reformism, of the united front', he warned, the 'etc' he added being particularly daunting.[43] It was Pollitt's more strategic perspective that prevailed, however, and in this he had by this time an intellectual counterweight to Dutt in Emile Burns, the Marxist theoretician who edited the *Busmen's Punch* and became Pollitt's King Street deputy. Possibly the decisive moment arrived later in 1933, when the busmen's unofficial leaders were faced with either signing a 'loyalty' document or risking expulsion from the TGWU. Urging compliance, Pollitt warned that, 'even if we have to stand out as a Party and... fight against the stream of militant busmen', the CP had to 'avoid at all costs any split'.[44] Thus, already in 1933, were defined the parameters within which the CP-led unofficial movements would operate.

Having pushed so hard for the new approach, Pollitt was thereafter far less directly involved in trade union questions. No doubt it was inherent in a strategy aimed at transforming the unions from within that it did not require his continual interventions as Party secretary. His steady flow of articles on industrial policy more or less dried up, and no longer did he turn up to offer his personal assistance in disputes as he had in the Yorkshire and Lancashire textile strikes. Instead, as from 1933 the CP gradually relaxed its self-imposed quarantine, Pollitt's was increasingly the political task of forging alliances on the left and building up the Party as their most dynamic constituent part. As orator, pamphleteer, negotiator and organiser, nobody was to be more closely identified with the CP's popular front initiatives. It should possibly be stressed, therefore, that Pollitt's pioneering approach to industrial questions had no early parallel in the political sphere. Indeed, if in the trade union controversy he seemed to anticipate Dimitrov's Seventh Congress dictum that the masses should be taken 'as they are, and not as we should like to have them', his contempt for the masses' political preferences remained vocal and tactless. If one had to detect any premonition of a more generous spirit it could only be in his indulgence of the odd maverick: his use at Seaham of messages from the veteran socialist and suffragist Charlotte Despard and

81

Birmingham ILP stalwart Joseph Southall, for example; or his welcome as allies in the 1931 crisis to John Strachey and W. J. Brown, both of them disaffected Labour MPs who had already flirted with Mosley.[45] As far as the organised left was concerned, however, there were no possible allies but only rivals, traitors and charlatans. The ILP in particular, as it leant towards revolution and disaffiliated from the Labour Party, he shamefully traduced. In April 1932 he took part in an extraordinary debate with Fenner Brockway, published afterwards by the CP in the semblance of a boxing programme. 'BUT NO POLITENESS! No mere "difference of opinion"', Dutt exhorted the willing pugilist. 'Treatment as CLASS ENEMIES throughout. You speak for holy anger... against the foulness that is Brockway. Make that whole audience HATE him.' While lacking perhaps Dutt's own richness of metaphor, Pollitt did indeed set about the 'opportunist poisoning' and 'foul corruption' of the ILP in the 'SMASH HARD-HITTING' way that Dutt had urged. '... with such a party there can be no talk of unity, no talk of anything in common, and there can only be war to the death', he declaimed. He did not know, of course, that it would be on Brockway and the ILP that he would, in less than a year, have to practise the first of his united front seductions.[46]

The turning point in the two parties' relations, as for the whole of the European left, was the victory of fascism in Germany and the crushing of its disunited opponents. Within weeks of Hitler's appointment as chancellor, as uneven instincts of unity and exculpation coincided, both the CP and the ILP invited the co-operation of other working-class bodies to stem the tide of reaction. As they alone responded to each other's advances, their fraught and wary rapprochement during the course of 1933 marked the beginnings of a real united front in Britain. For the CP the ramifications were to be far-reaching, although its initial tactical adjustments were modest indeed. Its approach to the ILP, with which it shared so many assumptions, required of the Party little in the way of ideological concessions. Moreover, its basic objective in the collaboration, of an eventual merger of the two parties on its own terms, was so baldly stated as to satisfy even the purest of Communist sectaries. Indeed, it was through the intervention of Stalin himself that the Comintern line that the CP followed on this question was 'very considerably' strengthened.[47] At the same time, the Party had as yet no real sense of the gravity of the setback suffered in Germany. With breathtaking complacency it presented its glib vindications of the humbled KPD, its malignant analogies between social democracy and fascism and a confidence in history's quickening revolutionary tempo that seemed quite impervious to reality. Pollitt was no exception. Behind closed doors he argued as early as March 1933 that the situation in Germany was now '100 times more difficult' than before Hitler's accession to power.[48] In public, however, he showed none of his later alertness to the distinctive threat that fascism posed, but only a tendency, when he mentioned it at all, to lump it together with the other forms of bourgeois dictatorship.

It was during the following year, 1934, that he began to emerge as a tribune of the anti-fascist left. In his willing adoption of this role one detects that interplay of national and international factors that shaped the transition to the popular front of the Comintern as a whole. Across Europe this was a year that saw not only the extending infamies of fascism but the first signs of serious workers' resistance. The core of this resistance, moreover, was more often the socialist workers than the Communists. So long as the focus had been on the heavily compromised German social democrats, the Comintern's Third Period sectarianism had conceivably had some justification. In embattled workers' Vienna that February, however, and the Asturias rising that October, the scorned social fascists displayed a courageous fighting spirit that virtually compelled solidarity. The moral was the more readily identified thanks to the arrival in Moscow that February of Georgi Dimitrov, the hero of the Reichstag Fire trial and himself an international symbol of proletarian defiance. Within weeks Stalin had him elevated to the very apex of Comintern affairs and Dimitrov there exercised his immense authority and prestige to hasten the advent of anti-fascist unity. Of particular importance were events in France to which, with the eclipse of the KPD, the Comintern's centre of gravity had now shifted. Urged on by the International, the PCF reached in July 1934 a first working agreement with the socialists and it thereafter developed with enormous gusto what might loosely be called the popular front strategy. Comintern sceptics remained, but as fascism cast its threat over both the USSR and the European working class, the logic of unity was inexorable.

Pollitt, of course, was closely in touch with these international developments and greatly influenced by their example. Indeed, it seems likely that he discussed these very questions with Eugene Fried, the Comintern adviser to Maurice Thorez who exerted such an influence over the policies of the French Party. In February 1935 Dutt proposed to Pollitt a special visit to discuss anti-fascist work with 'the fellow from Paris', and this connection most probably explains Pollitt's periodic visits to that city.[49] Pollitt was not only responsive to Comintern initiatives, however, but positively eager to push ahead with the new policy, and for this one must look primarily to domestic considerations. The Communist Party at the end of 1933 was still, in relation to the dangers and opportunities of which it preached, a negligible force: stubbornly reluctant to grow, as yet barely implanted in the unions and factories and having to make do with a quarrelsome unity of outsiders with the ILP. At the Thirteenth and last ECCI Plenum in December 1933, the Party came in for sharp criticism and, to judge by the fervour of Gallacher's denials, the rumours that Pollitt's leadership was now under threat must have had considerable currency. Indeed, faced with new charges of sedition along with Tom Mann, Pollitt complained in April of the Party's failure to develop a campaign around the issue and noted that some saw in his being put away 'a good way of getting a change in the Party without having a Party discussion'. Invariably at meetings, he went on, he himself had to draft a resolution demanding that the charges be withdrawn. Even the appearance of Mosley's Blackshirts seemed at first to promise only a perpetuation of the Party's fringe status, as rival groups of extremists battled it out in the streets. If the Party carried on as it had been doing, Pollitt warned at the start of 1934, then its opposition to Mosley would be seen by the workers not as a 'real political struggle' but as a 'brawl' and a 'dogfight'.[50]

Possibly it took events in France to reveal for him the mobilising potential of anti-fascism, and possibly too the immediate public outcry after Mosley's notorious Olympia rally in June 1934. This was the occasion for the Party's first properly organised counter-demonstration, and the Communists themselves were taken aback by the scale of the propaganda victory they achieved. Like other CP leaders, Pollitt never overestimated Mosley's significance and his main focus throughout was on the hated National Government; but as London CP organiser Ted Bramley put it to Stafford Cripps, Labour Party theoriser of so-called 'National' fascism, the Blackshirts provided a 'visible piece of evidence' that the British working class could identify with the spread of fascism. Within a month or two of Olympia the CP had initiated a Co-ordinating Committee for Anti-Fascist Activity, with the broadest Labour and trade union representation invited. Dutt, who with friends abroad had sketched out the new movement, described the prospects it opened in captivating terms. 'The decisive question is real living LEADERSHIP... and in reality that means YOU', he wrote to Pollitt. 'If you can for a period put all your preoccupation and activity into this... I believe you will not only make an enormous success personally, reaching a full Thaelmann position as the visible leader of the widest possible mass opposition movement against Mosley, Fascism and War, but also make the fortune of the party, establishing its mass leadership and drawing together our many scattered strands of influence into big mass organisation.'[51]

Such vistas flowed freely from Dutt's pen, but on this occasion they had within a matter of weeks a striking practical confirmation. On Sunday 9 September, in the first major action to be sponsored by the new committee, a derisory display of Mosley's Greater Britain was swamped in Hyde Park by a vast and orderly assemblage of anti-fascist workers. It was the biggest Hyde Park turnout in very many years and Ted Bramley would recall vividly Pollitt's euphoria as he turned the corner of Marble Arch to behold the sight of his dreams. 'September 9th, comrades, was a triumph', he proudly addressed the Comintern the following month. 'We have never, in our experience, witnessed such scenes... It was not merely the fact that 150,000 people were in Hyde Park, the Mosley demonstration was an absolute fiasco, but it was the fighting spirit of the workers, the discipline, the splendid anti-fascist banners they had made, and it was really a tremendous victory for our Party.' Here, in the teeth of Labour's disapproval, was a real display of independent leadership, just as the phrase itself was falling into disuse. Bramley would remember it as a turning point for the Party, and there is no doubt that in the struggle against fascism the CP found a new impetus and focus for its activities and what seemed an unanswerable argument for unity of the left. The mood of buoyancy in those early years of promise was irresistible. For Pollitt, the Party's Thirteenth

Congress, held in Manchester in February 1935, was the best yet: united in policy, agreed in its leadership, confirmed in a common sense of purpose and capped by an inspirational rally to which supporters came from all over Lancashire. 'What a Congress', he wrote to Dutt. 'From opening to end splendid.... I could sleep for ever if sleep would come, but it won't.' In the united front, to which his congress report was devoted, he had found at last the key for which he had been looking. 'The mass movement grows', he continued his letter. 'The Party does count now.'[52]

It was thus that, with the Comintern itself a prey to conflicting counsels, Pollitt came to identify himself with those within its ranks most committed to change. After extensive ECCI debates on the new approach in December 1934, he decided to take the battle against the retreating die-hards to the pages of the *Communist International*. Evidently the piece he drafted was a full broadside against sectarianism, identifying particular culprits and boldly raising the question of past Comintern mistakes. Dutt, to whom he sent successive drafts, was not impressed. Pollitt's criticisms of leading CI official Bela Kun and of the Polish CP he felt ill-advised, while the article as a whole he thought so negative and lopsided as to give a definitely distorted picture, 'like an echo of the ILP'. 'This is all the more worrying, because of the importance of your role', he reminded Pollitt. 'When you spoke here about raising questions more sharply in all international work, and we strongly agreed on the need, we did not for a moment take you as meaning a written theoretical discussion in the 'CI'... and I don't feel happy about the result.'[53]

The article never appeared, and one must assume that Pollitt took to heart Dutt's advice to 'stick to the positive ground' in public and communicate his more contentious thoughts only 'privately and orally'. He had by no means ceded Dutt's case, however, and with the rare prospect of a Comintern congress to set the seal on the new policy, he raised the issue again in a slightly different guise. In Pollitt the subjugation of the mighty KPD had, already in March 1933, prompted sombre reflections as to the Comintern's failure to foresee even the possibility of such a calamity.[54] He made little of it at the time, but as Communist attitudes changed he could not help but notice in each new call for unity an implicit condemnation of its earlier policies. Moreover, the German Party, blind to its predicament even in defeat, was the most resistant of its sections to the abandonment of old shibboleths. Remembering perhaps all the plenums and commissions at which his tiny British Party had been slighted, Pollitt led it now in pressing to tackle the issue head-on. 'we think it is important to raise in our statement the various international problems that have to be discussed at the Congress', he wrote, mentioning particularly, in view of its past and current failings, 'the problem of the leadership of the C.P. of Germany'. Dutt, to whom these guidelines were sent, was again dismayed at this presumption, 'coming forward from our own little party to put all the world issues and every other party right'.

His caution at first prevailed and the discussion statement he drafted steered clear of controversy. At the congress itself, however, intended by its choreographers not as a debating platform but as a taut display of Bolshevik unity, the British delegates introduced a distinct note of discord. In the discussion on Wilhelm Pieck's report for the ECCI, it was not Pollitt but J. R. Campbell who spoke, remarking pointedly that 'the Executive Committee must examine its own work in those seven years [since the last congress] in the same objective spirit as it examines the work of the various Parties'. Amongst the specific questions he mentioned were the imposition on the British Party of a sectarian trade union line, the 'half-hearted' pursuit of united front tactics in the first year after Hitler's accession to power and the need for 'a careful examination of our German comrades', the better to render them assistance. Pollitt's own contribution, destined for a much greater degree of publicity, was a positive exposition of the united front that dwelt little on these awkward questions. We can be sure, nevertheless, that he had agreed their overall approach with Campbell, with whom he was developing something akin to his relationship with Dutt in terms of their respective aptitudes. The two were not only in accord on most major issues but since Pollitt's estrangement from Dutt in 1930 had been close neighbours in Colindale. It is notable in this regard that, on leaving for Moscow two months before the congress, it was Campbell that Pollitt left in charge at King Street, 'as he is one of the best comrades that ever I have worked with'.[55]

The overwhelming feeling of the congress, however, was one of consensus. 'The important question now', Dutt had written to Pollitt, 'is, not whether past mistakes have been made, but whether such mistakes, if they have been made, are now corrected'. As the

87

congress rose as one to acclaim in Dimitrov the encapsulation of unity, probably Pollitt himself would not have dissented. The congress was the first he had attended since 1921 and it marked in many ways his coming of age as a Communist leader. It was a mark, not just of personal distinction but of his Party's crucial role in the new scheme of things, that in the main congress debate only Dimitrov and Thorez preceded him. Dutt too made a 'very very good' contribution on more theoretical lines, possibly marred by 'too many ands, ifs and buts' but destined in Pollitt's words to 'give universal prestige to *your* despised CPGB'. Only Dutt's delivery, in fact, left anything to be desired. 'I spoke too quick', Pollitt admitted, 'but Jesus Christ you were that slow it was like the bloody Pope addressing his Cardinal.'

What mattered more than his Party's new standing, however, was the validation at the congress of a political strategy that conformed to Pollitt's own basic predilections and released a whole set of new energies and enthusiasms on the left. It meant a decisive commitment to the Labour movement and yet seeking allies beyond it; taking up the battle on immediate issues, and yet always with a view to their further development; and waging the struggle against fascism and war, not in the abstract, but in the shape of Britain's unspeakable National Government. *Unity Against the National Government* was the title Pollitt gave his Seventh Congress speech, and the title would sum up the next half-decade of Communist achievement and frustration. The 'twilight of Comintern' it may have been, as E. H. Carr put it, but for one at least of its member parties the upturn was only just beginning.[56]

4 Against fascism and war

In confirming the CP in its initially tentative moves away from sectarianism, the Seventh World Congress set the scene for what might, too simplistically, be regarded as the Party's heroic period. While many would dispute its effectiveness or the integrity of its motives, few would deny that it was, in the late 1930s, the most dynamic force on the British left. While its numbers increased steadily,[1] its influence, now felt across a whole range of activities, grew dramatically. One result was that Pollitt emerged for perhaps the first time as a political figure of national importance. True, having in the 1935 election failed in the first of three attempts to win East Rhondda, he lacked the platform for his oratory that Parliament might have provided.[2] Given the impotence of the opposition benches in the years that led to war, however, it is at least arguable that Pollitt's talents were more usefully employed away from Westminster: inspiring campaigns of solidarity with republican Spain, for example, or enthusing the Left Book Club with its fifty thousand members. Certainly Pollitt saw it that way, and in the interests of unity proposed standing neither in the Rhondda nor anywhere else at the election due in 1940. 'It is not for Comrade Pollitt to say that he would be much more use up and down the country', one of his colleagues complained, 'but Comrade Pollitt would be much more use in the House of Commons than carrying out a propaganda campaign.'[3]

If Pollitt owed what authority he had to the Communist Party, it is equally true that the CP owed much of its credibility to its charismatic leader and to the trust and esteem in which he was held by many on the left. Certainly no other Communist, not even Willie Gallacher, the Party's sole MP, exercised anything like his influence over the well-disposed. 'Harry Pollitt is one of the few men thrown up in the last generation in England with a natural capacity for leadership', wrote the editor of the New Statesman in 1940. 'He is a man whom sincere Socialists want to follow whatever class they come from... because he is inspired with a moral fervour... utterly alien from the opportunism and Machiavellianism of current Marxism.'[4]

Quite apart from such tributes from the world at large, Pollitt enjoyed from about this period a considerable ascendancy over the opportunists and Machiavellians of the CP itself. Much later A. L. Morton was to refer to 'the Communist Party in the age of Pollitt' and his epithet describes no period better than the late 1930s.[5] One result of the Seventh World Congress, signalled already by Dimitrov in July 1934, was to free member parties from the Comintern's constant interference in their day-to-day affairs, and Pollitt gave every sign that he relished this greater degree of responsibility. It was a revealing sign that in mid-1936 Dutt at last returned to live in London, a move urged on him by Pollitt since the start of the previous year but postponed due apparently to further medical treatments.[6] The broad lines of Communist policy were still determined abroad and for Pollitt periodic trips to Moscow remained obligatory. By and large, however, he now felt that it was for the Party's national leadership to take its own decisions 'as responsible leaders of a political party in this country'.[7] It was under this illusion that he was to resist the Comintern's diktat when differences arose over the war in 1939; and for his contumacy on this occasion he was to find himself replaced by the more adaptable Dutt.

For the time being, however, Pollitt seemed indispensable to the Party in its efforts to promote left-wing unity. Indeed, when in 1937 the Comintern leadership took soundings to replace him with somebody less inclined to rock the boat, his colleagues are said to have stood by him to a man.[8] Pollitt was not only the Party's most effective propagandist but also its shrewdest and most plausible negotiator. As Communists sought out and seduced every potential ally on the left, he seemed able to win, if not always the hearts and minds, at least the co-operation of associates of considerable influence. Already his skills were demonstrated on the committee the CP set up with the ILP in 1933. Forgetful of his earlier calumnies, Pollitt now came 'cooing to the ILP like a sucking-dove'. The foulness that was Brockway remembered him as 'reasonableness itself' and even John Paton, the ILP's more antagonistic secretary, described his contribution with grudging admiration:

He was conciliatory, he was deft, he was diplomatic, he knew to a hairbreadth just how far to press and when to give way…. When one of his colleagues, less far-sighted than himself, seemed likely to over-press some point I was contesting, he'd suavely intervene with a decisive – 'We'll let that go', and the insistent voice was silent. He was very definitely the man in command of the Communist team…

He was, according to this witness, particularly adept at handling Brockway and managed to extract from him a commitment to 'day-to-day co-operation' with the CP which Paton at least had not intended.[9]

The CP's relationship with the ILP over the next four years was to be a tempestuous one. Nevertheless, along with the Socialist League, a left-wing ginger group within the Labour Party, they made in the Unity Campaign of 1937 a final despairing attempt to change the course of British politics. Pollitt's role was again a crucial one and yet from the start he had deep reservations about the whole project. His own aspirations by now centred very much on winning over the Labour Party, to which the CP vainly pledged its loyalty and sought affiliation. That indeed was the rationale for the Party not again contesting parliamentary seats and simply holding on to Gallacher's. In the fractious alliance of the outside left Pollitt foresaw a more likely hindrance than assistance in this basic task, inviting the suspicions and exclusions of the official movement. He was, he said, 'apprehensive of doing anything that gets us into the camp of the splitters': the ILP, a much diminished force, was now virtually beyond the pale, while Socialist Leaguers like Aneurin Bevan and William Mellor he suspected of hidden designs for an independent 'workers' party' of which the CP wanted no part. During the talks, moreover, the CP was subjected to just those rejoinders and reminders that came most tellingly from the left, particularly when they concerned Stalin's Russia. Nevertheless, Pollitt endeavoured to remain his usual equable self. '… a lot of you think I am an irritable old bastard', he reported back to his CP colleagues, 'but I believe I gave a model so far as good temper is concerned, because I never listened to so many studied insults of the Communist Party…' Bevan and Jennie Lee he found particularly provoking. 'At the right time, and the right place I shall let myself go', he went on, 'but I had to hold the chair etc. in order to relieve my tension a little.'[10]

91

The talks had been initiated by Sir Stafford Cripps, the Socialist League's chief spokesman and provider and a somewhat erratic and impressionable luminary of the Labour left. Pollitt himself described Cripps as 'the only clean man in the whole of that bunch' and it was for this connection alone that he thought the effort worth making. 'There was no doubt that Harry Pollitt understood Cripps's value', Brockway wrote afterwards. 'He wooed him assiduously, played up to him in committees, staying on for chats with him after committees.' Cripps had little grasp of the doctrinal questions that threatened to rend the campaign, only an impatience to get things moving; and it is not hard to imagine how Pollitt, with his own disregard for theoretical quibbles, must have impressed him with his eloquence and sense of urgency. In the emphatic disclaimers of any breakaway mentality when at last the campaign was launched, the influence of the Communist leader can clearly be discerned. Likewise, when the Socialist League dissolved itself to avoid the expulsion of its members from the Labour Party, and then when the Unity Committee itself folded for essentially the same reason, it was at the very least with Pollitt's vigorous assent.[11]

Pollitt maintained contact with Cripps until the war and through him exercised a perceptible influence over the weekly paper *Tribune* which Cripps founded in 1937 and subsidised thereafter. The CP's hand can, for example, surely be detected in Cripps's summary dismissal of the prickly and independent-minded Mellor as the paper's editor in 1938 and his replacement with the evidently pliant fellow-traveller, H. J. Hartshorn. In his flair for this sort of work Pollitt certainly stood out from the Communists who accompanied him. Dutt, for example, came across as 'a withdrawn and mostly silent personality, secretive, suspicious, waiting and watching'; while the aged Tom Mann complained after one Unity Committee meeting that with his hearing so bad he could 'scarcely get any sense from the speeches' and could see no further point in attending.[12]

From its formation in 1936 Pollitt also had a good deal to do with Britain's liveliest attempt at a People's Front, the Left Book Club. 'Though the platform had a faint tinge of the Popular Front, I was left under no illusion about the inspiration of the Club', the *News Chronicle*'s A. J. Cummings wrote of its first Albert Hall rally. 'The name of Mr Harry Pollitt... brought a bigger cheer than that of any other politicians; and when he approached the microphone to say his

piece the audience rose at him as if he were one of God's chosen.'
As with the Unity Campaign, the fervid oratory with which he held
rallies spellbound up and down the country was accompanied by a
quieter influence behind the scenes. Victor Gollancz, the club's
founder and ultimately its controller, had his publisher's offices only
just round the corner from the CP's King Street headquarters and
for the first two years of the club's existence both parties took full
advantage of the liaison and collusion this permitted. Pollitt in
particular, as he himself later recalled, got on well with Gollancz;
well enough, indeed, to get Gollancz to suppress at least one club
selection of which the CP disapproved. In private Gollancz himself
attributed the Communist influence over the club at least in part to
the force of Pollitt's personality.[13]

The club's other selectors, John Strachey and Harold Laski, were
also susceptible to Pollitt's influence, albeit to rather different
degrees. Assessing Strachey's eight-year sojourn with Communism,
both his biographers emphasise the dominant influence of Dutt.
Intellectually this was no doubt the case, although it is notable that
while Strachey looked to Brussels for help with theoretical
questions, it was to Pollitt and his assistant Emile Burns that he
submitted a more polemical text like *The Menace of Fascism*. In
political campaigns too, like those against Mosley and like the Left
Book Club itself, Strachey worked closely with Pollitt. His own
impact on the Communist leader is not to be discounted. There
survives from 1933, for example, a letter in which, with his broader
experience, he urged on Pollitt a subtler, more calculating approach
to propaganda if the CP was not only to demolish its opponents but
win some of them over. By and large, however, it seems that
Strachey too, while never afraid to put his own point of view,
deferred to Pollitt's authority. Certainly, when in the more divisive
circumstances of the outbreak of war he proposed remaining alone
in London to deal with the organisational side of the LBC, both
Gollancz and Laski opposed the idea, and both for the same reason.
'If you were up there in London... seeing Harry Pollitt every day',
Gollancz wrote to him, 'nothing in the world could prevent the whole
thing gradually taking on the King Street tinge...' Laski was blunter
still. What Strachey had to remember, he wrote to Gollancz, was
that 'he was very impressionable, especially to Harry, that we must
safeguard ourselves against his use by Harry as an instrument'.[14]

Laski himself, on the other hand, was by no means the sort of person to sacrifice his own judgement to Pollitt's. He nevertheless regarded him, as he later wrote, as 'one of the half dozen people on the Left for whose complete integrity I would have gone to the stake'. The two quarrelled bitterly during the CP's anti-war period and Laski again expressed his wariness of Pollitt's willingness to 'use' friendships for political ends.[15] His comments highlight the difficulty of assessing Pollitt's attitude to political relationships extending beyond the CP. Here, apparently, was an integrity worth going to the stake for alongside a perceived ability and readiness to manipulate even the closest of associates. Pollitt's position was indeed an ambivalent one. He was certainly not one to eschew Party advantage but this did not preclude a genuine commitment to the common objectives underlying his various associations. Possibly even the opposite was true: so convinced was he that the Communist Party was essential to whatever objectives he was pursuing that he could not, or would not allow himself to, conceive that furthering the Party's particular interests could conflict with those objectives. It is this mixture of moral fervour and opportunism, even Machiavellianism perhaps, that one has to grasp if one is to understand either Pollitt or the CP.

Laski's house provided the setting for a fascinating vignette that exemplified his diplomatic skills. The occasion was a private meeting between Pollitt, Laski's brother Neville, the president of the British Board of Deputies, and Herbert Morrison, leader of the London Labour Party and scourge of the Reds. Their purpose, in the immediate aftermath of the 'Battle of Cable Street', was to discuss how best to respond to the fascist presence in the East End. More specifically, Laski and Morrison desired from Pollitt an undertaking that his supporters would desist from physical confrontation with the Blackshirts. Pollitt was no enthusiast for such clashes but he insisted that his supporters would not be persuaded to surrender the streets to fascism. Nevertheless, his contribution to the discussion, as recorded in a note by Neville Laski, was both constructive and adroit. Surprising Laski by his moderation, he expressed sympathy with the police and support for the rule of law in 'almost identical terms' to those of Morrison. Moreover, although the feud between Morrison and the Communists had been bitter and protracted, Pollitt made not the slightest attempt to score points off his longstanding adversary. 'In fact I must commend his restraint', wrote Laski. 'He said much less than M and what he said was almost exactly the same as M.' Pollitt's moderation had a purpose, however, and by the end of the discussion he had in the deftest way possible raised the question of just the sort of joint activity that Morrison was sworn to eliminate:

> A suggestion was made by P, to which I made no reply – nor did M – but there is some genius in the suggestion, that a Communist, Jew and a Labour, and perhaps others including the Church, should be represented on one platform in the East End for a municipal meeting to denounce anti-Semitism.

No wonder Morrison had no reply! Quite apart from Pollitt's tact and cunning, however, it should be noted that Morrison had apparently the completest confidence in his discretion; for it would of course have been highly embarrassing to London's most vocal anti-Communist had any word of the meeting crept out. One wonders who else Pollitt might have met without a Laski there to record it.[16]

His rendezvous with Morrison notwithstanding, the question of Mosley was not one that very much occupied Pollitt by this time. Of far greater concern to him was the relentless spread of fascism on the Continent. The underlying rationale for all his activities during this period was, in his own words, 'the need to deliver powerful blows directly against Fascist aggressors like Hitler, and those who support him directly – the National Government – or indirectly like those who believe in accepting his false "Peace" gestures'.[17] It was the better to deliver such blows that Pollitt worked so hard to achieve unity of the left in Britain, and to an overwhelming degree his own speeches and writings were devoted to the worsening international situation. 'The questions arising from the danger of war overshadow everything else in the minds of the workers', he wrote in 1936. 'Wages, hours, workshop conditions, the fight against the Means Test, all are recognised as being urgent, but... even these issues give way before a situation in which the lives and destinies of millions are at stake.'[18] In ways that were as yet barely perceptible, this emphasis set Pollitt subtly apart from others in the Communist leadership. Commenting on a draft pamphlet of his in 1939, Dutt warned that Pollitt's disregard for domestic issues as

95

entirely secondary would 'only help those who attack us as a "foreign policy party"'. The criticism might just as well have applied to almost any of Pollitt's pamphlets of the previous three years. So too might Dutt's warning that his eagerness to 'strike the best blows against Hitler and Mussolini' might be taken as a declaration for war.[19] Certainly, from no other Communist leader did the rhetoric of peace come less convincingly nor, as one country after another fell to fascism, the language of hatred and vengeance so authentically. Like all his colleagues, Pollitt's primary focus was on the National Government with its own 'fascist' tendencies, but more single-mindedly than most of them he denounced it less for its domestic policies than for the crime of appeasement. The difference was as yet one of emphasis only and the tensions ran within Pollitt as well as around him. Nevertheless, when after the outbreak of war the CP was required by Moscow to practise its own form of appeasement, Pollitt was to prove the most recalcitrant of British Communists.

That Pollitt was in 1939 to resist the International's anti-war line, knowing full well the futility of his doing so, indicates very clearly that his anti-fascism was not simply a question of tactics, or of Party orthodoxy. There was here a deeper and enduring emotional commitment deriving above all from his involvement from 1936 onwards in the war in Spain. In a recantation that reads in parts like a justification, Pollitt was in 1939 to explain his initial support for the war against Germany by 'the strong personal feelings which had been aroused by what I had witnessed in Spain, and the respon-sibility I felt I had in regard to the sacrifice made by the British Battalion of the International Brigade'. His contribution to the recruitment and later the morale of the British Battalion was indeed a considerable one. In the first heady months of the war there was no greater stimulus to solidarity with the republic than Pollitt's passionate oratory and his regular appeals for recruits and donations in the *Daily Worker*. In due course ostensibly non-Party organisations were established to organise Spanish aid and support for volunteers' dependants. Recruitment, on the other hand, was from first to last strictly under Party control, and as general secretary Pollitt had a keen sense of his responsibilities towards the British volunteers. Five times between February 1937 and August 1938 he visited the British Battalion and he would be remembered warmly by the volunteers for the gifts, the messages and the sense of solidarity that he brought. 'Well you could say that it was the sort of thing that any adjutant in an army would do for his men', one of them recalled; but it was not every Communist leader who would take on himself the role of adjutant. Pollitt also had the task of dealing with those left bereaved by the war or unsettled by the rumours that moved so much more quickly than official information. While many shared Pollitt's own pride in their loved ones' sacrifice, others had an angry sense of having being manipulated by the Communist Party. Pollitt, to judge from his surviving correspondence, handled both types of situation with tact and humanity.[20]

What Pollitt saw on his visits to Spain evidently made a profound impression on him. It was in Madrid that he first witnessed the effects of sustained aerial bombing and drew inspiration from the fact that it seemed not to demoralise the population but to engender 'a fiercer determination than ever to be avenged for every crime'. The most searing memory of all was of his visit to the devastated Catalan town of Tortosa in April 1938. Thousands had fled the town, their homes reduced to rubble, and the few afflicted souls that remained – he recalled in particular one woman sat amidst debris, driven to distraction and dangling a child from her hand – called forth Pollitt's instinctive defiance and desire for revenge. 'I shall never forget that afternoon', Victor Gollancz recalled of his subsequent return to England. 'Pollitt strode up and down the room, with an extremity of passion in his face and voice – a passion of fury against Hitler and of deepest pity for the women and babies of Spain – and he said: "If there is war between us, and if it goes on for ten or twenty years, and if every town and village of Britain is razed to the ground, the working class of this country will never submit to him."' This terrifying image of the destruction of Tortosa was one to which Pollitt would return on many occasions, including the impassioned debate in September 1939 as to whether Britain should fight or shake hands with those who had ravaged Spain.[21]

That the crusade in Spain was no more a simple tale of valour than any other of history's crusades Pollitt had good enough reason to know. As Party leader he received from the political commissars with the British Battalion regular reports that gave witness to 'the void between the official version of events... and the reality'.[22] Desertions, indiscipline and sagging morale, along with personal jealousies and animosities, formed part of the fabric of this as of any protracted war. To these were added a breath of the cynicism and brutality then casting terror over Stalinist Russia and so damaging to the ideals for which two thousand Britons had enlisted. From Orwell onwards, many observers have indeed found in the treachery and mendacity of Communist functionaries the most meaningful and disillusioning image of the Spanish war. It is not surprising, then, that Pollitt himself has been cast in the stock role of Stalinist villain in cautionary tales scarcely less glib than the edifying myths they seek to displace. In these depictions the classic attributes of amorality and expediency rest mainly on a nasty rumour that in 1937 he told the poet Stephen Spender, then dallying with Communism, "'go and get killed, comrade, we need a Byron in the movement'". The story, oft-repeated, lacks any plausibility: there is no hint of it in Spender's published recollections of the meeting and it is in any case completely out of character. Even had he harboured such a thought, Pollitt was far too astute a politician to have revealed such unbridled cynicism to a poet of liberal pedigree and demonstrative sensitivity.[23] Nevertheless, on the basis of this sort of irresistible titbit, various literary pundits have depicted for us a Harry Pollitt for whom the volunteers in Spain were just so many means to an end, to be cosseted or sacrificed entirely as best served the Party's interests. 'No one', writes one of them with the smug and feeble irony that is their hallmark, 'no one ever accused the very efficient Pollitt... of idealism'.[24]

That Pollitt did of course ask Communists to risk their lives in Spain was something he made no secret of. 'I asked him to go, and explained that it meant facing death', he recalled in 1937 of an interview he arranged with one Cambridge Communist. 'Without a moment's hesitation Comrade McLaurin gave up everything he held dear and went the next day.' Comrade McLaurin was, in fact, killed in the defence of Madrid. Of course his death had its uses in propaganda as partial and romanticised as war propaganda invariably is. The objectives of this propaganda, however, McLaurin would have recognised as his own. Even where Party interests intruded, neither he nor Pollitt would have grasped the distinction between the cause of Spain and the organisation that was everywhere most active in promoting that cause. To hint at vulgar manipulation is in any case to overlook Pollitt's passionate identification with the struggle and its casualties. It was, for example, a measure of his deep

98

sense of involvement in McLaurin's death that on a visit to New Zealand some quarter of a century later he made certain to call and pay his respects to his mother.[25]

An authentic glimpse of Pollitt's role in the Spanish war, unconstrained by personal or political allegiances, was provided by Fred Copeman, ex-Invergordon mutineer and from mid-1937 commander of the British Battalion. By his own account Copeman was at this time a favourite of Pollitt's, although the two later fell out badly. Indeed, possibly because Copeman published in 1948 an unvarnished account of life at the Spanish front, Pollitt systematically expunged every reference to his former protégé on going through his own reports from Spain some years later. In this memoir and in a later recorded interview, Copeman certainly dwelt on aspects of the war that found no place in its official histories. More than anything else, his accounts seethe with the serving soldier's resentment at 'politicians': in this case commissars enjoying hotel comforts, meddlesome Comintern officials and, above all, Russians. 'There were too many bastards running round giving orders and not enough of them fighting', he remembered. 'And those that were giving orders, they were useless silly orders and irresponsible to human life.' From this harsh judgement, however, Pollitt was apparently exempt. Far from holding the soldiers' lives cheaply, he 'was very determined to look after our lads, he wouldn't let us be pushed around'. Thus, for example, his indignation at the frightening extent of British losses at Brunete in July 1937. Moreover, he had, it seems, a mature and humane understanding of the pressures to which such bloody slaughter as that at Jarama and Brunete subjected the men:

> You don't necessarily discipline people in a voluntary army of that type as you do in an ordinary army. They still think they're volunteers. And volunteers means what it says. 'I volunteered to come out. I volunteer to go back.' And bloody sound common sense if you've been wounded enough times. So that I had a great deal of sympathy with that. And so did Harry Pollitt.

More specifically, Pollitt fought with Copeman and others a long though ultimately unsuccessful battle against the introduction into the British Battalion of the death penalty for desertion.[26]

Against this one must set the more hectoring approach to recruitment that the Party adopted during the latter stages of the

99

war when, as Pollitt admitted, the romanticism had rather gone out of things. Moreover, Copeman had another story to tell of the alleged misappropriation of Dependants' Aid funds for Party purposes, or at least the repayment of its earlier Comintern grants as supposed loans. Whatever the truth of this, it is important to keep in mind that by 'Stalinist crimes' in the British context we mean not a murderous disdain for human life but the funding of Party activities through petty acts of defalcation. It is an important distinction. Copeman also recalled that in Spain the Russians and some of the other European CPs were 'up to all the tricks in hell... of having people bumped off and things like that'. One victim, he alleged, was the British commissar and friend of Pollitt's, Wally Tapsell. The British Party itself, however, thankfully less steeled in the class struggle than some of the others, 'wouldn't be that deep in that type of thing'.

The tragedy of the Spanish war lay not just in its mingling of heroism and idealism with a cruel, corrupting cynicism but in the inevitability, short of dramatic upheavals elsewhere, of a Franco victory. It was in fact the view of Communists that possibly only a change of government in Britain could so alter the balance of international forces as to save the republic; and it was this perception of Britain's pivotal role in world affairs that aroused in Pollitt such bitter feelings of shame and frustration. Visiting Spain, he wrote in 1937, 'wherever I went the same question was repeated. What is British Labour doing? What could I reply?' he went on. 'They can never be beaten except by our passivity and inactivity.' If Pollitt accused the Labour leadership not only of passivity but of a positive 'identification with every fundamental aspect of the foreign policy of the National Government', this was as nothing compared to his denunciations of the National Government itself. 'Whatever was good in British traditions', he told the Party's Fourteenth Congress in 1937, 'the National Government has abandoned and betrayed while they have added new examples of reaction and treachery to every infamy that has previously sullied the name of Britain.' What this involved was not weakness towards the dictators or mere indifference to the plight of Spain but active collusion in the promotion of fascist interests. 'The main responsibility for the increase of the war danger, for the menace of Fascism to the democratic countries and to all mankind lies upon the

National Government.'[27] How much more serious the charge, then, when the following year first Austria and then Czechoslovakia fell victims not so much to the German war machine as to Chamberlain's appeasement.

The late 1930s were in fact for Communists years in which the initial euphoria associated with People's Front successes in Spain and France gave way to a grimmer preoccupation with the defence of the status quo. As the hopes of sweeping social advances released by the Seventh World Congress were replaced by more basic instincts of self-preservation, the 'two camps' so central to Communist thinking came to be defined almost exclusively in relation to the fascist war offensive. Just as opposition to anti-fascist unity defined the camp of reaction, so was almost anybody alive to the threat posed by Hitler admitted to the ever more laxly defined camp of 'peace'. In March 1938, for example, Pollitt published a pamphlet on the imminent *Anschluss* from which it was barely deducible that it was not a democratic Austria that Hitler threatened, but Schuschnigg's clerical dictatorship. Within Britain the same narrowing perspective was expressed first in the CP's endorsement of a proposed 'United Peace Alliance' embracing the Liberals and later in 1938 in its explicit extension of this concept to include the likes of Churchill. During the crisis over Czechoslovakia that September, it would seem that Pollitt was even persuaded that the treacherous Chamberlain was at last about to stand up to Hitler and raised the question of whether he should in that case receive Communist support. A row ensued backstage at the Party congress then taking place in Birmingham and Dutt has described his own and Salme's role in holding the Party to a line of absolute scepticism as to Chamberlain's intentions.[28]

Dutt's stance was of course vindicated, as Czechoslovakia was forced with the shameful connivance of the British and French governments to cede to Germany the territory that Hitler coveted. The message of Munich was, apparently, that under no circumstances would Chamberlain come to align himself with the anti-fascist camp. In an internal Party document shortly afterwards, Dutt lost no time in chastising the unnamed Communists, Pollitt included, who had shown 'tendencies to capitulate to the war scare (speculations on imminent war, "should we support Chamberlain if he fights Hitler?" etc)'.[29] The episode was evidently taken by Dutt's

101

comrades as a salutary warning against any further such speculation, with one curious and significant result: if over the next few months nobody made more noise about the coming war than the Communists, this only served to divert attention from their almost superstitious refusal to discuss where exactly they stood if and when the war did eventually break out. Once bitten, the CP fought shy of any suggestion that the sequel to Munich might find Chamberlain unable to draw back from confrontation. Pollitt himself later claimed to 'have given more thought and more study to this question of our tactics in war, long before it broke out, than I have done to anything else in my life'.[30] The gist of these thoughts was not, however, made public. Only in the very last month or two of 'peace' was it that the CP leadership, with Pollitt dragging his heels, began at last to prepare in earnest for the long-predicted war.

In retrospect Munich was to the anti-fascist campaigns of the 1930s not so much the climax as the decisive setback. In his own disappointment Pollitt succumbed at last to ill-health and exhaustion brought on by years of relentless political activity. On doctor's orders, and apparently thanks to Party benefactors, he set off in November on the sort of tropical cruise that occasionally figured in his diatribes against the ruling class. 'I have made the most of every minute, and now feel my old self again', he wrote to Tom Mann from Costa Rica, 'and hope to more than repay the comrades who have made this trip possible.'[31] The Europe to which he returned offered gloomier prospects than ever. More or less directly, Munich led not only to Hitler's annexation of Czechoslovakia in March 1939 but to Franco's final victory in Spain. The latter in particular left Pollitt almost pathetically defiant even in defeat. 'Those who worked closely with him then', one colleague recalled, 'know the agony of mind he went through at that time, for Spain perhaps was the cause dearest to his invincible heart.'[32]

If, as the Comintern was by this time asserting, the second imperialist war had already begun, it seemed in Europe at least to be fought on one side only. With Britain's decisive influence still apparently exercised on the side of fascism, a note almost of desperation entered into the CP's calls for extraordinary measures of political mobilisation to displace Chamberlain. To those who mattered, however, especially in Transport House, the placid routines and ritualised alignments of peacetime politics remained sacrosanct. With gaze fixed not so much on the 1940 election as on the one after, just about the only decisive action of the Labour leadership during the whole of 1939 was to expel Cripps for campaigning around proposals for a cross-party alliance very like the CP's. However, even Cripps, as likewise Gollancz who refused to confer with the CP during the Munich crisis, now seemed less responsive to Pollitt's influence than previously. Instead of the vigorous political campaign against expulsion that Pollitt favoured, Cripps put forward a rather feeble technical case; and when the June Labour Party conference dismissed his lawyer's quibbles by a huge majority, the Cripps campaign simply folded.[33] No wonder that in August Pollitt likened the situation to banging one's head against a brick wall.[34]

The CP itself was by this time in a state of some considerable confusion. If the second imperialist war had already begun; and if, as Pollitt insisted in speech after speech, the 'hot, foul breath of war' could now be felt on British cheeks, then the Party's well-worn assurances that resistance to fascism meant peace were past believing. Moreover, as the campaign for a 'people's government' ran out of steam it became increasingly difficult to see by whom, if not the existing government, such resistance might be organised. For Communists this posed an impossible dilemma, confronting not only their assumptions as to Chamberlain's foreign policy but their perception of his every feeblest preparation for war as an instalment of fascism on the home front. 'The plain fact is that Britain to-day is ruled by a Government which prepares a way for the advance of fascism in Britain as well as supporting fascist aggression abroad', Pollitt wrote in February 1939. 'The group [Chamberlain] represents will as surely betray Britain as the Fifth Column in Spain have betrayed the Spanish Republic.'[35] To preach military resistance as the one hope for peace and deny at the same time the means of resistance was not a policy easily sustained. So tightly interwoven were the conflicting strands of Communist policy, however, that they produced not the clear-cut alignments of earlier controversies but differences of emphasis and tone whose significance was often elusive. There was no fiercer antipathy to fascism than Pollitt's, for example, and he struck more often than most the bellicose note for which Dutt had once to reprove him.[36] The strength of these sentiments he later demonstrated by his stubborn resistance to the

Comintern's anti-war directives. It is a mark of the period's complexities, however, that in a similar controversy only four months earlier he held out just as stubbornly against the enveloping war atmosphere to which he felt his colleagues were succumbing. Indeed, so important did he consider the issues raised by the conscription controversy that he proposed already his own replacement as Party secretary.

The row over the Party's opposition to conscription was apparently instigated by the French CP, whose leaders could see no reason why the British should be exempt from obligations willingly accepted by themselves. Evidently they raised the matter with the Comintern with the result that the British representative in Moscow, then J. R. Campbell, returned to London to set the Party right. Ostensibly its basic line of opposition to Chamberlain's war measures, on grounds of his fascist inclinations at home and abroad, was reaffirmed. What Campbell challenged was the tendency of some British Communists, apparently in response to the PCF's criticisms, to embellish this with 'dubious arguments of a technical character' extolling Britain's distinctive traditions of voluntarism. These, he argued, made a mockery of the Party's calls for collective security, which had necessarily to rest on overwhelming force if it were to deter Hitler. Instead, the Party had now to make perfectly clear its ready acceptance of measures of compulsion under a progressive government. Moreover, with the passing into law of the Conscription Bill, it should campaign not against the principle of conscription itself but against Chamberlain's reactionary purposes in introducing it.

On the face of it, the debate did little to dispel the Party's confusion. As Arthur Horner observed, 'nobody says clearly what our policy is now in light of the fact there is a National Government, not another government of the kind we state is necessary'. Horner also noted, however, that the practical effect of Campbell's proposals was in reality 'that we are prepared to tolerate conscription even with this National Government'. That was Pollitt's understanding too, and over four sessions of the Politbureau and one of the Central Committee he remained steadfastly opposed to the Comintern's instructions.

There were a number of elements in the case that Pollitt put to the Central Committee and, by contrast and analogy, they throw a fascinating light on his later rebellion against the anti-war line. First of all he reasserted for the British Party the absolute primacy of its struggle against the National Government. '... in all my work I am actuated by one motive in leading this Party', he said, 'that is to utilise... every tradition, every expression, every mood, in any circumstances to try to bring about the defeat and downfall of this government'. Secondly, he insisted that this was best done on the basis of those indigenous traditions that united the Party with the rest of the Labour movement in its opposition to the government. Pollitt was indeed one of the Communists who had lauded the voluntary tradition and he had already had certain formulations to this effect excised from the pamphlet on the subject he wrote for the Party. As he pointedly remarked, 'we have the responsibility of looking from the point of view of the situation here as well as other comrades looking at it from the point of view of the situation in their country...' Still more intriguing was his rejection of any adaptation by the Party to the developing war situation. '... what we are talking now is war language', he warned:

> We have given up hope of peace. We don't believe that the Peace Front means peace. Johnny [Campbell] cannot put his pen to paper without talking about overwhelming forces and that sort of stuff. Does not want 12 million Russians to fight and 200,000 children. The policy I am fighting for is the policy that will prevent any of them fighting.

That on the very eve of war even Pollitt nurtured such illusions says something of the enormous problem the CP had with the question of war and peace. It also provides an extraordinary contrast with the relish for combat that he later showed during the Party's debates on the war itself. If Pollitt was consistent in one thing, however, it was his resentment at the Comintern's arbitrary interference in the British Party's affairs. Quite apart from the PCF's unwarranted intervention, Campbell arrived with instructions not to discuss but to impose on the CP the CI's decisions, and he entirely pre-empted the Politbureau by inserting in the *Daily Worker* an editorial conveying already the new position. It was, as Peter Kerrigan put it, 'a contemptuous flouting of the whole of the leadership', and particularly of course of Pollitt as Party secretary. It was thus undermined in his authority that Pollitt proposed to the Politbureau 'certain organisational changes in view of the opposition that he in particular had to the [conscription] resolution', and that he alone then voted against a counter-proposal 'that all members of the P.B. retain their present positions in the Party leadership'. Pollitt was no prima donna and the offer of resignation is not one that he would have made lightly.[37]

He did not however take long to overcome the setback. Indeed, it seems in some ways to have been offset by the opportunity he had at last to give uninhibited expression to his more basic anti-fascist instincts. Possibly the influence of Campbell, who remained in Britain, had something to do with this. The quasi-pacifist note that Pollitt usually scorned was now forgotten, and in the pamphlet *Will It Be War?*, published early in July, he invoked for the first time in the context of Chamberlain's Britain the passion and indignation aroused in him by the struggle in Spain. Despite its ritual invocations of the 'Peace Front', the pamphlet was in effect Pollitt's and the CP's first declaration of support for the looming war. Against 'the mealy-mouthed pacifism which would lie down humbly and let fascism wipe its boots upon our bodies' Pollitt counterposed the resilience and combativeness of the common people:

> And so to the fight, inspired by consciousness of our latent power, strength and dignity as a free people ...
>
> For our defence is... enriched by the collective experiences we have assimilated from the titanic struggles of those who hundreds of years ago saw the gleam of socialism...
>
> We are the inheritors of their fighting traditions... We will never besmirch their proud records... or sully the flag of liberty they held so proudly aloft.
>
> Our country and our people will never fall victims to fascism. The people of Britain will fight if necessary better than any other people in the world.

With its inescapable message, this pamphlet was intended by Pollitt to form the basis of his report on the war situation to the Sixteenth Party Congress, due in October. 'Should we deal with question of our policy if war breaks out and a Chamberlain Government in power?' he wondered in planning out the report. Campbell answered with an emphatic affirmative. 'This is speculation but it has a basis different from last year', he wrote to Pollitt, outlining the policy of a 'war on two fronts' with which the CP would initially respond to the outbreak of war a month or two later.[38] Like Pollitt,

Campbell looked to the Comintern special commission on the British Party arranged for August to settle the matter once and for all. After years in which it had combined the rhetoric of armed struggle with that of peace and denounced not only Hitler but some of his likeliest foes, the CP seemed at last to be sorting out its priorities.

As it turned out, Moscow was that August to witness even more momentous events than a commission on the British Communist Party. The cruelly undeceiving Nazi-Soviet non-aggression pact, signed in the Russian capital on 23 August, not only cleared the way for the annihilation of Poland and European war but, as if at the touch of a switch, cast a mocking light on the hopes and dogmas of half a decade. Pollitt was as little prepared for the blow as anybody. For years his main propaganda activities had been devoted to a conception of international politics upholding the Soviet Union 'as the Workers' State and principal guardian for maintaining peace for the peoples of the world'. In this context peace had not connoted a genial diplomacy tending towards compromise, but stern resistance to every reactionary manoeuvre and 'an army ready to throw its full, dynamic weight into the scales against German, Italian and Japanese fascists'. It was against this background of seemingly irreconcilable enmity between Communism and fascism that Pollitt had pledged British Communists to 'support 100 per cent., and without any reservations everything that the Soviet Union does in its foreign policy, because we understand that this foreign policy is in accord with the interests of the international working class as a whole'.[39]

On the surface, and not just in the eyes of Communists, events in the late 1930s seemed to bear out this misapprehension. In the Moscow trials were revealed fiendish Nazi plots to undermine the Stalinist edifice; in Spain, Pollitt encountered widespread enthusiasm for the USSR as the one country to come to the republic's aid; and of the great European powers, the workers' state alone had no part in the grim farce played out at Munich. Pollitt later revealed that he had, even before the pact, been disturbed by the disappearance of internationalism from Soviet pronouncements,[40] but no warning signals could have prepared him for so severe a shock as a Soviet-German rapprochement. To an incredulous public, however, as he was called upon to explain Stalin's volte-face, he gave no hint of the 'nasty taste in the mouth' that this left.[41] On the contrary, he hailed

107

the Bolsheviks' 'swift masterpiece of a stroke' and insisted again that their every act was 'consciously directed, not only to the good of their own citizens but to advance the interests of all sections of progressive mankind'.[42] In no sense had the fascists gained a victory, he explained. The Franco-Soviet pact remained operative and an Anglo-Soviet pact feasible, while the parties of the Comintern were as far as ever from relaxing their efforts to restrain the dictators. Over the next painful month Pollitt was to learn better.

The precise sequence of events by which the CP came to oppose the war and demote Pollitt has recently become much clearer.[43] On the outbreak of war the Party's initial response was a call for a 'war on two fronts', expressed with characteristic vigour in Pollitt's pamphlet *How to Win the War*. 'To stand aside from this conflict', he wrote, 'to contribute only revolutionary-sounding phrases while the fascist beasts ride roughshod over Europe would be a betrayal of everything our forbears have fought to achieve in the course of long years of struggle against capitalism.' On 14 September, however, the very day that these words were published, there arrived from Moscow a press telegram employing precisely those distracting phrases about imperialist war that Pollitt had had in mind. Dauntless, he had the telegram suppressed. Dutt, however, and possibly one or two others more readily attuned to signals from Moscow, began immediately to argue for a reorientation of the Party's policy. Over the next fortnight or so Pollitt stuck to his guns, initially as part of a large Central Committee majority which then faded away when the Party's new CI representative, David Springhall, returned on 24 September with instructions to oppose the war. At the adjourned Central Committee called to resolve the question on 2-3 October, only Pollitt and Campbell finally voted against the anti-war policy. Gallacher, for his part, could hardly find the words to express his disgust at Dutt, Rust and Springhall, the 'three ruthless revolutionaries' he felt were conspiring against Pollitt. Eventually, however, he registered his vote in favour of their thesis, presumably at Pollitt's behest so as to retain his seat on the Political Bureau. Pollitt and Campbell, on the other hand, were both relieved of their duties, as Party secretary and editor of the *Daily Worker* respectively.[44]

That this notorious episode has so often been personalised as a clash between Pollitt and Dutt is not surprising. Dutt it was who first took up the new refrain from Moscow; who then presented the new Comintern line, and implicitly the case against Pollitt, at the adjourned Central Committee; and finally took over from Pollitt responsibility for the Party's affairs. Moreover, their dominating contributions to the debates on the war revealed just how far the conceptions of Communist politics held by the two old comrades had diverged during the 1930s. As so often, differences of emphasis and approach acquired with the loss of shared objectives a sharper significance. Where Pollitt relied on gut feelings, Dutt displayed doctrinal athleticism. Where Pollitt was concerned with practical results, Dutt wanted to get things worded right. Most importantly, where Pollitt never forgot to consider the Party's standing with British workers, Dutt was above all interested in getting things straight with Moscow.

First and foremost, Pollitt's resistance to the new line was not a cerebral matter but a question of fundamental 'class instinct'. Back in 1914, he explained, he had known nothing of Bolshevism or of the Marxist analysis of imperialist war, but had been guided by 'a class instinct which was sound' to denounce the pointless carnage. The same instinct now told him that, 'whether it is the Second Imperialist War or the Third one', if a chance now existed to destroy fascism then 'that, and that alone is justification for the line we are putting forward'. While drawing on his deeply felt memories of the Spanish war, he now expressed the same instinctive solidarity with the workers and peasants 'fighting in Warsaw against the bastards'. 'I am ashamed that because of what we have heard about the line', he reproached his colleagues, 'we have not been able to treat the Warsaw resistance in the same way that we treated Madrid and Valencia and Barcelona.' Unimpressed by this emotionalism, Dutt dismissed the Polish workers airily. 'There are moments', he intoned, revolving his globe, 'when it is necessary to be hard because you see the whole world situation and where the forces go.' How very different this from Pollitt's visceral utterance: 'Smash the fascist bastards once and for all.'

Dutt's casuistries appalled Pollitt as much by their wild unreality as by their cynicism. Since the Seventh World Congress and earlier, Pollitt's constant endeavour had been to maximise the CP's impact on British politics. What this required at all times was a sober assessment of the political situation and particularly of the Party's own marginal capacity to shape events. In presenting the new line, however, Dutt seemed first to posit a sharp revolutionary turn that had no objective basis and then blithely to refashion reality to fit his thesis. No wonder Pollitt taunted him. 'Common sense is needed now as never before', he noted, 'and English common sense.' Hitler had not been weakened by recent events but immeasurably strengthened, and as to glib talk about revolutionary prospects, well, '1917 in Russia was a bit different from France in 1917. They only shot 17,000 French soldiers who mutinied.' Moreover, even had Dutt's prognoses been sounder, his proposals took not the slightest account of the Party's weakness. 'Even if you are going to carry out the perspective of the thesis', Pollitt warned, 'you cannot do it with 18,000 members, and cannot do it if you are going to be separated from the labour movement and the Trade Unions.'

Pollitt's instincts, as in previous years, were to make contact with Cripps, with Lloyd George, with anybody in fact whose voice could be made to count against the National Government. Dutt, on the other hand, seemed disposed to turn away from those who wielded influence in British politics to the more nebulous concept of a 'united front from below'. He was indeed unconcerned with the practicalities of replacing the government. Pollitt held that to be taken seriously the Party had to indicate some alternative government to Chamberlain's, necessarily based on the Labour movement. Dutt, on the other hand, was content that this alternative be defined not in terms of its origins, support or composition but simply 'by the aims that it should accomplish'. He was no more to be swayed by Pollitt's avowal that the very fact of performing the somersault required by Moscow augured ill for 'a leadership that can command the confidence of the Party, the working class and the majority of the people'. These were not indeed constituencies with which Dutt had a very direct relationship. As his fellow theoretician Emile Burns pointed out, his 'persistent underlying sectarian tendencies' were rooted in 'his formal approach to problems, not understanding the problem of getting a line across. All he is concerned with is the thesis form of the line.' That at least could not be said of Pollitt.

Pollitt's expressions of national feeling were a further indication of how he had internalised many aspects of popular front politics to which Dutt had only a tactical commitment. 'As English as a

110

Lancashire rose or an oak' was how Dutt would later describe the genial boilermaker,[45] though probably on this occasion some rather different simile struck him. Certainly, there was no confusing which of the two had emerged from the bowels of the British Labour movement and which had spent half his adult life enmeshed with the Comintern apparatus abroad. 'My remarks may be coloured by thinking about the British people', asserted Pollitt, not at all apologetically. 'We had the right to make the British people think about the people of Abyssinia, Austria, Czechoslovakia and Spain, and we have the right also to make them think about the danger they now face themselves from fascism.' There was more than a hint in his attitude of Robert Blatchford, graphically illustrated by his proposal that the Party campaign around the slogan 'Britain for the British', the title of one of Blatchford's most popular books. Worse still, by the standards of the Comintern's debased internationalism, these patriotic sentiments engendered in Pollitt a resentment of 'Soviet-Fascist' collusion amounting almost to heresy. How, he wondered, would recent pronouncements from Moscow read on the Siegfried Line? 'I tell you there is enough thinking about the poor German people and not enough about the poor British people.' Given that on these grounds Pollitt was in effect urging the British Party to defy the Comintern's authority, it is not surprising that Dutt complained of 'anti-International tendencies', 'anti-Soviet tendencies' and 'talk of our being an independent Party', all reflecting 'enemy outlooks'. What Dutt wanted, and what he got more or less, was 'absolute identity on the international line'.

As if the political setback were not enough, the discussions were conducted with a rancour which Pollitt would not easily forget. In particular he resented Dutt's aspersion that in the more difficult circumstances now facing the CP 'any member who... deserts from active work for the Party will be branded for his political life'. Pollitt could have had no doubt as to whom this referred, for he had that very morning received a letter to similar effect from Salme. 'All the young ladies in the Party will undoubtedly admire you if you retire to your Popular Pals', she jeered, 'it is dramatic and tragic.' Either one accepted the fact of a 'centralised world party', with all that that entailed, or else 'one finds oneself outside at the best, but most often in the camp of the enemy'.[46] Pollitt replied with vehement feeling, but despite his pledge to abide loyally and

111

publicly by the decision he so deplored and 'take every knock that is coming', it was felt wiser to remove him from the inner leadership. Slighted and discarded by his oldest political associates, it was with bitter experience that he reflected that 'in politics there is neither friendship or loyalty'.

That Dutt's innuendoes were phrased in terms of 'desertion', and that Pollitt responded as if this was indeed the issue, gives some idea of their shared conviction that Party membership brought with it irrevocable obligations. Agnostic readers nowadays may well wonder just why it was that Pollitt did not 'desert'. After all, the policies he was now required to uphold he regarded with shame. 'I spoke better than I have ever spoken in my life', he confessed of his first public oration of the new themes, 'and I despised myself.' In the *Daily Worker*, edited once more by Rust, he even began to detect a note of 'pure Goebbels type of fascist propaganda' which he felt must be 'offensive to every sincere anti-fascist in the country'.[47] Moreover, his being summarily dismissed without even a chance to give public voice to his views must surely have hurt a man of Pollitt's pride. In a letter he would treasure, his mother wrote to reaffirm the notions of self-respect she had instilled in him. 'One thing I do know', he read. 'I would not lose my dignity by having an office boy's job and being dictated to by someone half as competent, because the tools are still in the vaseline.'[48]

Sadly, however, Pollitt did allow himself to be dictated to. When, for example, he sent Dutt his thoughts for a pamphlet giving the anti-war line, Salme in her reply addressed him as if he were still the political tyro of years gone by. His emphasis on his 'own people' and their needs, albeit now for peace, was 'absolutely incorrect', she wrote, and a sign of 'suppressed chauvinism'. It is not surprising that Pollitt apparently refused the early meeting she requested to put him right.[49] Even more humiliatingly, Pollitt's initial statement accepting the new line was apparently deemed insufficiently self-critical. Eventually he had to submit, for publication in the *Daily Worker* and elsewhere, a longer and less dignified recantation, humbly admitting to an 'impermissible' breach of discipline.[50] What will surprise many is not that Pollitt's relations with his one-time mentors took some time to thaw,[51] but that he put up with these indignities at all. In other circles and amongst other associates, after all, the objectives to which he had clung had not been abandoned.

Possibly for the last time, as he must surely have been aware, a career in mainstream Labour politics still lay open to him, and with it the chance to play his own part in Britain's war against fascism.

Pollitt's disciplined allegiance to the Party in these circumstances must of course be seen primarily in terms of the compulsions and taboos we associate with Stalinism. Campbell recalled of this episode that 'if you didn't live through that time you can't understand what the pressures were to convince ourselves that the line of the International... was right'.[52] This is not to say that Pollitt's submission had quite the sort of nightmarish quality we associate with Darkness at Noon. For him the Communist Party was not, or not simply, Rubashov's 'embodiment of the revolutionary idea in history', but a living political organisation which for twenty years he had sweated blood to build up and to which innumerable ties of friendship and loyalty bound him. Amongst the most heartwarming of the messages he received at this time was one from Sam Wild, fellow Mancunian and ex-Battalion commander in Spain, expressing 'confidence that the Pal and Comrade I loved and trusted for his devotion to the Battalion will emerge from this fully conscious that the line he takes is for the benefit of the class he has sacrificed so much for'.[53] It was because he knew that nothing was so certain to split the pals and comrades like this who made up the CP that Pollitt could not countenance the idea of defection. Moreover, if he did indeed feel that the Party had some essential call on his loyalty almost regardless of its particular policies, this owed as much to his trade unionist's conception of democracy as to the imported theories of democratic centralism he had grafted onto it. 'For him, not to have supported a party decision with which he disagreed', one Communist wrote of this episode, 'would have been like blacklegging on a majority decision to strike no matter how ill-judged he might think the strike to be.'[54] The analogy is particularly apt inasmuch as, just as Pollitt perceived the struggle of worker against exploiter even in periods of industrial truce, so despite their diplomatic entanglements did he remain convinced of the fundamental antagonism between Communism and fascism. Already at the October Central Committee he had expressed fears for Soviet security and scepticism as to the prospects of Stalin's friendship with Hitler. It was this conviction that the two camps would eventually form again on more recognisable lines that gave him heart even in the darkest days of 1940.

113

The pattern of the following twenty-one months was one of Pollitt's gradual restoration to a position of leadership in the CP. At first, with the newly found time at his disposal, he settled down to write his splendid autobiography *Serving My Time*, the modesty and humanity of which compare so favourably with the pompous and self-serving volume that Thorez had had ghosted a couple of years earlier. That Pollitt was called on to produce its British equivalent, concluding with his proud reflections on becoming Party secretary, may indicate that his demotion was regarded even then as only an interlude. At his own request he spent the winter months working at the Lancashire and Cheshire district offices in Manchester, returning to London to fight the Silvertown by-election in February 1940. The proposal that he contest Silvertown had been put by the Party's prospective candidate for the seat and London district organiser, Ted Bramley, in the hope that this would secure Pollitt's early return to a leading position in the Party.[55] The calculation paid off inasmuch as Pollitt stayed in London to work at Party headquarters and before long was again contributing regular articles and pamphlets to the Party press. At some unpublicised point in 1940 he was re-admitted to the Politbureau; and when at the height of the invasion threat in September the CP issued a 'call to action' to its supporters, Pollitt was one of the four signatories.[56] It was thus as once more part of the CP's inner leadership that in April 1941 Pollitt returned to his trade as a plater at the London Graving Dock as a precaution against possible government moves to intern leading Communists.[57] Two months later the news of the Nazi invasion of the Soviet Union led to his almost immediate reinstatement as general secretary, a position with which, indeed, no Communist had been publicly identified in the period since his demotion. There was no existing Party leader for Pollitt to displace but rather a form of collective leadership to the head of which he could now return. It was very much as if they had been keeping his old job open for him.

If it would thus be quite misleading to suggest that Pollitt spent this period in the political wilderness, it remains true that these must have been amongst the unhappiest months of his life. As if the political blows were not enough, there came at the beginning of November 1939 the terrible news of his mother's death. Right to the end she had been to Pollitt not only his closest friend and wisest confidante but a symbol of the dignity and resilience of his own class, of all those exploited but never cowed or brutalised by capitalism. The deep sense of loss he felt is conveyed best by the affecting dedication to her with which *Serving My Time* begins. With the further loss of his much-loved comrade Tom Mann in March 1941, Pollitt was robbed of his principal surviving link with that formative and partly mythical period of uncomplicated socialist fervour to which his thoughts so often returned. Possibly this double loss helps explain the tremendous efforts made by Pollitt on behalf of the old socialist propagandist and idol of his youth, Bill Gee. It was before the war that he first came across Gee down on his luck, but it was on seeing him again in 1941 that he felt moved to organise on his behalf an appeal to well-wishers which soon became an annual responsibility willingly undertaken.[58]

To personal griefs were added political frustrations. It is true that in print and on the platform Pollitt gave full expression to the CP's evolving anti-war line. Indeed, it was more than once his invidious task to put the Communist case against those socialists most nearly occupying his own original position on the war, and he did so with such vituperation as surely to betray an uneasy conscience. The integrity of old colleagues like Laski and Gollancz was impugned, and scurrilous references to Pétain and even 'police snoopers' showed that when the occasion required Pollitt had little to learn from Dutt in the way of calumny and innuendo.[59]

There was, of course, much in the anti-war line with which he could fervently identify. Denunciations of the British ruling class and its hypocrisy, never so evident as in wartime, came as easily as ever. For a while too, as the electors of Silvertown had every opportunity to discover, Britain's threatened involvement in the Soviet-Finnish war took him right back to the days of the *Jolly George* affair. Here indeed was a cause to renew his enthusiasm, and he described addressing a mass rally at the Free Trade Hall the day after Churchill had spoken there as 'an inspiration I will never forget'.[60] There was too, as for all Communists of his generation, the memory of struggles against the First World War and the wretched peace that followed it, of the simpler anti-militarism and anti-capitalism of the pre-Hitler period relived by Pollitt as he wrote *Serving My Time*. The CP drew constantly the parallel between the first and second imperialist wars and it is no surprise to find that during his spell in Manchester Pollitt spent his dinner breaks reminiscing about events

115

some twenty-five years earlier.[61]

By the second half of 1940, however, as the bombs fell on Britain as previously on Spain and the threat of invasion loomed, such historical analogies can have offered little comfort to one so deeply marked by the struggle against fascism. Back in London, Pollitt witnessed the Blitz at first hand and would later recall in particular a dreadful night of devastation spent in the East End. 'I can see now the air-raid Wardens pulling people out of the debris in Commercial Road', he wrote, 'and I will never forget witnessing the bits and pieces of two dear friends of mine being put aside for identification.' In a *Daily Worker* feature prompted by these scenes, however, Pollitt drew on conventional anti-war images simply to indict the British government.[62] His feelings of defiance towards those directly responsible for the carnage received forthright expression only in private.

In particular, despite his inevitably diminished contacts on the left, Pollitt struck up at this time a friendly relationship with the Beaverbrook journalists Frank Owen and Michael Foot. Through the *Evening Standard* and their bestselling polemic *Guilty Men*, their radical version of the Dunkirk spirit had reached far and wide, and their conception of a people's war was one with which Pollitt still privately sympathised. Foot later remembered him as 'a frequent, frustrated, drinking companion of those wretched months', desperate that Nazism be resisted and impatient to play his own part in that resistance. Another Beaverbrook journalist, Trevor Evans, recalled a similar pledge of defiance, while the Communist Alan Winnington remembered asking Pollitt in May 1941 whether he still felt the war should be supported:

> 'My opinions haven't changed', he said. 'The war hasn't begun yet. Resistance to the Nazis is growing everywhere. That's the side we have to be on....
> 'Don't quote me', he grinned and went off down Fleet Street...

Sadly, the 'don't quote me' was as significant as the sentiments expressed.[63]

What hint of these attitudes Pollitt gave to other Party leaders, we shall probably never know. There is, however, amongst Dutt's papers a fascinating document from about August 1941 in which Pollitt at last gave vent to frustrations and resentments that had been incubating for two years. The subject was Dutt's *Crisis of the British*

People. This vast and untimely work, intended as the definitive exposition of the analysis underlying the CP's anti-war policies, received its final touches just as the Party decided after all to support the war. Mindful of his own labours and the advance subscriptions, and possibly resistant to recent developments in Party policy, Dutt apparently remained keen to publish. Pollitt's objections are like a recitation of grievances, recent and longstanding:

> How is the mistake of the Party treated in September 1939 – completely glossed over – Yet this was a mistake of great consequence & over which there will always be endless discussion....
>
> Let R.P.D. read what he is writing now about Hitlerism & what he wrote in Nov 1939.
>
> Dishonest to pose as leading Marxist in Europe and not give attention to a political mistake of such importance in a book purporting to prove we have always been right.
>
> Can see value of such a comprehensive sweep of world events in peace time, but not in this war... when aim of everything we write is mobilise for victory over fascism, over Hitlerite Germany. When no Soviet leader goes over past only in order to whip up anti-fascist feeling, when fundamentals of Communism are not touched upon...
>
> God knows we have had enough battles of Quotations – Dare we afford another one now, when Party got its feet on ground & masses not interested in past, but only the terrible present & future.

What resistance Dutt put up, and how he answered back, is not clear; but the book was never published.[64]

Probably the story is apocryphal that at a meeting at this time Pollitt held up *How to Win the War* and claimed to stand by every word of it.[65] Certainly these were his sentiments, but by and large the question of 'who was right' at the beginning of the war, and of the CP's conduct thereafter, was simply shelved. Not a whisper of the controversy over Dutt's book reached the public, for example, and its eventual non-appearance was blamed, with brazen implausibility, on printing difficulties. Pollitt himself put the Party's perceived interests before any desire to have his own stance formally vindicated and did nothing to disturb what amounted to a conspiracy of silence on the issue.

Following his acquiescence in what he now described privately as a mistaken policy, this calculated evasion threw a stark light on Pollitt's most obvious political limitation. It took his old associate

Tom Wintringham to point out that both the Communists' integrity and their future effectiveness required that they now 'admit fully how wrong their policy has been, and seek out the reasons why it has been wrong'.[66] Pollitt's instincts were the opposite. To open such a debate, focusing as it inevitably would on Stalin's diplomacy and the question of 'orders from Moscow', was simply unthinkable. In earlier years, to advance changes of whose necessity he was convinced, he had been more prone than most Communists to open such discussions. In 1941, however, the Party's policy was corrected virtually overnight and without resistance: the resurrection of past controversies seemed likely only to hinder its implementation. It was thus that, in what was his great political strength but also a debilitating weakness, Pollitt threw himself unreflectingly into the campaign to 'smash Hitler now', casting aside all the 'insignificant things of past history that have no place in the titanic events of the present time'.[67] It was with precisely the same instincts that, when in 1946 Stalin pronounced the war to have been anti-fascist from the start, the Party leadership again decided to let the matter lie. At this time there was of course nothing more titanic to inhibit them than their campaign to affiliate to the Labour Party. In the longer term, if not quite within Pollitt's lifetime, this atrophy of the CP's critical instincts would reduce it to virtual irrelevance in British politics. But before that there lay an extraordinary halcyon period in which Pollitt's triumphant conception of a people's war would draw workers in their thousands to the CP to flesh out its claims to represent the future.

5 'A fine working man type'

Pollitt's was a generation in which the Communist Party attracted to it many 'fine working man types' of considerable ability.[1] In a number of cases these acquired reputations well beyond Communist circles: Gallacher as an MP, for example, or Hannington among the unemployed, or Arthur Horner representing scores of lesser trade union figures. None, however, could match Pollitt's authority and standing simply as a Communist Party leader. 'To most adult people in this country', an obituarist wrote, 'he was the British Communist Party.'[2] For some three decades he not only represented the Party to the world at large, but embodied for Communists themselves the values the Party stood for. In this he had neither predecessor nor successor, nor was he replaced during his temporary loss of office. 'The biggest applause of all', a Mass-Observer noted of the People's Convention of January 1941, 'was received by Harry Pollitt simply on announcement of his name... more people were trying to *see* him than had been in the case of any other speaker'.[3] What sort of person was it that made them crane their necks?

First and foremost Pollitt was one of Britain's finest mass orators, even during that Indian summer of the art of public speaking. The 'monster' rally or meeting was a vital feature of all the period's campaigns, assembling the curious and the committed to win or sustain their enthusiasm for the cause. Always, whatever the venue or the occasion, Pollitt's speeches were meticulously prepared and delivered with fervour. He was, in the words of Michael Foot, who spoke many times alongside him, 'a magnificent platform speaker'. 'Most of the speech would be extremely well argued and prepared, a detailed presentation of a case', Foot remembered. 'But then the last ten or fifteen minutes of the speech, he would absolutely take the roof off and the whole thing would be extremely exciting.' A Manchester Communist gave a similar report from the floor of the hall. 'Pollitt really was the best speaker by far that I've ever heard', he recalled, 'and I think that his effectiveness was that he was so very simple in everything he said: a very simple argument put together, and suddenly he'd bring it all together in a sentence and it was incredible, it really was wonderful.' Individual testimonies apart, Pollitt's meetings were notable for the extraordinary number of people who signed up for the Party under the influence of his rhetoric: 305 during a tour of South Wales in 1935, for example, and 683 after a single meeting in 1941! Part of his secret was that he strove always to present a case that actually drew people to Communism as well as blasting its enemies. In particular, none knew better than he how to 'lift the curtain' and give a glimpse of the glorious future by which even the dreariest of present tasks was ennobled. 'Nine of our speakers out of every 10 in nine-tenths of their speeches devote nine-tenths of their arguments to a denunciation of everybody's line and no explanation of our own', he complained in 1932, extolling instead the simple socialist expositions of Tom Mann and the 'street-corner propaganda of years ago'.[4]

However appreciative his audiences, there was none perhaps who received as great a boost from his performances as Pollitt himself. A letter to Dutt after a rally at Shoreditch in 1935 conveys something of his effervescence the morning after. 'D.W. anniversary meeting wonderful', he wrote, 'and your old pal, whose deviations and going off the deep end sometimes make your hair turn grey, delivered the goods, although he says it who shouldnt.... I went home, having missed the bus, soaked with sweat, my shirt, singlet, trousers literally wet, but it was worth it.... I set them on the roof and it brought the money rolling in.'[5]

Within the Communist Party it was not alone the orator's distant charisma that Pollitt exercised, but a vibrant force of personality that commanded allegiance. To the formal obeisances due any Communist leader was added in Pollitt's case a deeper and more spontaneous regard for his loyalty, his integrity and his common humanity. With his contemporaries in the movement there was the comradeship born of long years of shared struggle, but it was possibly over the younger recruits of the 1930s that Pollitt exerted the greatest influence. By the war years he was fully twenty years older even than the average congress delegate, and this pullulating movement of youth he viewed almost as if he had fathered it. His feelings of pride, authority and protectiveness would be remembered by Communists in different ways: his solicitude for any of his own in distress, for example, sometimes overlapping with his considerable powers of patronage; or the responsibility he felt for the young men who fought fascism in Spain and in the wider global contest that ensued. On the opening of the Second Front in 1944, for which he more than anybody had campaigned, Pollitt sent out a message to all Communists serving in the Forces. 'I nearly lost the use of my hand signing every one of them, and they ran into thousands', he wrote to a colleague, 'but I thought the lads would understand that it was not some hurried dashed off thing on a duplicator...'[6]

It was a typical gesture, at once deeply felt and flamboyant, and it was precisely this human touch that so endeared Pollitt to those who knew him. The wife of one of the *Daily Worker*'s early editors recalled on his death 'how he used to come into the... office, gay and full of humour but bringing a dynamic influence which put us all right on our toes; how in a few words he could solve any problem which we had been chewing over vainly for hours; how with his deep sincerity and determination he never lost his humanity...' Another Party worker remembered him for his 'wonderful sense of humour, and a big warm heart'. 'Nothing was too much trouble for him, and he was always available to comrades with a problem', she explained. 'His sympathy and understanding has helped me personally several times when I have faced family tragedies.'

It was Pollitt's special charisma to combine these human qualities with the willpower and firmness of purpose that middle-class recruits in particular sought in Communism. An early instance was his relationship with Esmond Higgins, a university-educated associate from the days of the nucleus. After returning to his native Australia in 1924, Higgins maintained with Pollitt a regular correspondence, confiding to him his tendencies to dissolution and disillusionment. The language and roles they adopted were extraordinary: Pollitt as 'my father confessor', 'your poor old father', 'a Self-Made Communist to his Son', Higgins as 'my lad' and 'your nephew'. Pollitt, it should be remembered, was only six years the elder. It was the prototype of a relationship that was to be repeated countless times in subsequent years. Gabriel Carritt, one of a famous family of Oxford Communists who came to Communism in the 1930s, placed Pollitt vividly in his period setting. 'Harry had

121

a personality which attracted people to treat him as if he was a gospel, almost like a confessor', he remembered:

> My wife, Joan MacMichael, used to treat him as if he absolutely knew about everything: all her problems, personal problems, social problems. She would go and consult him, like going to the oracle. He didn't intend to, but he did create that feeling of knowing and authority and integrity which made people go and talk to him; because he would listen, because he was wise, and because I think a lot of the intellectuals and perhaps many of the workers too wanted the Party to be the authority, to lay down how it should be.

One gets a glimpse here of the compelling personality to which not only Communists but at various times the Crippses, Stracheys and Gollanczes succumbed.[7]

If Pollitt's was thus a responsive and accessible style of leadership, it was by no means a democratic one. Whatever he may have discarded of his and Dutt's early report on organisation, he remained committed to its basic centralising credo and thus to laying down for Communists 'how it should be'. While this discipline and cohesion gave the Party an influence on the left out of all proportion to its size, it also drained its formal democratic procedures of all but the most vestigial significance. The 1935 Party Congress, judged by Pollitt such an outstanding success, was the first that was entirely free not only of internal division but of meaningful debate. In this it set the pattern for those that followed: great stage-managed affairs that left hands sore from clapping. Even the Central Committee, meeting monthly as the Party's leading body, was reduced to what some wryly described as the 'exhortation committee'. Its members were in 1938 encouraged for once to vent their grievances, and these turned out to be considerable: the issuing of pronouncements in its name without it having met; the inhibiting presence of the stenographer; and most of all its domination by the few exalted figures who opened its proceedings having reached their decisions elsewhere. 'One comes here without any feeling that anything depends on what he does or says', Horner observed, contrasting its rather intimidating atmosphere with the livelier debates of the 1920s. 'I feel I am doing more service if I have a point to raise, in seeing Pollitt, etc. than spending a whole day in this executive.'[8] It was this travesty of democratic organisation that Pollitt upheld even when its consequences were most distressing to him. He might be driven to the point of resignation or removed by his colleagues from office, but never could he conceive of putting to the Party itself any question that might divide it. Unity came above all else, and nothing could have underlined that more than Pollitt's stoical acceptance of his own personal setbacks.

Pollitt's impatience with mere discussion was also evident in his indifference to matters of theory and Marxist analysis. The Dutts, paradoxically, had encouraged him from the start not to concern himself too much with these questions, seeing in Pollitt a talent complementary to their own. It was thus, for example, that on one of his first trips to Moscow Dutt advised him 'not to be afraid about making mistakes in theory, but to speak in a rough, practical strong way so that they should see that here is the movement, and the party'. The division of labour that underlay this advice Pollitt adhered to all his life, not only in his relationship with the Dutts but subsequently with Emile Burns and later still with James Klugmann. 'Here', he used to say to Klugmann, handing him some draft or other, 'now you put the Marxism in that.' Initially he stood somewhat in awe of his more theoretically minded collaborators. With each new proof of their own limitations, however, particularly perhaps their failure to anticipate the coming of fascism in Germany, he became more sceptical as to the value of their work. When Dutt returned to Britain in the late 1930s he had to wage with Pollitt 'a most prolonged and epic fight' to be given time for anything but the most immediate tasks. Eventually, indeed, he had 'to take strong measures to compel a changed decision', presumably going over Pollitt's head to the CI. There was a tension here that Pollitt articulated most fully during the sharper conflict on the outbreak of war, deftly citing the works of Lenin. 'Being disinclined to abstract theories and taking pride in their common sense', he quoted, somewhat out of context, 'the English often approach practical questions *more directly*, thus helping the Socialists of other countries to find real contents under the cloak of phraseology of every kind (including the "Marxian").'[9]

Particularly after the events of 1956, Pollitt's name would be very much identified with this vein of anti-intellectualism. According to Gollancz in his memoirs, 'he distrusted, despised, disliked and occasionally even hated intellectuals as such'. The reality was much more complex. From his heady association with Pankhurst, through

123

his liaison with the Dutts, to his benign supervision of a younger generation of Klugmanns and Margot Heinemanns, Pollitt had no difficulty getting on with intellectuals 'as such'. The influx of middle-class recruits into the Party in the 1930s he welcomed with open arms and a number advanced as his protégés to leading positions within it. Stephen Spender gives a fine account of first encountering Pollitt with 'something paternal in his friendly twinkling manner' and yet making Spender quite aware that his intellectual pilgrimage lacked the depth and authenticity of Pollitt's own lived experience. Like hundreds at Pollitt's meetings, and with as little lasting effect as so many of them, Spender joined the Party on the spot.

What Pollitt expected of such recruits, despite his initial concession to Spender of a limited right of dissent, was the same loyalty and discipline as of the ordinary, unassuming working-class Communist. He rather resented, even when they were useful to the Party, any who by virtue of their background thought to give themselves airs. Hewlett Johnson, for example, the clerical enthusiast for Soviet Russia who rather paraded his sanctity, Pollitt rechristened 'that bloody red arse of a dean'. His fiercest antagonism was to those who, passing through or close to the Party, thought to exempt themselves from its collective disciplines. Especially during the early war years, when such individuals were able to quote at him policies he still supported, while he loyally defended those he did not, this produced in him an unreasoning sense of betrayal. 'This type like to see long letters and longer replies because it gives their bourgeoisie souls the personal belief that they are important people', he wrote to Ivor Montagu of Strachey and Gollancz. 'Don't waste any further time on [them]. They are going to eat more than a plateful of vomit, after a Black Fast celebration.' It was not intellectualism as such that aroused this antagonism, but the egocentricity that would not subordinate itself to the Party. With Montagu himself, author, aristocrat and film producer, Pollitt maintained a cordial, Communist friendship until his death.[10]

Also setting Pollitt apart from certain progressive milieux was his distaste for anything that reeked of faddism or affectation. Meticulous in his own appearance, he 'used to be absolutely furious with people who didn't have clean collars and ties and things, and say that it wasn't respectable, we'd got to look respectable'. He had no time either for casual promiscuity — 'do what you like all year and share out the kids at Christmas', he described it — or artistic experimentation. Addressing a meeting of Party intellectuals in 1946, Pollitt quoted for them the lines of the Chartist poet, Ernest Jones:

> War to the palaces and peace to the cottages
> That is the battle cry of terror which may resound throughout our country
> Let the wealthy beware.

'I don't want poetry and writing to go backward', he conceded, 'but I do remind [you] that [that] thought which I have just quoted would leave the modern intellectual stone cold, but wins the warm approval... of every miner, engineer, transport worker and farm worker who hears it, even in these days of a new format, typography, and sequence of an Auden or Spender.' To Spender himself he put the question whenever they met: 'Why don't you write songs for the workers, as Byron, Shelley and Wordsworth did?'[11]

Pollitt himself was widely read in English literature, his tastes as broad as the divergent strands of his own personality. His 'greatest craving' was for the romantic poets, but he also read with huge enjoyment those novelists whose appetite for life matched his own: Smollett, Dickens and the plebeian entertainers of his youth like Wells and Bennett. To the abstract appeals of music he was, characteristically, entirely unresponsive: if ever he chanced to hear any, he admitted, it only set him thinking about what to put in his next article or speech. Far more attractive to him were the demotic appeals of music hall and balladry. His special fondness was for homely domestic recitals at which, notwithstanding the uproarious character of his own contributions, the more sentimental offerings of his sister Ella would reduce him to tears.[12]

In his tastes, manner and appearance, Pollitt was thus indeed, as his Russian hagiographer put it, 'a true son of the British working class', with what one colleague recalled as a 'curious conventional streak'. For Pollitt, however, these were not matters of blind convention but of self-respect, of 'pride in the Party' and pride in one's contribution to its work. 'This is no new thought on my part', he told a 1946 meeting of professional workers. 'The old organisation of the most skilled craftsmen in the land knew what it was doing when its initiation ceremony exhorted new members "so to conduct themselves in the workshop that the employer would be prompted to ask where others like them could be obtained".' Rooted in the old discredited labour aristocracy as they were, under Pollitt's leadership these notions were to leave a lasting imprint on the Communist Party.[13]

In his home life, too, Pollitt was the very picture of conformity. His marriage to Marjorie Brewer in 1925 was what one might call a 'Party marriage', into which there no doubt entered an element of convenience. With his surpassing charm Pollitt was evidently attractive to women, but his all-absorbing political commitments made for rather tempestuous relationships. He described for Salme in 1923 the upsets that occurred when a lover failed to see the 'gleam', or possibly sought a different one. 'My best girl is thoroughly fed up with me', he wrote from Manchester:

> She has been looking forward to seeing the best lad in the world for such a long time, and I have been with her exactly 10 minutes and instead of talking about the things ardent young lovers are supposed to do, all I could do was to explain the best way of organising the nuclei...
>
> She hates the Party, oh if ever the Fascisti want a Murderess who will stop at nothing to annihilate the entire Party, only sparing me, I know where such a lady can be found.

A subsequent attachment, and a more compatible one, was to Rose Cohen of the Labour Research Department, by whom Pollitt claimed in his frustration to have been spurned fourteen times. It was 'on the rebound' from these multiple rejections, and 'feeling autumn in the air' as he himself put it, that in his thirty-fifth year he married Marjorie.[14]

Their marriage, according to a number of witnesses, was not a particularly close one, and in Marjorie's recent memoirs the references to her more illustrious husband seem somewhat niggardly. No doubt this was more or less inevitable given Pollitt's constant round of engagements at home and abroad and the activist's temperament that caused him to thrive on this. During the Blitz he bemoaned to Tom Mann the lack of activity 'in the meeting and conference line'. 'Just like you, you cannot sit in your own home ten minutes together without wanting to be off', Marjorie told him. But if Pollitt put his politics first, he also encouraged Marjorie to develop her own capabilities, and he retained from his Lancashire origins a keen sense of his domestic responsibilities without always necessarily fulfilling them. Indeed, he spoke feelingly on occasion of the 'amazing amount of domestic unhappiness' within the CP, with its cadres being looked upon as 'wife deserters'. His solution, characteristically, was that more wives should be recruited for the Party. It was nevertheless a mark of some sort of enlightenment that he used to protest in the mining districts at the 'back to the middle ages attitude' taken towards the womenfolk. 'They won't lift a teapot off the hob to pour themselves out a cup of tea', he wrote of the South Wales miners. 'The women are almost chattel slaves...' It was one of those touches that so won the hearts of the Party faithful that when staying in such homes Pollitt himself was always first up from the table to start upon the crocks.[15]

Because he looms so large in our mental picture of the period, one thinks inevitably of Orwell in writing of Pollitt. How many of Orwell's themes does his life illuminate, though not as the easy polarities with which we are familiar but so jumbled together that one hardly knows what moral to draw: decency mixed with doublethink, integrity with expediency, 'totalitarian' notions with a passionate anti-fascism, and a transferred allegiance to Stalin's Russia that Pollitt combined with the organic links with the English people that Orwell spent years trying to cultivate. 'Naturally the people who could be attracted by such a creed, and remain faithful to it after they had grasped its nature', Orwell wrote of British Communists in 1941, 'tended to be neurotic or malignant types, people fascinated by the spectacle of successful cruelty.' So sweeping a judgement is not of course open to the historian. Pollitt himself resembles less this caricature than the sort of working-class intellectual of whom Orwell wrote in *Wigan Pier* that 'not even the most hidebound Tory could help liking and admiring'.[16] Was it not, after all, the Reverend Francis Coveney, formerly of the Special Branch, who on Pollitt's death wrote to the *Times* to testify that 'most of my old colleagues whose task it was to keep abreast of subversive movements would agree that Harry Pollitt was essentially a good man'. One or two of them he apparently saved from physical violence, while with the reverend himself Pollitt shared, if not his secrets, a convivial drink or his seat on the bus. And yet it was this 'essentially good man' who led the British Communist Party through the entire Stalin period, installed by the dictator himself and

127

resigning at last when Khrushchev formally brought his era to a close. Pollitt was not what is ordinarily regarded as a complex man, but there is nothing simple about the problems that his life raises. It might disturb our cruder notions of both Englishness and Communism, but how very English a phenomenon was Stalinism in the shape that Pollitt gave it.

6 Not standing aside

The great patriotic war, as Pollitt might well, with the Russians, have remembered the years 1941-45, marked in obvious ways the apogee of his and the CP's fortunes. For once, not only were Communists convinced that history was on their side, but history seemed aware of it too. With Hitler's reckless plunge into Russia's daunting vastness and then the explosion of US-Japanese rivalry at Pearl Harbor, a world anti-fascist front, like a People's Front writ large, emerged to bear the hopes of millions. Truly this was, for the first time, a world war, but one in which for month after temporising month the brunt of Hitler's blows were borne on the Russian front alone. Grim images of Leningrad and Stalingrad humbled observers with their heroism, and it was not only Communists who credited their achievements to the awesome figures who gave these cities their names. In all countries Communists acquired a new prestige, both as the bearers on national soil of the creed that inspired the Russians and because of their own generally exemplary contributions to the struggle against fascism. In Britain Communists became the most impatient partisans of a total, offensive war against Germany and the most fervent and intolerant critics of those who disrupted 'national unity'. So attractive was its new policy, coinciding as it did with a contagion of Russophilia and a pervasive discontent with Tory politics, that the CP almost trebled in size in less than a year. As the Party's official historian put it, Communists 'had spent years swimming against the stream, and now suddenly found themselves swimming with it – a new and exhilarating experience'.[1]

None was more exhilarated than Pollitt, nor could many have matched the almost religious certainty with which he viewed the unfolding struggle between good and evil. '1942 – and the whole world in arms', he wrote at the start of that year:

129

> The issue is clear: Victory over the fascist barbarians, and social progress; or defeat and a return to slavery for mankind. Victory over a bestial monster to whom democracy, culture and peace are poison; or defeat and the rule of terror, violence and endless bloody struggles...

It was with the issues thus clearly delineated that Pollitt felt strongest his vocation for leadership, for rousing people to action. With Communism and fascism locked in mortal combat, the scholastic Marxist analyses he rather despised could be set aside. Surveys of the past and speculations as to the future alike he discouraged as obstacles to the fullest mobilisation for immediate tasks. All, in fact, boiled down to one question alone: who was for or against the creation of a national and international front to defeat Hitler?[2] The policy was that of Communists worldwide, but it nevertheless came to Pollitt naturally and even spontaneously. On the very day, indeed, of the German attack on the Soviet Union, he apparently headed a minority in the British Party leadership favouring unconditional support for the Churchill Government. It was no accident that the adoption of this policy shortly afterwards should coincide with his own reinstatement as general secretary.[3]

That Pollitt would in the next year or two adopt a series of postures seemingly as uncharacteristic as his support for Churchill shows perhaps how fundamental were his instincts of solidarity with Soviet Russia. The hint of cynicism detectable at the time of the Nazi-Soviet Pact was forgotten as the Soviet resistance fulfilled and exceeded the expectations even of Communists. To this struggle 'everything else in life' was subordinate, as he spelt out in 1942 in a letter to the Indian nationalist leader, Jawaharlal Nehru. Even the victims of colonialism, he urged, should not press their claims to the point of confrontation with their oppressors:

> I assure you, Comrade Nehru, that I hate British Imperialism as deeply as you yourself do, that my whole upbringing and experience has taught me to regard the ruling class with a hatred that no circumstances will ever damp down...
>
> But at this moment when Socialism is being butchered and battered as it is in the Soviet Union, when our Soviet comrades are dying in their millions to hold the one-sixth of the earth that is ours, I am ready to co-operate with all who are prepared to fight against fascism.[4]

In other circumstances, and even at this time for Pollitt's Indian comrades, such loyalty could jar badly with existing class and national allegiances. For Pollitt, however, if only for a few years, everything seemed to pull in the same direction, as his anti-fascism, his pro-Sovietism and his radical patriotism combined to release in him a passion and hatred rarely encountered in British politics.

It was as an unofficial propagandist on the home front that Pollitt made his chief contribution to the war effort. Immediately on his resumption of the Party leadership he applied for release from his job at the shipyard; and on 8 August 1941 he laid down his tools again, this time for good. For the remainder of the war he set about doing not just 'his bit' but rather more than that through the effect of his words on others. He was, perhaps, the war's most prolific pamphleteer, with every few months the same message renewed under titles reading like gunshots: *Into Battle! Speed the Second Front! Deeds Not Words! Smash Hitler Now!* Thanks to vigorous distribution methods, sales sometimes exceeded 150,000 although, as Pollitt himself conceded, many of these no doubt went unread.[5]

More people still were reached by the gruelling schedule of public meetings he set himself. In 1944 alone, 'the busiest year of my life', he addressed over a hundred large meetings all over the country, which given wartime conditions of travel was no mean achievement.[6] Largest of all were the Second Front demonstrations in Trafalgar Square, with reported attendances pushing sixty thousand. These platforms brought together Communists, fellow-travellers and Beaverbrook journalists, with the odd intrepid Labour or Liberal MP thrown in. It was Pollitt, however, who received as usual the most rapturous receptions. Of the July 1942 rally a typically painstaking Mass-Observer noted that, whereas only a third of the crowd clapped the MPs D. N. Pritt, Haden-Guest and Wilf Roberts, Pollitt was acclaimed by cheers and 80 per cent applause on finishing his speech.[7] The audiences at these rallies were of course highly partisan – at this one 70 per cent joined in singing the *Internationale,* hardly anybody in *God Save the King* – and the numbers Pollitt reached by speech and pamphlet were obviously negligible as compared with mass newspaper readerships and wartime radio audiences. It is nevertheless clear that to a greater extent than ever before he now had the ear of the 'serious-minded workers' in factory and pit whose influence on war production was of such significance.

In addressing these workers, Pollitt took to an extreme the approach he had developed in pre-war years. His main concern as a propagandist had never been to stimulate intellectually, but rather to promote action according to the imperatives and certainties of the Party line. Now the need for action was greater than ever, and even his monthly Central Committee report came across as 'not so much the occasion for a searching debate as an uplifting *tour de force*... to communicate his unquenchable confidence in Soviet victory'.[8] What Pollitt sought was less to inform and elucidate than to 'sear, rouse and inspire the people' with 'white-hot anti-Fascist propaganda'. 'In a people's war', he wrote, 'propaganda is one of the mightiest weapons, as important as any R.A.F. Bombing Squadron...' In terms of the force and subtlety of his own words, the comparison was indeed an appropriate one. With his call for the daily exposure of Nazi atrocities by those with 'feeling, passion and hate' to convey to others, there was added to Britain's chorus of resistance a new and distinctive voice, as if Robert Blatchford had found a job with *Soviet War News*.[9]

One of the recurring motifs in Pollitt's war of words was the need in Britain for a new 'spirit of sublime sacrifice'. 'This is a people's war', he wrote in 1942. 'It is an honour to sacrifice and suffer to carry it through to its victorious conclusion.' Later on, with British troops engaged in Western Europe, he would, as so many had in this and previous wars, draw on stock images of frontline heroism to invoke this spirit amongst those enjoying civilian comforts. For three long years before this, however, it was not British exploits but the terrible events on the Eastern Front that aroused in him feelings of guilt with which he sought to inflame British workers. Speech after speech of his would climax with the utterly unreal images of warfare churned out by Stalin's propaganda machine: young children hurling insults at their sneering executioners, for example, or the nightmarish Soviet teenage girl who swore to:

> wreak cruel vengeance on the enemy, mercilessly and with every drop of my blood. If one of my arms is shot off, I shall fight with one arm. If I am left without legs, I will crawl to the enemy camp and smite them with grenades. If they gouge out my eyes...

To Pollitt these were 'sublime and rousing' sentiments to which Britons too could aspire with 'a little more hatred... a little more fierceness... [and] a burning impatience that we are doing so little'.

In the meantime, however, and until the opening of a Second Front, such scenes of inhuman valour stood as an indictment of Britain's more leisurely way of warfare. 'Here we are wondering if we can live with dog racing only on one day a week', he reproached one audience, 'and expecting the Red Army to go on killing the Nazi dogs every day.... What hypocrisy. Why the word "sacrifice" has no real meaning or significance for the overwhelming majority of the British people.' Entirely disregarding the vast differences of political culture, Pollitt extolled a way of war as total, as ferocious and unflinching, as the Russians'. 'Everything for the Front must be the rallying call', he wrote on one occasion. 'Every single person at the disposal of the State for victory.' Here Pollitt betrayed his extraordinary immunity to liberalism and its scruples. 'We therefore ask again', he wrote with a disconcerting bluntness, 'if we have not got the production, where is it, and who is going to be shot for us not having it?' On other occasions too he called for conscious or just objective 'traitors' to be 'shot out of hand'. There was little sign here of the 'gentleness of the English civilisation' which Orwell noted and which writers like Priestley saw as the key to Britain's superiority over Nazism. Pollitt's message was more brutal: 'To destroy Fascism we must learn to hate and sacrifice.'[10]

If this had been all that Pollitt was saying, there would have been little but his sincerity to distinguish him from the *John Bull* type of demagogue. The themes of hate and sacrifice were, however, accompanied by an emphasis on the growing sense of initiative and responsibility of the common people that was much more widely shared on the left and probably made a far greater contribution to the CP's increased popularity. Where the hate propaganda was peripheral, the unleashing of democracy was fundamental to the concept of a people's war. It initially derived its force from the instant myths and disenchantments of Dunkirk and its aftermath, but like so much else that was dynamic in wartime politics it came also to draw on romanticised perceptions of Soviet achievements. Certainly this was true for Pollitt, who never tired of the lesson that, where they held power, the workers had shown a 'creative ability and constructive capacity' unknown to capitalism. If this engendered dissatisfaction with a Britain beset by Munichites, parasites and Blimps, it also suggested remedies. Nothing was

133

unattainable given only a bold leadership, not fearing the common people but 'prepared to draw upon their inexhaustible resources of genius, creative energy and initiative'. All the failures, dead-heads and fascist sympathisers had to be cleared from government positions, along with 'the thousands of non-producers floating around factories, impeding production by their... so-called "expert" opinions'. 'We have had a redundancy of "experts"', he wrote on another occasion. 'The *real* organisers are to be found in the ranks of the people', for they alone had 'drive, ideas and the complete confidence of their workmates'. It was imperative that they 'feel their own power, and be confident in the exercise of that power'. For Communists this was partly a question of 'personal responsibility' – of 'self-denial weeks', for instance, or factory shock brigades tackling production bottlenecks – and partly one of exercising to the full the collective strength of their class. The latter now involved not only the traditional institutions of the Labour movement but the officially recognised joint production committees on which both workers and management sat and by which the CP set great store. It was, all in all, a question of ending 'any remaining sense of dependency on others to win the war', and thus of securing the greatest say in the peace that would follow.[11]

If Pollitt expounded his views to one group of workers above all, it was to Britain's miners. The CP had considerable clout in certain coalfields and on its executive sat the presidents of the Welsh and Scottish miners' unions, Arthur Horner and Abe Moffat. During the war, however, it was Pollitt himself who emerged as the Party's chief spokesman on mining issues, an indication no doubt of its justifiable fears that coal shortages might cause the war effort to falter. If Pollitt was an outsider to the industry on which he contributed half a dozen pamphlets in as many years, he was certainly an informed and sympathetic one. For the miners as the rugged embodiment of proletarian dignity and solidarity he felt an affinity and great respect: 'the most class conscious, the best organised section of the working class', as he called them, 'the indestructible rock upon which the working-class movement is founded'.[12] He felt comfortable with mining audiences and had indeed addressed hundreds of them, especially in South Wales. Very often mining communities regarded interlopers with suspicion, as clattering saucepans announced to Pollitt when he contested Clay

Cross in 1933, but Pollitt was never so adept as at winning over those he saw as his own people. His experiences provided a sound basis for the more sustained interest he took in the industry during the war.[13] He paid monthly visits to the mining constituency of Rhondda East, to be contested again in 1945; he had regular meetings with the CP's leading mining comrades, who fed him with information as to internal union affairs; and he enjoyed the assistance of Margot Heinemann, the Labour Research Department's mining specialist and author of a Left Book Club selection on *Britain's Coal*. Will Lawther's preface to this book was actually written by Pollitt himself, and Pollitt also helped Lawther with various speeches and pronouncements as the mining union's national president. So assured was he of his authority, indeed, that in February 1944 he announced, without the prior or subsequent approval of leading mining Communists, not only the CP's discontent with government handling of the Porter Award but an altogether new demand for the industry's immediate nationalisation.[14]

During the strikes that followed the Porter Award and indeed throughout the war, Pollitt offered cogent and constructive opinions on the huge problems besetting coal production. The need to overcome wage anomalies and disincentives to work in the mines, to activate pit production committees, to overhaul the entire industry in fact, was spelt out persuasively. What stick in the mind, however, are not so much these common-sense proposals as Pollitt's emotional appeals to the miners to give their all, cherished customs and hard-won rights included, to defeat fascism. Here truly were 'the Commandos of war industry', as Pollitt flatteringly addressed them, with proud anti-fascist traditions, but with memories too of neglect and bitter class struggle that no froth about national unity could efface. Pollitt confronted these memories with the crueller contemporary image of Lidice, the Czech mining village that Hitler's thugs decimated out of sheer sadistic spite. 'Miners of Britain!' he wrote. 'We live in 1943. 1921 and 1926 have gone for ever. But Lidice remains.' The appeal to the miners' internationalism and instincts of class solidarity Pollitt now fused with the rhetoric of recruiting platforms everywhere. Valiant fighter pilots, mere lads bearing arms, intrepid convoys, beleaguered Stalingrad: were British miners with their easier tasks to let them down?

135

How can any decent man voluntarily lose work at a time like this! To do so is a crime. The soldier at the battlefront who decided to take a day off would be regarded as a deserter....

Avoidable absenteeism, lock-outs, or strike stoppages... are daggers stuck in the back of men of our own class in Europe, of the workers and soldiers of the Soviet Union, of the people in Britain who depend on us...

It was on these lines that in 1944 Pollitt exhorted striking Welsh miners to be less 'selfish' — 'We are so taken up with our own problems that we are getting out of focus with the problems of the Armed Forces', as he told one meeting. It was an intriguing fusion of Bolshevik and Blimp.[15]

Lest one incline too readily to deride these wartime aberrations, one should reflect for a moment on the numberless tragedies of fascist Europe which eclipsed even the cruellest torments of British capitalism. In Lidice, after all, we have a town that was murdered in a literal sense that British socialists, for whom Peterloo remains the definition of a massacre, can scarcely even comprehend. Even given Pollitt's priorities, however, it is far from clear that the CP's were the most effective means of achieving them. Indeed, in his preoccupation with external foes Pollitt in particular seemed to sacrifice the intuitive grasp of British political realities with which he had tempered the Comintern's excesses in earlier periods. Thus, for example, in his concern to maintain production he not only deplored strike stoppages but positively exalted those who in these circumstances defied the decisions of their workmates. 'What courage', he boasted of one Communist blackleg, 'what a sacred spirit of real class consciousness, to walk on the ship's gangway and resume his job'. No doubt such a departure from traditional principles did require courage; and Pollitt, in whom as in few others such principles were deeply embedded, no doubt spoke with feeling of the 'greater readiness to face the bayonet than... to stand up in a mass meeting of angry workers, badly treated, remembering all that has happened to them in the past, and call, not for strike action, but for the ordinary methods of trade-union negotiation'. Clearly what this involved was not scabbing as ordinarily understood, or not as far as Pollitt was concerned;[16] but it took not so much courage as the common sense that had apparently deserted him to appreciate that others might see it differently. The recollections of the CP's local organiser of the 'total time' strike on Tyneside in October 1942 are very much to the point:

> Our members spoke and voted against the strikes... but we would have advised them to come out with the strikers if they lost the vote had Harry Pollitt not come up and instructed them to go to work. I did not quarrel with his decision but it was an emotional not a political one. The Party shop stewards who worked through the strike were isolated and instantly deprived of their positions, yet the workers would have been willing to listen to them had they not blacklegged.... Few of the Party stewards were reinstated after the strike and the Party never regained the influence it had previously exercised on the Tyne.[17]

Thus, through a dubiously courageous and certainly empty gesture, was the CP's ability to influence production questions in the Tyne yards permanently impaired; and it is interesting to reflect that a Party official with no background in industry should see this more clearly than his vastly more experienced leader. What this pattern of events meant more generally was that in the years in which it implanted almost its first cadres in higher union structures the CP also encountered during disputes the sort of resistance from rank-and-file workers that Croucher has described in *Engineers at War*.

The Party's approach to by-elections betrayed the same lack of judgement. However impassioned its criticisms of particular government policies or personalities, the CP consistently supported the official nominees for parliamentary vacancies. The famous by-election upsets that dented the government's complacency were thus, in most instances, achieved in the teeth of implausible Communist campaigns for rather bemused Conservative placemen.[18] That these tactics went against the grain is perhaps indicated by the pent-up enthusiasm with which, in mid-1944, Communists wilfully misconstrued their leaders' call for a progressive majority at the next general election. 'There was nothing wrong about that formulation, "End Tory Domination"', Pollitt complained. 'What was wrong was that [it] was taken out of its context and immediately became the main slogan on some of our posters up and down the country...'[19]

Quite apart from any effects on Party morale, the CP's exaggerated regard for the electoral truce deprived it of its best chance of making its campaigns bite. Sporadic electoral setbacks were never seriously going to weaken the government, as

Communists claimed. Had the campaigns fused popular discontents with Communist organisation, however, they might have given ministers, especially Labour ministers, considerable food for thought. Those who feel that all Communist activity had the Party's own advancement as its sole *raison d'être* might well ponder on its self-effacement during the one period in its history when it might, on a credible platform of progressive unity, actually have won a few elections. As it was, the emasculation of the Party's campaigns was almost pitiful. 'We now have to agitate, fight and organise, to compel the Government to open the Second Front', Pollitt blustered at the CP's National Conference in 1942. 'Meetings, deputations, resolutions, demonstrations – every conceivable form of political pressure must be brought to bear.' But of course, 'every conceivable form of pressure' included neither industrial action nor electoral contests, both of which Pollitt specifically repudiated in the same speech.[20] No wonder the Second Front campaign made so much noise to so little effect.

All that was left to the Communists was reliance on the power of public opinion, however combatively Pollitt chose to express it. Characteristic of the Party's dilemma was his response in December 1944 to Britain's military intervention against the Greek resistance. With yet further memories of the *Jolly George*, he swept a protest rally in Trafalgar Square with a 'new sense of power and responsibility', as the *Daily Worker* put it. 'None knew better than Mr Churchill that pressure of public opinion could now force a change in the policy of the Government', he said, though the role of organised Labour in effecting this change in 1920 was not one he wished his listeners to emulate. He was, in fact, desperate to avert a political crisis over the issue, and when restive Greek seamen approached the CP with plans for protest strikes Pollitt successfully urged on them a more cautious response.[21] Not surprisingly, Churchill modified his Greek policy not at all; and within weeks Pollitt was, in the euphoria of the Yalta settlement, reaffirming his commitment to national unity in more fulsome terms than ever.

During the war the drift in Communist policy seems to have provoked little overt criticism from within the Party. In general terms, the overriding need for unity against fascism, and whatever tactical adjustments this required, was never questioned. As Hitler's downfall drew nearer, however, and with it the challenges of the post-war world, it became apparent that tactical necessities were developing, inexorably and with minimal discussion, into doctrinal heresies. The trend was encapsulated in the Party's scenario for the post-war election, for, far from predicting Labour's historic victory, Pollitt called in March 1945 for a renewed national government to oversee the transition to peace. The dismay that this and similar developments caused Party members was, for once, given forthright expression at the Party's first post-war congress in November 1945, the stormiest since 1929. Encouraged no doubt by the repudiation of the still more flagrant heresies which led Earl Browder actually to dissolve the American CP, resolutions and pronouncements critical of the British Party leadership came pouring into King Street. Pollitt was especially implicated, for it was in his writings, especially the long pamphlets *How to Win the Peace* and *Answers to Questions*, that the CP's revisionism received its fullest expression. Before turning to the 1945 congress, the vision of the post-war world articulated in these writings is worth recapturing, for it represented the most drastic transformation of Pollitt's political outlook since his 'Bolshevisation' in the 1920s.

For Pollitt's generation of socialists there was no more decisive question, nor one more complex and uncertain, than the relationship between socialism and war. On the one hand, the carnage of the First World War in particular had exposed for all who would see it the sheer bloody futility of imperialism and its rivalries. On the other hand, it was in its organisation for war that capitalism itself seemed to demonstrate, with all the conclusiveness of practical achievement, the potential benefits of collectivism. As surely as the earlier war evoked in Pollitt the first response, the Second World War, with its egalitarian notions, cult of planning and radical-democratic perspectives, evoked the second. The new forms of democracy he saw emerging all over Europe, he admitted, 'we never thought possible without the revolution and the establishment of the dictatorship of the proletariat'. Within Britain, the Tories themselves had been responsible for introducing measures 'the like of which, if we tell the truth, none of us thought would be possible... until we had complete power'. Moreover, the war had released new energies that could be directed into more positive channels. As he pondered on the tasks of reconstruction, his mind dwelt on images of D-Day:

139

I thought of all the planning and sifting of ideas, the inventive genius, bold conception and execution; of the myriad brains that had been at work; of the training, scope and perfect unity of action achieved between vast land, sea and air forces. I thought of the courage and daring, the heroism and selflessness displayed by... officers and rank and file alike....

One thought kept hammering in my brain. If all this... is possible for war, why not for peace too?[22]

It was a moral that Pollitt would draw time and time again in the years to come. The war was not for him a catastrophe from which to escape as quickly as possible to some banal conception of normality. On the contrary, he was never happier than when the issues of politics matched in their simplicity and urgency the intensity which he brought to them. The spirit of Dunkirk and D-Day he hoped in vain to see Britain through to post-war recovery and thence to socialism. In nobody's prescriptions for the new world to come was the imprint of the war more clearly detectable.

Pollitt's hopes of turning the dynamics of warfare to constructive ends rested first on expectations of a new and peaceful world order under Allied auspices. Not only did his vision of a new Britain presuppose this harmonious setting, but in a cruder sense it was from Stalin's diplomatic manoeuvrings to this supposed end that the whole new orientation of Western Communism ultimately derived. In particular Pollitt took his cue from the gatherings of the 'Big Three' at Teheran in November-December 1943 and Yalta in February 1945. The Yalta communique, whose Wilsonian platitudes he swallowed whole, had an especially intoxicating effect on him. 'Here you have got a categorical statement', he told the CP's executive, 'a formulation hitherto only found in Marxist literature... in which the greatest perspective ever given to world humanity stands before you – the abolition of the causes of war.' 'For the first time in history', he wrote elsewhere of the proposed United Nations organisation, 'the Governments of the greatest States in the world have made practical plans for the establishment of permanent peace.' Discarded in his excitement were the very fundamentals of Communism, according to which the major imperialist powers were, by their own internecine rivalries and their resistance to the forces of change, driven inexorably towards war. Instead he saw in the maintenance of the Allies' cohesion and the development of international economic co-operation the guarantee of world security. Far from squabbling as before over restricted markets, for example, the main imperialist powers were to collaborate in the enlightened development of 'more backward' countries to provide ever-increasing markets for the benefit of all. It was a vision combining utter credulity as to the motivations of great powers with an almost Cobdenite faith in the beneficence of international trade.[23]

Only one cloud darkened the horizon, and that was the threat allegedly posed even in defeat by the erstwhile aggressors, particularly Germany. This emphasis too could be traced to the 'Big Three', on whom Stalin, like a latter-day Clemenceau, was urging a punitive peace settlement. However, it is also clear that Pollitt's detestation of fascism had over a number of years engendered in him something of an anti-German outlook. If this had been implicit in some of his utterances even before the war, it was frankly stated even now only in private. Thus in a letter in 1944 he noted with satisfaction the erosion of public scepticism as to atrocity stories from the Eastern Front. 'Everywhere there is a tremendous growth in the hatred of fascism', he wrote with seeming approval, 'and not only against direct Nazis, it applies to the Germans as a race.' It was to this spirit that Pollitt looked to 'prevent any patched up peace'. Indeed, with his jibes about 'false sentimentality' and 'namby-pamby treatment', there was no keener advocate than Pollitt of a 'Carthaginian' peace settlement. 'Those who heiled Hitler as he rode roughshod over Europe must be made to understand that there is a price to pay and they have got to pay it in full', he wrote in defence of reparations by forced labour. It was as if Versailles had to be outdone as much in vindictiveness as in facile optimism. It was certainly a dubious basis for a new world order.[24]

In the domestic sphere, too, Pollitt's belief in the long-term viability of wartime alignments reflected the spirit of the Big Three. After all, if Stalin intended getting on with Churchill, who was Pollitt to disagree with him? The orientation towards a constructive engagement with progressive capitalism was indeed one with which Pollitt fervently identified. He took it to its greatest lengths in his post-Yalta pamphlet *Answers to Questions*. Society's problems he now attributed not so much to capitalism itself as to the 'hitherto chaotic aspects of capitalism' which the war had at last brought under a measure of public control. Even his traditional foes he felt would see the benefits of this development. 'Capitalism, in its pre-1939 set-up', he wrote, 'had become such a "fetter on production" that the capitalists themselves find these very fetters a nightmare.' In a return to pre-war conditions they saw the danger of such a slump as to imperil not only their profits but the profit system itself. To avoid this grim prospect, they too pinned their hopes on planning, state intervention and international co-operation providing full employment and buoyant markets. In this 'ordered and really creative advance' there was therefore, Pollitt concluded, for the first time in this positive context, 'a common interest between the working class and the progressive sections of the capitalist class'.[25]

The contrast with the doom-ridden prognoses of pre-war Communism need hardly be stressed. Such was Pollitt's breezy iconoclasm, indeed, that he laid to rest at last the vague spectre of insurrection which, in the absence of anything more precise, had lurked behind even the blandest Communist pronouncements. The Russian Revolution itself he now adduced as evidence that Communists had 'always endeavoured to avoid using force and violence'. That their opponents had in this case nevertheless forced violence upon them was not, of course, a scenario that Pollitt would definitely rule out for the future. Even so, the transformed conditions brought about by the war he now stated to be 'objectively more favourable for the peaceful transition to socialism than they have ever been'. Just as in 1943 the Comintern had been scrapped, so now, in theory as already in practice, were the revolutionary conceptions that had brought it into being. In their place Pollitt posited a united working class advancing to an ever greater say in the nation's affairs until in socialism there lay a practical and peaceful culmination to all its efforts. His cheerful fantasies about the nature of a world free of fascism would soon perish in the icy blasts of the Cold War; but this underlying perspective would survive, and six years later inform the CP's new long-term programme, *The British Road to Socialism*.[26]

With its comparatively modest proposals, the CP slotted comfortably into a position some way in from the left of Britain's emerging political consensus; so comfortably, indeed, that some Communists and others were beginning to wonder just what special contribution to British politics the Party had to offer. The answer, if there was one, lay perhaps in the 'new conception of democracy' which Pollitt took to be the legacy of 'people's war' and which gave his agenda for the new Britain a distinctive radical slant.

Since adopting a popular front strategy in the mid-1930s the Party had, through all its bewildering changes of policy, placed a consistent emphasis on the organised activity of the common people as the mainspring of political change. With an upsurge of popular initiative and the grudging sanction of the authorities, these ideas acquired during the war a more general currency. Pollitt himself mentioned the Home Guard and civil defence, evacuation and shelter committees and above all joint production committees as examples of effective democratic organisation. It was thus too that the people were to win the peace, not slipping back into apathy but exercising 'the same leadership, initiative, talents and power' as they had in defeating fascism. Pollitt's was thus an activist, participatory conception of democracy. 'It has not been a matter of voting in a Town Hall or a House of Commons what ought to be done by some other person', he wrote of Britain's wartime achievements; 'the people themselves have been doing the job.' This determining influence of those actually on the job breathed life into even the tamest of his proposals for post-war Britain. Against the '"neutral" plans of experts', for example, he posited a democratic system of planning driven by the 'independent democratic activity of the people' working through their own organisations. Nationalised industries he conceived not as 'centralised bureaucratic machines' run from Whitehall, but rather proposed that they 'draw the people into their administration at every level, and... submit their record and their plans for popular approval, so that the strengthening of production and the extension of democracy proceed side by side'. It was on this steady advance to the 'full participation of the people in the administration of things' that Pollitt based his hopes for a peaceful dissolution of capitalism.[27]

All the isms, Pollitt's pamphlets seemed to confirm, were now wasms. If he did not go quite as far as the born-again Browder in the USA, and indeed claimed later to have resisted attempts to smuggle 'Browderism' into Britain,[28] he nevertheless seemed happy to dispense with the fundamentals of Communism as understood even a year or two earlier. He did so, moreover, in a high-handed manner that, as if in deference to the memory of the Comintern, committed British Communists to the international line without so

143

much as a by-your-leave. There were no long discussions or consul-
tations, no special congresses or commissions, not even a formal
programme to be examined, amended and hypothetically rejected.
Instead there would every so often appear to great fanfares the latest
thoughts of the Party leader, to be studied and regurgitated and
disseminated according to demanding district sales quotas.

Pollitt's new conception of democracy did not in this respect
transform the internal life of the Party, and even leading
Communists complained at times about his cavalier methods. Idris
Cox, for example, an EC member and the South Wales district
organiser, referred in February 1944 to concern on the executive at
the perceived 'tendency to impose decisions from the top and to
stifle discussion on controversial points'. Pollitt's sudden announcement in a public speech of a policy of immediate coal nationalisation
was a case in point. 'I was rather amazed that such a tremendous
change in our mining programme was passed over so lightly',
grumbled Cox. 'The way in which the Political Bureau has dealt
with this... tends to confirm the impression that one or two leading
comrades at the Centre decide all policy questions, and that
members of the National Executive have no voice in the matter.'[29]
What this meant, of course, was that there was little, except
perhaps its stagnating membership figures, to indicate how far Pollitt
took the rest of the Party with him in his pursuit of respectability.
Only on the question of a post-war coalition were Party members
specifically consulted, and even then there were to be complaints
about the allegedly 'undemocratic manner in which branches were
stampeded into hasty acceptance of this policy'. Nevertheless, a
tenth of those voting either abstained or rejected the leadership's
position.[30] 'On Churchill the healthy distrust seems to be coming an
obsession preventing people from thinking clearly', Page Arnot
wrote to Pollitt in March 1945. 'There is the idea that Crimea
having Churchill's signature is bound to be a sham; and therefore
only fools would be enthusiastic about it.'[31]

Pollitt's Yalta perspective further lacked the sort of theoretical
underpinning required to give it substance and credibility. Partly this
was due simply to the speed and finality with which it was adopted,
almost as a reflex response to international developments. At a more
personal level it would also seem that academician Dutt, having for
twenty years performed dazzling variations on traditional

Communist themes, found little in the new outlook to stimulate him. It was not, of course, that he failed to expound the Party line, but that for the first time he declined to engage his considerable intellectual powers in doing so. Possibly, with his guiding notions of crisis and revolution all but forgotten, he lacked intellectual commitment. Possibly too he felt that to reveal the underlying consistency of Communist policy was now beyond even him; and no doubt he also felt chastened by the fate of *Crisis of the British People*.

Whatever the explanation, Dutt was not until well after the war to attempt another book of substance. When the young Lawrence Daly put it to him that he should supplement his *World Politics* (1936) with a sequel covering the war years, Dutt's rather feeble reply was that he was too busy. Even his 'Notes of the Month' had no longer their sweeping audacity. 'The *Labour Monthly* in particular has lost a great deal of its value as a theoretical journal', one Communist noted in 1945. 'The "Notes of the Month" have lost their liveliness, and become more a recital of events, than penetrating analysis.' Another went so far as to accuse the journal of 'dull practicalism'. Moreover, there is little to indicate a revival of the pre-war collaboration by which Dutt sharpened Pollitt's populism with his theoretical insights and Pollitt tempered Dutt's scholasticism with his plain common sense. Certainly, those who came to work at King Street in this period had no sense of any particular intimacy or understanding between them. The result was that the Party's revisionism bore all the hallmarks of the boilermaker's somewhat livelier practicalism. The assistance he received from younger, university-educated Communists notwithstanding, Pollitt was never going to make much of a theorist. There was no profound analysis of developments in British society or world affairs to give weight to his pronouncements, but simply an appearance of opportunism and of his characteristic over-enthusiasm.[32]

To provide a focus for the discontent simmering in some sections of the Party, there was not only the Browder fiasco but the CP's sorry performance in the 1945 election. The *Daily Worker*'s fanciful notions of a Communist electoral breakthrough were punctured as a score of two confirmed the Party's marginal status. Pollitt himself, in whom expectations were particularly high, failed narrowly at Rhondda East, as much as anything, apparently, because the Forces vote went to his Labour opponent.[33] Even the celebrations of

Labour's coming of age were tinged with renewed embarrassment at the CP's earlier misjudgement of the mood of the people. The Party's advocacy of national unity had, after all, involved far more than an electoral miscalculation. Certainly that entered into it, and Pollitt erred particularly in his assumption that generalissimo Churchill would command the Forces' allegiance. This was, however, incidental to the coalitionist orientation inherent in the CP's Yalta perspective and indeed in Pollitt's new, unitarian conception of democracy. All over Europe coalitions embracing Communists were coming to power; and it is notable that Pollitt, previously so careful to respect indigenous political traditions, should be led astray by the perceived 'contradiction between policy of National Front in Europe and our own reluctance to write about National Unity after war'.[34] Despite the absence in Britain of a powerful Communist Party or legacy of resistance to fascist occupation, he it was who took steps to bring the British Party into line with the international movement. Perhaps his passionate identification with the broader struggle against fascism had dulled for a time his sensitivity to national peculiarities. One of Pollitt's critics at the post-war Party congress noted long afterwards that in his 'absurd "national unity" line' as in other matters, Pollitt 'always went over the top with any "line"'.[35] Accurate as the assessment is for the war years, it had not always been the case.

Whatever the misgivings their leaders' excesses caused Communists, the Party's culture and organisation were hardly such as to encourage their ventilation. There were, after Yalta, mutterings from Wal Hannington on the EC. Even this hero of many bitter struggles, however, Pollitt reproached not with his intransigence but with 'looking at me so pathetically for the right not to vote'. It was further symptomatic of the disinducement to serious debate within the Party that Pollitt should anathematise Hannington's well-founded reservations as 'the policy of 1928 – Class Against Class'.[36] However, this particular chapter was not to close as one might expect with the usual dreary *mea culpas* on the part of a fossilised leadership. Instead, the executive's rather complacent discussion statement for the November Party congress prompted not a thousand paraphrases but a livelier and more wide-ranging controversy than for many years past. Not only did the Party weekly *World News and Views* invite an exchange of opinions, but for the first time branch resolutions, many of them sharply critical, were printed with the congress agenda. The impenetrability which has been the bane of Communist Party historians was for once broken down from within.

At the heart of the discussion was the feeling expressed in one resolution 'that our Party during years of war has made more wrong assessments and consequent mistakes in policy than is compatible with our claim to be a scientific leadership of the Labour movement'. The mistakes that critics had in mind were, by and large, the more recent ones. Some challenged the whole Yalta perspective from a traditional Marxist standpoint, in one case to deride its 'almost fatuous optimism' and in several to regret its superficiality. Others found it ironic or humiliating as the revolutionary vanguard to have been left behind by the working masses.

The mood of the critics was not, however, one of mere captiousness. In one of the most telling indictments it was noted that the Party leadership had, in its usual fashion, confined itself to the 'mere stating of errors... without an analysis of what led up to the errors'. How refreshing, then, that the pre-congress debate should in contrast reveal a genuinely critical attitude, as restive spirits touched on questions of role, culture and structure that had a crucial bearing on the Party's future. The perennial problem of the CP's position vis-a-vis the Labour Party, more acute than ever with the blurring of the CP's own distinctiveness, cropped up in a number of guises. However, whether aiming at a mass Communist Party or just to leaven the Labour movement with Marxism, whether valuing a robust independence or the benefits of integration, all seemed agreed on one thing: that what the Party needed was a strong, reviving dose of internal democracy. For the critics, the leadership's failure to involve the membership in important decisions was, if not the cause, then a symptom of the Party's malaise, and they gave frank expression to their diagnoses. According to a former CP representative to the CI, the atrophy of Party democracy led Communists either to 'the acceptance of leads without thinking' or to 'suppress their individual opinions and fall into inactivity'. Another grievance was the 'tendency to stifle expression of minority opinion within the Party', while several critics ascribed the recent errors of judgement to a cumbersome bureaucratic apparatus divorced from the daily struggle. 'From the Centre to the Districts

147

the Party is riddled with bureaucracy', wrote one; 'everybody from full-time comrades to the most capable comrades in the branches just sit at desks writing letters, which in the last lap go to the rank and file who never bother to read them'. One has only to remember how the Party first supported, then opposed, then supported again the war, with scarcely an audible expression of discontent, to appreciate that in their scope and their bluntness these criticisms were something rather out of the ordinary.[37]

At the congress itself the critical resolutions were, according to the *Daily Worker*, overwhelmingly rejected. However, the voicing of grievances from the congress floor was in itself enough to create a fractious atmosphere and sting Pollitt into a spirited defence of the leadership's conduct. To demands for democratisation he retorted that the Party was already 'the most democratically run political organisation in the world'. To calls for fuller consultation on critical issues, 'so far as I am concerned', he replied, 'you have another think coming'. More broadly, he was not be budged from his Yalta standpoint, now translated into support for the Attlee Government, and insisted that the Party's stagnation had other causes. 'You can talk about objective and subjective factors as long as you like', he expostulated:

> You can talk about under-estimations and over-estimations as long as you like. But the fundamental reason why our Party does not grow is that you comrades do not want it to grow! That is the reason! The Party wants to be a narrow Party, it wants to be a Party of exclusive Marxists.

It was not the sort of profound or, to use the appropriate jargon, self-critical analysis that the Party required if it was to move on from its wartime plateau.[38]

Pollitt's somewhat tetchy performance may in part be attributable to tensions within the leadership itself. Indeed, the Eighteenth Congress provided a rare glimpse of a tremendous personal rivalry at the head of the Party dating back to the 1920s. For several years Pollitt had a potential Brutus in William Rust, a man to whose memory it is hard to be kind. More than any of his British contemporaries, Rust was everything that Stalinist means as a term of abuse, without a hint of Pollitt's redeeming generosity and humanity or even Dutt's revolutionary asceticism. Unlike most of the CP's ablest leaders, Rust never really experienced life as

148

anything but a Party functionary. While undoubtedly possessed of considerable talent and energy, he emerges from most accounts as a terrible man: vain, self-important, manipulative, hypocritical – Charlotte Haldane has a dreadful story of him as a commissar in Spain feeding himself up in black market restaurants – but above all personally ambitious. His ambition was bound up with a sort of political sycophancy towards the CP's overlords. A Communist who witnessed his fawning in Moscow likened him to a 'mobile jelly', and within Britain he was notorious amongst Party workers for his subservience to the Russians. 'He was the man who wanted every little thing done just as Moscow said', one of them recalled; 'Pollitt was a different character'.

That much had been demonstrated at the start of the war when, as one of the triumvirate that humiliated Pollitt, Rust replaced Campbell as the editor of the *Daily Worker*. It was a position that Rust had occupied several years earlier and this time he had no intention of relinquishing it. Instead, he is alleged by a number of witnesses to have built up at the *Worker* his own little fiefdom, and from his editor's chair was known to covet Pollitt's job. Not all Party workers were conscious of, let alone willing participants in, the contest; when, for example, it was put to the *Worker*'s popular cartoonist 'Gabriel' that he was a 'Rustie boy' and not a 'Pollitt boy', it was the first that he had heard of such matters. Pollitt himself, on the other hand, was fully aware of Rust's antagonism; that presumably was why he so rarely set foot in the *Daily Worker* building. Moreover, he well understood the oblique methods by which in Communist politics a leader's position was undermined. 'Harry once said, "When Bill Rust was making that speech, of course he was getting at me"', one Party worker recalled. There were, she went on, a succession of such speeches, and the most conspicuous of these was that at the post-war Party congress.[39]

If Rust had a role model in 1945, it was no doubt William Z. Foster, the American Communist who with Moscow's approval had ousted the over-zealous Browder. Rust had no particular leftist inclinations but was anxious then as ever to interpret correctly the trajectory of the international movement. Just as at the time of Teheran, for example, he had formed part of a 'right' minority on the EC resistant to the slightest breach of national unity,[40] so now with the worsening international situation he began to see the virtues of a switch to the left. Moreover, he appreciated no doubt, and possibly exaggerated to himself, Pollitt's vulnerability. As one of the critics at the Eighteenth Congress later recalled, 'there was a lot of dissatisfaction in the Party over the way Pollitt (and it centred on Pollitt) handled such issues'. Probably it was at this congress that Pollitt passed a note along the platform to two EC colleagues whose support was evidently a mixed blessing. 'Ivor and Isabel', the note ran, 'Don't clap so much. I am in the shit enough.'[41] As defiant about the present as he was unrepentant about the past, Pollitt gave little ground to those in the Party clamouring for a sharper treatment of the Labour Government and particularly a denunciation of its foreign policy.[42] On the latter point, indeed, he had, after a 'long and friendly chat' with Bevin at a Soviet Embassy function, been for further discussions with the foreign secretary only days before the CP congress. True, they ended in a mutually enjoyable slanging match (how one would love to have been a fly on the wall!) but Pollitt's commitment to working with the government was nevertheless clear.[43]

There was thus no mistaking Rust's intent when, replying to the congress for the EC, he seemed suddenly to side with the leadership's critics in demanding Bevin's removal from office. From the floor of the hall his remarks were greeted with the loud cheers that he doubtless anticipated. Moreover, while it was his attack on the government that the press seized upon the following day, causing Pollitt to issue an official repudiation, Rust was also to be accused of having 'implied a different view from that of the EC re our mistakes'.[44] His intentions were further underlined when, in a *Daily Worker* article entitled 'On Guard in 1946!', he shortly afterwards ruled out the possibility of 'a swift transition to prosperity and a world free from the menace of war'. Instead he insisted 'that peace-making is no cakewalk, that imperialism is in all essentials unchanged, and that fine words are no substitute for the united political action of the people'.[45]

There was no question as to whom Pollitt had to be on guard against in 1946. The *Daily Worker*'s Sam Russell recalls well Rust's determination to be on the CP's first post-war delegation to Moscow and there give his own slant on recent events and personalities. His manoeuvres got him nowhere, however. There were not now the same mechanisms for outside interference as in

150

1939, whilst amongst British Communists Pollitt was still held in an affection and esteem that Rust would never match. 'He had his followers', one remembered, 'but they were usually among the place-seekers.' The majority even of the leading Party functionaries – Campbell, Gallacher, Kerrigan, Bramley, Gollan – were, if one can so put it, 'Pollitt boys'. It was to be another two years before the Party was decisively to change course, and then it would be Pollitt himself who would oversee the transition to sectarianism.[46]

The intervening years of broad identification with Labour's postwar objectives were arguably the last in which Pollitt found in the challenges of domestic politics an adequate outlet for his own constructive impulses. Already evident in his enthusiasm for the popular front and his disdain for mere posturings at the start of the war, these instincts found a worthy object in the tasks of victory and reconstruction. 'Concentrate on the positive', he had exhorted Communists in mid-1941, when support for their own government was still a novelty. 'Our Party history shows on many occasions an aptitude for criticism to the neglect of unfolding our positive policy.' In the subsequent period this accent on the positive was to transform the Party's outlook, the tone of its propaganda and even its organisation. In 1943, for example, Pollitt was closely involved with the decision to set up a number of standing committees to formulate constructive Communist policies on all the issues of postwar politics. 'This is particularly necessary for the coming period', it was claimed, 'when the questions of positive measures of advance will be so important – rather than the fight *against* reactionary measures.'

In the carefully argued policy memoranda that these committees produced, Pollitt saw the evidence of his Party's new standing in the affairs of the nation, and it was a position from which he would not readily withdraw to the carping oppositionism of earlier years. All over Europe, Communists were emerging from illegality to participate in reconstruction at every level, up to and including the new national governments. Within Britain, moreover, 1945 was the year in which, after years of frustration, Pollitt's own generation of socialists at last assumed responsibility for the country's future. Of the new government's leading figures, all were born within a decade of the Communist leader; and it is clear that as old associates and adversaries proceeded to put into effect many of the CP's own policies, Pollitt was not disposed to stand aside contributing only revolutionary-sounding phrases. 'Are we never going to learn?' he lashed out at critics at the Eighteenth Congress. 'I have been in too many campaigns which had as their main motive *against*, and not sufficient with the main motive *for*, and comrades, especially the younger comrades... would be well advised to assimilate that experience too.'[47] Despite growing impatience with the government, it was an outlook to which he remained faithful until the Cold War decreed otherwise.

In the meantime the CP's attitude to Attlee's government was akin to that it had taken to Churchill's. There were some harsh criticisms, especially regarding its foreign policy, and a sort of creeping disillusionment, but not as yet such as to consign the government to the camp of reaction. Even as the Cominform was taking shape to shepherd all Communist parties to the far side of the Iron Curtain, Pollitt could confidently assert of Labour Britain 'that the essence of the period we are now in is that of a transition stage towards Socialism'. Accordingly, the CP was happy to support government candidates in by-elections and as late as September 1947 it opposed to the Yorkshire coal strikes the more responsible conception of trade unionism it felt this nascent socialism required.[48] The call for 'an entirely new, constructive approach' from the unions was but one aspect of a concerted campaign over production, which the Party saw as central to Britain's problems. The fuel crisis, the housing crisis, the balance of payments crisis, economic dependence on the 'dollar imperialists' and the maintenance of a huge and costly unproductive sector in the Armed Forces: all the themes to which Pollitt kept returning seemed to touch on this basic question of production. Moved in 1947 by the concerns about communication and motivation that had some ministers slyly manoeuvring Ernie Bevin into Attlee's shoes, Arthur Horner went so far as to propose Pollitt's inclusion in the government 'to organise and direct all aspects of production'.[49] The odd technicality apart, there was certainly no role to which Pollitt's exhortatory fervour and willingness to court temporary unpopularity were better suited. In his writings on production he dealt not only with the need for more planning, investment and wage incentives but warned that 'we, the workers... also have to pull our socks up... Sectional and craft interests must be subordinated to the interests of the movement and the nation as a whole.' Specifically, this involved things like building workers dropping their traditional resistance to piecework; and miners, newly blessed with the five-day week, working voluntary weekend shifts. Not surprisingly, Communist trade unionists who followed Pollitt's lead, among whom Horner himself was foremost, did not always win friends by doing so. Most extraordinary of all, perhaps, was Pollitt's advocacy on the East European model of 'great weekend volunteer brigades' to help out in the key industries. 'There are tremendous possibilities here, if only these are exploited', he wrote. 'All that splendid initiative and sacrifice that was shown during the war by the Home Guard, the ARP, the Fire Watching Parties, can once again be called forth and enrolled in a constructive drive to help the nation in peace as in war.'[50]

Pollitt's wartime analogies were carried furthest during what Labour's chancellor later dubbed the *Annus Horrendus* of 1947. The multiple crises that hit Britain in that year Pollitt considered graver even than those of 1940. Repeatedly he expressed the hope that Attlee would, as he had after Dunkirk, introduce emergency legislation according the government 'complete control over persons and property', and then make good use of these powers. Emigration should be blocked, pleasure trips abroad prohibited, passenger transport curtailed as necessary and labour directed to essential industries, especially the labour of monied parasites who ought otherwise to be deprived of their ration books. In his demands for equality of sacrifice, one detects the authentic note of class hatred that, whatever the trappings of the current Party line, was peculiarly Pollitt's:

When the Ritz, the Savoy and Claridges are used to house workers on holiday in London; when Simpsons, the Criterion and Oddeninos are turned into British Restaurants; when the great country houses are rest homes for miners and agricultural workers; when Harrods, Debenhams, Fortnum and Masons and Bond Street shops cease displaying the luxury goods that at present insult the eye and mind alike when you think of the shops in Tonypandy, Ashington, Bellshill, Wigan and other working-class centres... when silence reigns in the Stock Exchanges of our cities; when the rich and their families queue up at the Labour Exchange for jobs – then you can believe that at last the rich are being soaked and we are at the beginning of a Socialist policy for Britain.

Had Horner's wish to see Pollitt in the government magically been granted, the vermin clubs and housewives' leagues of Labour Britain would have had themselves a hate-figure more threatening perhaps even than their lurid image of Aneurin Bevan.[51]

Pollitt's overall mood in these years is best summed up as one of grim optimism. The confidence expressed in the very titles of pamphlets like *Britain Will Make It* was offset by a stark depiction of the sacrifices required to 'make it' and of the catastrophic consequences of not doing so. With each month of dampened expectations and international gamesmanship the note of foreboding was accentuated. By August 1947 the brighter scenarios he sketched in *Looking Ahead* seemed somehow forced and artificial, even according to the book's own internal evidence. More believable than the 'new British road to Socialism' he mapped out was the alternative road allegedly favoured by Wall Street, the Tories and those Labour leaders inclined to capitulate to them. It was a road that meant 'the return to the full anarchic chaos of capitalist economy, the surrender of all economic planning, the colonisation of Britain by the US trusts and the establishment of the British Islands as a base for atomic warfare on European democracy';[52] and it was a road, too, that within weeks Pollitt was to be forced by Moscow to conclude that Britain had quite definitely embarked upon. After all the grandiose hopes he had believed in and struggled to achieve, it was like finding himself back where he started. The tone of the coming period was of a mean and wayward sectarianism, akin to the anti-war line Pollitt had so fiercely resisted or the discredited excesses of 'Class Against Class', without even that period's revolutionary fervour. Henceforth, Pollitt's constructive impulses would again receive only vicarious satisfaction, from the triumphant socialist regimes of Eastern Europe and beyond. That this seemed only to strengthen his allegiance to Stalinism in power was not the least unattractive feature of the period that followed.

7 Looking backwards, looking east

In December 1947 Pollitt declared that, with the world now divided into two camps and Labour Britain active in the imperialist camp, 'important changes' in Communist policy were again required. The cue for the announcement was the unveiling in Sept-ember 1947 of the Communist Information Bureau or Cominform, an afterthought to the Comintern to which lesser parties like Britain's were not even admitted. Pollitt, not for the first time, was a little slow or else unwilling to fall into line. For some weeks even after the Cominform's founding declaration he 'clung to old formulas and approaches', as he himself later put it. His October report to the EC still maintained that, just as during the war, objections to govern-ment policies should not be allowed to hinder the campaign 'for the utmost possible increase in production'. By December, however, clarification of the Cominform policy must have got through to King Street, and the Party now obliged with a recitation of past errors and promise of sharper struggles to come.[1]

Thus was effected the last of the spectacular reversals which punctuated Pollitt's leadership of the CP. Henceforth, and for the rest of Pollitt's life, Communist policy was very much a reflection of the Cold War version of the two camps theory; and as the shifting alignments of great-power politics gave way to this sullen antagonism between East and West, the CP's postures came to acquire a certain predictability. It is true that over specific issues like the denunciation of Tito there would be further major upsets. It is also true that the intensity of the CP's feelings of alienation, stuck there in the heart of the enemy camp, tended to fluctuate with the ebb and flow of the Cold War. The waspish sectarianism exemplified by its challenge to allcomers in the 1950 election gradually gave way to a more pragmatic orientation towards the Labour left, but no further somersaults were involved, nor any dramatic developments of programme or ideology. Now one

155

campaign was to the fore, and now another; but the basic compo-
nents of Cold War Communism – the anti-Americanism and anti-
colonialism, the peace campaigns and 'fighting trade unionism', the
panegyrics to the other camp – remained, for year after year,
essentially unaltered. Far from springing any great surprises on its
much put-upon membership, the Party was indeed in danger of
becoming rather dull. 'We get about the same resolution each
Congress', one comrade complained before that held in 1956. 'To
say the least, this is an uninspiring document', another agreed; 'the
general reaction to the resolution is "Read it all before"'.[2] That same
year a great deal more than this was said to reveal a deep-seated
malaise within the Party, buried under layers of habit until the
Khrushchev speech and then Soviet intervention in Hungary caused
thousands to rethink their habits. An early casualty of these events,
much too old now to have second thoughts, was the Party's general
secretary. In May 1956, just as Khrushchev's revelations about Stalin
were being made public, Pollitt resigned from his post on grounds
of ill-health.

The poor health that certainly was amongst the factors influencing
Pollitt's resignation had by 1956 dogged the ageing revolutionary for
several years. His was a robust constitution which succumbed less to
his indulgences in food, drink and tobacco than to his enormous
appetite for hard work. 'Harry certainly did the work of three or
four men in those days', recalled one of his closest associates. 'He
went to the very limit in overworking himself, and I am afraid we
let him do it...'[3] As early as 1923 he suffered some sort of
breakdown and spent part of that spring convalescing in the Schiff
Home, Cobham, Surrey. He had a further breakdown in the
immediate aftermath of Munich, attributed by Gallacher to his
having 'worked himself almost to death for the Party',[4] but it was
after the war that more serious problems arose. First in 1947 he
injured his knee in a car accident and then, two years later, he was
set upon in a notorious fracas a few days after the shedding of British
blood in the Yangtse River incident. Previously arranged meetings in
Dartmouth and Plymouth provided the occasion for the assault, and
it is a tribute to Pollitt's rather reckless courage that he should even
have attempted to fulfil these engagements in the Navy's heartland.
Trouble was anticipated and it was no surprise that some brave
young sailors should have decided that what they could not take out

156

on the Chinese People's Army they would take out on this man of sixty instead. But for the burly Glaswegian presence of 'Big Peter' Kerrigan, a fit match indeed for the Royal Navy, Pollitt's injuries might well have been worse. As it was, the kicks he received would later in the year have him in hospital, as doctors diagnosed a prolapsed disc and fitted him with a corset to strengthen his spine.[5]

For the treatment of this condition and the general effects of overwork, Pollitt relied not just on Britain's fledgling health service but on the people's clinics of Eastern Europe. The VIP, or rather apparatchik, treatment he received, in Czechoslovakia in 1949 and in the USSR in 1950 and 1954, can hardly have helped to engender in him a more critical and disinterested approach to the problems of those countries. Nevertheless, the visits were not without some effect on his fundamental preconceptions. 'Carrots, cabbage, radishes, beetroots, prunes', he wrote from a Soviet clinic in 1950, 'and then again carrots, cabbage, radishes, beetroots, prunes... Never again will I, a boilermaker who likes his pint, his dram, and fish and chips, laugh at vegetarians... for the results speak for themselves.' His disc was back in place, he went on, and his corset in the Revolutionary Museum. He would need it back again, but without these treatments, and the provision as from 1947 of an assistant secretary to bear some of his pressures and deputise when necessary, Pollitt might have been forced to retire somewhat earlier than he actually did.[6]

There were other signs than his deteriorating health that by the 1950s Pollitt was getting to be an old man. He felt, as which Communist did not, a sense of disenchantment as Labour's blissful dawn turned out to have heralded not the glad day of socialism but the dreary, soggy afternoon we remember as Butskellism. What distinguished and rather dated Pollitt, however, were his repeated invocations of the loftier, purer ideals of his youth to damn the bloodless heresies of an upstart generation. His admiration for the 'pioneers' had, of course, long found expression in his writings, but never before so insistently nor with so transparent a sense of loss. How to recapture the 'gleam' of socialism that had inspired this earlier generation was a question that constantly troubled him. 'It is necessary to give an idea of what Socialism is and what it is not', he echoed Blatchford to James Klugmann, who was drafting parts of his *Looking Ahead* in 1947:

157

What was it that prompted Morris to go to the street corner? What was it that prompted Will Thorne to go every Sunday morning and never miss, wet or fine, to speak at Beckton Road in Canning Town extolling his conception of the gospel called Socialism. And do not be afraid of being sentimental in your approach even if you did go to a university. For alas in these days when pineapples and peaches pass for a British socialist epoch, we need to recapture once again something of the spirit that dominated this type of man.

What Pollitt sought was not just a revival of the idealism and the bitter class feeling of days gone by, but a perpetuation even of the methods of propaganda used. How often in these days did he call for a 'return to the soap-box to blazon the principles and the cause of the workers at every street corner, market place and public hall'. Fired by the rhetoric of socialism, the assembled crowds would, in Pollitt's reverie, then make their way home clutching pamphlets expounding the same principles with all the 'bite, sting and satire' of a Blatchford, a Tom Mann, a Harry Quelch. It was a vision not of the future but of the past. 'You can listen to the radio and watch the television until you are blue in the face', he wrote in a paean to the penny pamphlet, 'but they will not answer the questions which are a life and death matter for the workers.' Sadly, however, these 'instruments of capitalist propaganda', together with the roar of traffic as workers began to shoot round street corners in motorised capsules, were cutting the ground from beneath the old agitator's feet. Increasingly, the decisive say in the propaganda war lay with the smooth-tongued professionals he distrusted and even detested.[7]

It was from the same standpoint of an idealised Edwardian socialism, and with a scorn which he yearned for a Tressell to express,[8] that Pollitt viewed the post-war colonisation of the Labour Party by middle-class parvenus. His images of the golden age, 'when self counted for nothing, when careerism was not thought of, when cutting a figure in Parliament was not the only aim', were of course too good to be more than part of the truth. His sense of a movement born of the sacrifices of working men and now succumbing to a Trojan horse of Oxford accents was no less powerful for all that. It was a note that first entered into his utterances with his growing disappointment in the Attlee Government. The 1947 reshuffle by which, as the *New Statesman* put it, 'the old type of working class leader gives way to the disinterested expert who had studied

Keynes', evoked from Pollitt a characteristically acerbic response. 'All the old-timers in the Movement', he wrote, 'those who, whatever differences there may be between them and the Communists, at least have helped build up the Movement, do know its struggles and are part of them – these are the people who have been removed'. Their replacements, by sorry contrast, were men with 'no mass experience of the Movement... most of whom have never smelt a grease rag, oil or pit dust in their lives'.[9]

The old-timers, like the pioneers, had in Pollitt a tireless champion, and their disapproving presence could often be felt as over the next few years he excoriated the revisionist currents we associate with Gaitskell, Crosland and *New Fabian Essays*. 'The Labour Party type of "new thinking"', he declaimed with ringing contempt, 'is peddled with such a patronising, pompous, "You were never at Haileybury, Winchester, Oxford or Cambridge" air on the part of alleged Labour leaders who have never been in a strike or lock-out, hunger march or dole queue... never preached the gospel of divine discontent or socialism at a street corner or market place, never known what it is to feel hunger or anger, and to passionately desire the overthrow of the capitalist system...' Feeding off one another and apparently quite inextricable were his disgust at the interlopers' social mannerisms and his dismay at their political postures. 'We have Labour leaders who ape the fashions and manners of the rich', he wrote, 'who don't eat their peas with their knives, whose striped trousers and hats are equal to anything Anthony Eden sports. Some might think these affectations irrelevant, but Pollitt knew better. 'It explains', he went on, 'why we are murdering innocent people in Malaya and Korea.'[10]

Despite the absurdity of this particular claim, many may sympathise with Pollitt's basic sentiments. The view that parliamentary socialism was emasculated by its willingness to play by the establishment's rules has, moreover, a respectable academic pedigree. Nevertheless, Pollitt's dismissal of Labour's 'new thinking' in such crude terms was simply an evasion of new post-war dilemmas which the revisionists had, however inadequately, at least begun to address. Pollitt, on the other hand, seemed content to mouth the unchanging verities he found in his fading pamphlets. 'We have... reached a stage now where it is not only necessary to look into the future, but to remember the past', he wrote. 'The Labour movement was built up on the basis of hatred against those who rob the poor'; and 'as long as one man robs another of the full fruits of his labour, there will always be need of struggle against it'. However true or deeply felt they might be, these platitudes were inadequate to the challenges of the post-war world.[11]

Perhaps Pollitt himself had some inkling that by the 1950s he had indeed served his time. 'I do not like the reference to Bob Smillie as being spent and done', he wrote after reading one of Page Arnot's mining histories. 'After all I am getting old myself, and would not like such a reference to be made to me.'[12] But if domestic politics conveyed to him a brutal message, exemplified by the CP's annihilation in the 1950 election, Pollitt managed to find in the wider pattern of world events the confirmation he needed of the pioneers' teachings. If, for example, capitalism at home bore a somewhat more benign aspect than heretofore, which Pollitt could in any case hardly bring himself to admit, its impact on Britain's colonies and ex-colonies remained absolutely devastating. The Empire had never really been a dominant concern of his and only on his Caribbean health cruise in 1938 had he witnessed colonial oppression at first hand. However, on the occasion of the Indian CP's Third Congress in December 1953 he paid a month-long visit to that country, and the poverty he witnessed there did nothing to dispel his hatred for those who were its beneficiaries. 'The most depraved human being in Britain would not keep a dog under such conditions', he wrote of the Calcutta slums, so much the worst he had ever seen. 'Human beings with hearts that can beat and minds that can think were never meant to live in such conditions.' While the sight of such deprivation sunk him for a time into an uncharacteristic depression, the unparalleled contrast between rich and poor restored to him his healthy sense of anger. 'There is only one thing I wish I could do to them', he wrote of his compatriots swanking it in Calcutta's opulent West End. 'Not murder, not violence. Only just go and make them eat and sleep in the conditions of the working people who live in the other Calcutta.' In India, as right across Africa and Asia, capitalism was perpetrating old-fashioned evils and meeting with the sort of bitter resistance that Pollitt sought in vain in Britain. 'All the bombs, terrorism, starvation, concentration camps and policies of deliberate murder cannot intimidate our colonial brothers and sisters', he said shortly after returning to Britain. 'They are fighting back in an unconquerable spirit that has no parallel in world history...'[13]

What really sustained Pollitt in his political faith, however, was the knowledge that under the leadership of his party a third of mankind had left capitalism behind to forge for themselves a more glorious destiny. During this period, when he judged it 'particularly necessary to overcome any feeling that the world is against us', he derived from the global advance of Communism the assurance that, as he put it, 'we are on the winning side'. In a country like Britain where this was far from self-evident, the thought was no doubt a great comfort and the victories overseas a compensation of sorts for domestic humiliations. 'Above all, we are part of [a] great world force, hundreds of millions strong', he wrote during the disastrous 1950 election campaign. 'We draw strength and encouragement from the mighty forward march of the world movement...' Michael Foot recalls a similar display of bravado after a categorical by-election defeat in 1949. 'We may have lost St Pancras', Pollitt conceded, 'but we've won in China.'[14]

The epic proportions of the victory in China and the supposed romance of socialist construction in Eastern Europe did indeed provide a refreshing contrast with the British Party's pettier concerns. 'Reckon yourself lucky', Pollitt told the journalist Alan Winnington, who for his misdemeanours was unable to re-enter Britain and was escorting Pollitt on a tour of China in 1955. 'You've survived the Korean war and now you're living through the Chinese revolution instead of being stuck in our King Street rabbit-warren.' One can well understand how, with his hunger for a 'sense of drama... spirit of adventure [and]... feeling that great things were happening', all of which he complained were absent in post-war Britain, Pollitt should view with 'joy and understandable envy' the more momentous challenges history was posing his foreign comrades. No speech of his, it seemed, was complete without a peroration depicting the starkest possible contrast between East and West, politically, economically, morally and culturally. As Pollitt himself pointed out, the 'splendid reality' of socialist achievement played the same role in his effusions as the 'gleam of socialism' had for the pioneers; except, of course, that Pollitt's splendid reality was so very much more far-fetched. Repeating the preposterous claims in which, if nothing else, the People's Democracies fulfilled all

161

quotas, he came increasingly to adopt the required language of Wellsian fantasy in describing the socialist bloc. 'Consider', he taunted the timid and the parochial denied this vision, 'consider the "new thinking" that has gone into the gigantic projects of construction in the Soviet Union, where the face of geography is being changed, climates regulated and the secrets wrested from the bosom of Mother Nature.' Here was the proof the pioneers had lacked 'that the lily does indeed bloom; that men like ourselves are performing greater miracles in the realms of Socialist and Communist construction than it was thought that even Gods could ever do'. How long ago this faith in man's superabundant capacities seems, a survival into the nuclear age of illusions that at least one of the world wars should have shattered. 'Literally miracles', Pollitt once described the achievements of socialism in power. The old freethinker should have remembered that there is no such thing as a miracle.[15]

If they now seem almost as remote to us as the Anabaptists or Southcottians, these expressions of quasi-religious fervour served even in the 1950s to set the CP and its penumbra apart from the sceptical millions. Back in the 1930s the cult of Stalin's Russia, though scarcely better founded, had united Communists with a broad swathe of humane opinion, precisely because it answered to the most pressing concerns of the time. Beset by stagnation and reaction, Western progressives found in the Socialist Fatherland, with its optimism and its rationality, exactly the utopia they might have had to, and to a certain extent did, invent. Two decades later, it was an altogether more esoteric matter for workers spawned in the cradle of the industrial revolution to excite themselves over the stirrings of factory life in the Balkans. 'See this feature', the *Daily Worker*'s cartoonist complained of a typical piece he had to illustrate, 'we've got another bleeding Russian tractor on here. That's no bloody use, we've got thousands of tractors in Britain.' It was indeed a strange obsession. No doubt because of the finite appeal of foreign tractors, most British people found little to attract them to the proliferation of societies for friendship with the new socialist countries, most of which had thus to resort for their 'non-Party' figureheads to the same, few, long-rumbled 'celebrities'. The multiple presidencies and chairmanships of comrades D. N. Pritt KC and Commander Edgar Young RN (retired) expressed as well as anything the CP's isolation during the Cold War period.[16]

162

Its unconditional allegiance to unpopular dictatorships was just the most visible of the idiosyncrasies that undid much of the Party's work to establish itself as an integral part of British political life. Amongst the other exogenous curiosities so characteristic of the period, Harry McShane, a veteran of three decades in the Party, instanced compulsory standing ovations and the tendency to regard the secretary as 'almost infallible'. 'If one opposes policy', McShane complained on leaving the Party in 1953, 'he is often met with the remark: "That is an attack on Comrade Pollitt."' During these years there was indeed a half-hearted attempt to give the Stalinist cult of personality a native dimension in the shape of the British people's own affable and stocky incomparable genius. It is to Pollitt's credit that his endearing bent for bantering self-deprecation singularly unfitted him for the solemn encomiums that went with this role. The personality cults, however, rarely clung too closely to the characteristics of the individual concerned; indeed, the very last thing they required was a personality. Pollitt, for example, was nobody's idea of an 'outstanding Marxist theoretician', but it was to hail him as such that in 1953 there appeared, chronologically arranged just like Lenin's and Stalin's, the first volume of his selected works. It was presumably an indication of the CP's inability to confront its own past that only two of the projected four volumes appeared. Like a television thriller, the story was left hanging in mid-air with the nail-biting question *Will It Be War?* in July 1939.[17]

Possibly the most outlandish manifestations of the miniature Pollitt cult were the celebrations organised first for his twentieth anniversary as general secretary and then for his sixtieth birthday. Just as the Soviet Communist Party had in 1949 mobilised the entire Soviet population, its writers and its troubadours, to salute Stalin's birthday, so the following year British Communists gathered to pay tribute to their leader amongst the pomp and splendour of Lime Grove Baths, Shepherd's Bush. The presentations, the *Daily Worker* reported, took 'well over 30 minutes': an overcoat from the London CP, a teaset from Communist lawyers, a cake from Communist bakers, rose trees, coffee tables, pottery, whisky – as the gifts piled up, Pollitt began to disappear from sight. If this was rather like a traditional trade union presentation taken to the Communists' usual extremes, the tributes that accompanied the gifts were such as to defy comparison. Not only his modesty, his courage,

163

his links with the masses were celebrated, but also his erudition, his 'brilliant grasp of strategy and tactics', his unequalled mastery of Marxism-Leninism. Peter Kerrigan's eulogy of 'the greatest leader of the British people' was a prime example. 'In our General Secretary we have no detached and distant leader', he slobbered. 'Leader yes, but also bone of the bone, and flesh of the flesh of the toilers. That is a most important part of his genius.' One can only wonder what Blatchford's disciple felt as he read this tripe in his Party's theoretical journal.[18]

The sadness of it was that Pollitt had by his very humanity earned the deep respect and affection of Communists, whom he in turn regarded almost as an extended family; and that these laboured genuflections, attributing to him virtues he did not even acknowledge as well as those which were genuinely his, served only to cheapen this relationship. Of the dozens of greetings he received on these occasions, one prefers to remember not those pledging to emulate their 'beloved leader' (the Hackney Party's nauseating phrase) but the many more expressing an altogether more human and spontaneous regard for their comrade and spokesman. A letter from Rowton House in Whitechapel, for example, provides a glimpse not only of this warmth of feeling but of the sort of response Pollitt's propaganda could evoke in the old-timers who meant so much to him:

> I have always found you true to the core   I know it as been a hard life by my own experience being victimised i fired and threths of all discrip-ions... I should like Harry to have half a hour with you sometime before I go back to Doncaster   I was very much struck by your article in the Daily this morning   It made tears come in my eyes how my poor old farther had to fetch us up on 17/10 per week   I had to get up every morning go with the Paper the Huddersfield Examiner 3d per week till I was ten then start half time 2/6 per week till the old Man died then I Had to face the World... and I have been traveling ever sinse

One can imagine perhaps how, as similar views and experiences were put to Pollitt during his travels round the country, they must have fortified him in his own most fundamental political instincts.[19]

Pollitt's personal contribution to the CP's partial retreat into its own private world is difficult to gauge. Over a period of fifteen years, after all, he more than anybody had striven to shake off the Party's sectarian legacy. Moreover, as its main contact with those wielding influence on the non-Communist left, he could not but feel keenly the CP's returning political isolation. 'We watch men pass in the Lobbies of the House of Commons whom we have known all our lives, fearful to stop and say, "How do, Harry"', he wrote in 1950, although there was of course more to this ostracism than just fear of guilt by association.[20] The hostility to Communism during the Cold War was immense, and although Pollitt could bear with fortitude the attacks of the capitalist press or a jingo mob, the defection of traditional constituencies must have disheartened him. 'I wish those who came... would try it in East London or Glasgow', he challenged his assailants at the ill-starred Plymouth meeting; but it was precisely in one of the Party's few proletarian citadels, the Rhondda Fach, that in the 1950 election Pollitt's supporters abandoned him in their thousands. Over five elections the Communist vote in the constituency had laboriously been built up to a rough equivalence with Labour's; and then, as if overnight, the Party suddenly found itself in a position worse even than when it started its Sisyphean task in 1929. It was the last of Pollitt's eight parliamentary contests and a setback of some symbolic importance.[21]

In the contrast between inflated rhetoric and dismal reality, the 1950 election exemplified the CP's partial regression to the follies of the 'third period'. That the final crisis was, had anybody still been counting, now entering its seventh or eighth period only made the rhetoric seem hollower still. The election campaign itself the Party conducted on the basis that there was not the slightest thing to choose between the two main parties. 'Tweedledum and Tweedledee' was how Pollitt described them to Rhondda electors, some of whom might, had they only the memory for these things, have recalled William Rust using the very same phrase at Mardy during the 1931 campaign. Pollitt's skewed logic and pure fantasy as he sought to rationalise the defeat might also have derived from Lewis Carroll. The decision to contest a hundred seats, losing deposits in 97 of them, he insisted was 'absolutely correct'. After all, by every criterion – recruits made, meetings held, leaflets distributed, *Daily Worker*s sold – by every criterion except votes the campaign was a thumping success. The more leaflets distributed, one might have thought, the more presumably were read and disregarded or simply used to light the fire with; but it was from these statistics, so lovingly recited, that in his wilder utterances

165

Pollitt drew the inference that the Party's message had begun to take hold of the masses. Under the improbable heading 'Forward with confidence' he taunted the election's gloating victors with their underlying fear of the Communist Party. 'They understand perfectly well that events are going to prove us right in the eyes of millions of workers', he wrote; 'that we are the alternative force which is going to develop and increase in strength... [and] bring our country out of the camp of war and imperialism and into the camp of peace and democracy.' It was all as inevitable – and how often was Pollitt tempted by that treacherous word – as the looming slump and the rending political crisis that would give the Communists their long-awaited opportunity. 'The crisis of British imperialism will inevitably deepen with every day that passes', he asserted just before the election. 'The contradiction between the growth in the productive capacity and the consumption of the working people will sharpen. There will be still fiercer attacks on the workers and the rights they have won... Every development will drive home the need for the revolutionary way out of the crisis.' One could quote at length without ever being quite sure whether this was 1949 or 1929.[22]

For the sectarianism and sense of unreality typified by this passage Pollitt must, in the end, bear the primary responsibility. The cult of the general secretary in Cold War Communism gave him an unrivalled authority within the Party, and it was his congress and EC reports, indeed his every public utterance, that set the tone for its activities up and down the country. Within the leadership, too, his was very much the dominant role. With the death of his rival William Rust in February 1949, Pollitt's old sidekick Johnny Campbell took charge at the *Daily Worker,* while his younger protégés Gollan and Matthews took the positions of assistant editor and assistant secretary respectively. Dutt, of course, remained, but with a much reduced influence except in the realm of international affairs.

There was, in other words, nobody inside the British Party capable of foisting upon it policies against its leader's better judgement. Only the Russians could do that, and it is to this relationship that one must inevitably trace the inadequacies of the Party's understanding of the post-war period. In effect the CP allowed itself to be used in a global propaganda war of extraordinary virulence and crudity, as incapable almost of a critical view of British politics as of one of the Soviet Union. Its constant warnings of a slump that never seemed to materialise or its failure to see in the Tories' recovery anything but the treachery of social democracy were the necessary counterpart to its idealisation of countries going through the worst traumas of Stalinism. The classic dichotomies of war propaganda, combined in the CP's case with the dogmatic immunities of 'scientific socialism', stifled in it any critical understanding of the realities behind the conflict. It was to this detachment from the real world around it that the 'deep-rooted sectarianism' which Pollitt acknowledged to be the Party's principal weakness should have been attributed. To blame it, as he did, on attitudinal defects, was a characteristic evasion of deeper political problems that he did not quite know how to address. His calls on Communists to display more modesty, openness and friendliness in their dealings with others, commendable though the advice was, were not going to transform the Party's standing in British political life.[23]

Nevertheless, in the importance that he attached to these matters Pollitt did at least show his enduring instinct to bridge the gap between Communists and those they purported to lead. Sometimes, indeed, he was so blunt as apparently to give some credence to the routine allegations of anti-Communists. 'We must prove by our methods of approach, contact and activity that we are not out to dominate, not out to form cliques to push through things that others disagree with', he told one Party congress. 'And it is high time that we stopped creating the impression that... we are some kind of human beings who never eat, sleep, play or dream – but somehow or other that we are inhuman people unlike in every respect those we are in daily contact with.'[24] His ambition to embed the British Party in its native soil showed no sign of abating, even during periods when his overriding loyalty to the international movement made it so much more difficult to achieve. This ambiguity was at the heart of what was arguably the CP's last despairing effort to carve for itself a niche at the centre of British politics, *The British Road to Socialism*. This long-term programme was in later years to acquire a talismanic value for Communists, and their bickerings over the cryptically designated and otherwise unread 'BRS' were to encapsulate their diminishing sense of common purpose. It was a sad end to the hopes that Pollitt had invested in the programme as its chief British architect back in 1950.

167

The initial impetus for the programme was provided by that year's electoral debacle, which persuaded Pollitt that the CP had somehow to rediscover its sense of identity and direction. Since 1945, he noted, Communists had had less to say about their basic socialist goals than ever before, and in the absence of any clear alternative perspective they had been unable to counteract the immense feelings of loyalty that the Labour Party commanded. This more sober judgement was at first only an undercurrent to his prevalent triumphalism, but during Pollitt's stay in the Soviet Union that spring the gravity of the setback to his Party was evidently impressed upon him. After discussions with no less a person than Stalin, amongst others, he returned to Britain a chastened man. 'We may try and excuse ourselves for both an inadequate analysis and political conclusions by the fact that it was necessary to tone up the Party', he reported on his return, 'but this is not a Marxist approach to the situation…' Indeed, observers in Moscow had managed to drive home to him what the British electorate apparently could not, that 'there is evidently a gap between what the workers are thinking and wanting, and what we believe they are thinking and wanting'. To bridge this gap and end the CP's 'present living from hand to mouth stage', Pollitt returned to London committed to the idea of a new long-term programme, based on British institutions and conditions. Only thus, he argued, would the CP secure acceptance as a 'serious political party' with a serious contribution to make to solving the country's problems. The drafting of the programme required months of discussion and possibly two further visits by Pollitt to the USSR. Eventually, the following February *The British Road to Socialism* came rolling off the printing presses in tens of thousands. It was the CP's first formal statement of long-term policy since *For Soviet Britain* way back in 1935.[25]

Despite the extravagant claims made for it, there was little about the *British Road* that was particularly new. It marked, in fact, a partial return to the conceptions of the 1945-47 period, though without abandoning the more sectarian language and postures of the intervening years. The programme's central claim, that the British people could advance to socialism through the transformation of their existing democratic institutions, had already been adumbrated by Pollitt in 1947.[26] Likewise its rejection of the inevitability of a third world war and espousal of peaceful co-existence merely expressed in the gloomier terms appropriate to the Cold War the CP's earlier hopes of international concord. The claim that, far from aiming 'by underhand subversive means' to undermine the British Empire the CP advocated a 'new, close voluntary and fraternal association' of its liberated peoples, had a similar pedigree. Back in 1947 there had been much talk of 'new fraternal associations, devoid of all taint of imperialism', by which the motherland and dominions would draw closer together to withstand American imperialism and assist in the economic development of the colonies.[27] Even the programme's title, which so succinctly conveyed the desired impression of something home-grown and practical, had already been used as the title of the key chapter in Pollitt's Looking Ahead in 1947.

One should be careful therefore not to exaggerate Stalin's legendary contribution to the British Road, first made public in a speech of Khrushchev's in 1963. Indeed, the possibility of using Parliament to achieve socialism, the point that Khrushchev specifically attributed to Stalin, had been advanced in the British Party press as far back as 1947, and under the very heading 'British road to socialism'.[28] Some of the programme's sharper formulations, such as the categorical denial of any intention to establish Soviet power in Britain, may well have been Stalin's; or at least Pollitt would not have inserted them without the necessary authority to do so. It was, moreover, clear from the day it was splashed all over Pravda that the programme bore the imprimatur of the Kremlin; and it was the blatancy of this derivation that was to prove its greatest weakness.

It would be unrealistic, of course, to think that even a much better programme could have revived the CP's flagging fortunes by this time. The more accurate its appraisal of British conditions, it might be argued, the less likely any such programme would have been to accord to the Communist Party a central role in changing them. Nevertheless, in bearing so clearly the marks of its foreign origins the British Road was singularly ill-fitted for its stated purpose. It might, as one Communist later remarked, more aptly have been entitled The Russian Road to Socialism, Done into English.[29] Its leaden formulas, so much more numbing than Pollitt's livelier personal style, did not so much distil the lessons of the British experience as plagiarise those of Eastern Europe. 'People's Democracy for Britain' was the refrain, at a time when the very words were enough to conjure up images of prison camps and show trials. Certainly there

169

was nothing in the *British Road* to disabuse people of these notions, no mention of press freedoms or guaranteed rights of organisation or contested elections. Even in the manner of its adoption there was something fraudulent about the whole affair. For several months a handful of Party leaders met in secret conclave, guided only by the advice they received from Moscow and never dreaming to consult their own British Party membership. Even so compulsive a political fixer as Dutt had later to admit that the issue 'might have reasonably been considered to merit a full prior discussion and special Congress'.[30] Insouciant of such niceties, the Party struck out boldly on the independent path ordained by Moscow with its fundamental problems untouched. *The British Road to Socialism* simply perpetuated them pending a more serious crisis.

It is not surprising, then, that the programme failed to galvanise the Party. Reported initial sales figures of 200,000 testified more to its energetic launching than to any spontaneous welcome for it by British workers, and the gently descending curve of Party membership figures continued uninterrupted. Even within the Party's ranks, as Pollitt himself admitted, the enthusiasm the programme generated was 'terrific but temporary'. If anything, indeed, its effect was the very opposite to that intended. While designed to bolster the Party's sense of historic mission, its acceptance of a parliamentary road to socialism, along with its growing congruence with the outlook of the Labour left, resigned many Communists to a much more modest role for their Party than Pollitt would countenance. At the 1956 Party congress he deplored this '"ginger group" conception of the Communist Party', but his own efforts to reconcile the CP's conflicting impulses lacked coherence. 'The Communist Party and the Left in the Labour Party are not opposing alternatives', he noted in 1955, before adding that 'an individual Left in the Labour Party can do the most effective work for his cause by joining the Communist Party' and moreover that 'the Left in the Labour Party will be strengthened, not weakened, by such action'. How much simpler life was in the 1930s when Communists joined both parties and kept mum. Raymond Williams no doubt oversimplified matters when he wrote that 'until 1957, the only major dividing line between the Labour Left and most Marxists was in attitudes to the Soviet Union'. The traditions of discipline and authority that were bound up with this allegiance so affected every facet of Communist Party life that it is impossible in reality to isolate this one factor. By the same token, however, when once that basic allegiance was called into question, then the entire edifice resting upon it would surely begin to crumble. That, for thousands of Communists, was what happened in 1956.[31]

The Khrushchev disclosures did not have quite this effect on Pollitt, but they did bring about in particularly painful circumstances his resignation as general secretary in May of that year. The precise reasons for his decision, against the express wishes of his colleagues, are not entirely clear; but the journalist Trevor Evans, in whom Pollitt often confided, would have had something to go on when he ascribed it to the Communist leader's 'highly developed sense of loyalty'. 'For Harry thought it despicable to kick the corpse of Stalin', Evans wrote on the day the news was announced. 'Harry found that he was too old to go into reverse and denigrate the man whom he had admired above all others for more than a quarter of a century.'[32]

Three months earlier Pollitt had, with Dutt and Matthews, formed the British contingent at the CPSU's Twentieth Congress where, within the very walls of his Kremlin fortress, the father of the peoples was knocked from his pedestal. Already Pollitt cannot but have been aware of the first tremors of de-Stalinisation, but this was no preparation for the shocks that were to follow. He left no personal memoir of the congress, but the atmosphere that he and other foreign delegates encountered is vividly conveyed in the diary of the Italian Communist, Vittorio Vidali: the bewilderment not to see Stalin's picture or hear his name but to learn obliquely of his 'mistakes'; the whisperings of shootings and rehabilitations, and the missing faces that accused their survivors; the feelings of repugnance as, with the unanimity which he had taught them, Stalin's creatures turned against their safely embalmed creator. No doubt Pollitt was among those who burst into applause when, in apparent defiance, first a spokesman for the Chinese Party and then Maurice Thorez invoked the memory of their departed leader.[33] Like the other foreign delegates, he was not present at the secret session on 25 February at which Khrushchev provided the damning details of Stalin's tyranny that would rock the Communist world. 'Where do you reckon I was when Comrade K. made that speech?' he said afterwards. 'I was being conducted round a French-letter factory. At

171

my age, I suppose that was a compliment.' Probably Pollitt, unlike some other leading foreign delegates, was not yet apprised of the contents of the speech. Even so, he must have returned to Britain knowing a good deal more than he was prepared to divulge. Sam Russell, the *Daily Worker*'s Moscow correspondent, learnt on the very day of the secret session that Khrushchev had 'dotted the Is and crossed the Ts' as to the cult of personality. He mentioned the fact over lunch with Pollitt and Nikolai Makovsky, who liaised with British Communists for the CPSU. Neither of them took up the subject and there was an uneasy transition to some more acceptable topic of conversation.[34]

It was with obvious reluctance that Pollitt brought himself even to acknowledge the issue. Neither the piece on the congress he cabled from Moscow nor his subsequent statement on behalf of the British delegation made the slightest reference to the cult of personality, which the luckless George Matthews was left to explain instead.[35] No doubt Pollitt needed time to get his bearings and to ascertain more fully the official Soviet position. Possibly also he allowed himself the forlorn hope that even so momentous an issue could be dealt with in time-honoured fashion, bureaucratically and from the top downwards. Typical of the leadership's response was Campbell's initial guillotine on the correspondence on Stalin in the *Daily Worker*, ostensibly because it was becoming 'repetitive'. When a few days later, on 18 March, the Party received from Russell in Moscow a summary of Khrushchev's revelations, it suppressed it and printed instead a sunshine bulletin, *That Krushchov Speech*.[36] With the leaking of its details elsewhere, however, Pollitt was compelled to address the issue head-on, first in the *Worker* and then at greater length in the CP weekly *World News*. In doing so he gave no sign that this was other than a necessary labour dutifully performed. There was no question of going beyond the standard rationalisations that were emerging to consider the profounder causes and implications of the Stalin cult, as for instance Togliatti did, in however circumscribed a fashion. The more searching questions that he could not entirely avoid, Pollitt parried with a complacency and lack of imagination that suddenly seemed quite as naive as cynical. As to the CP's uncritical solidarity with Stalin's Russia, for example, he was quite unrepentant, while he paid only lip-service to the idea of democratising the British Party. 'We have nothing to be ashamed about in the field of Party democracy', he wrote. 'Our right-wing Labour critics would do well to learn from our methods and to begin to put their own house in order.'[37] For Communists struggling to come to terms with their own unwitting acquiescence in a murderous despotism, the old stock responses and pitiful point-scoring must have been exasperating. Some, the first of many, apparently said as much at the Party congress at the end of March. 'He was', Evans wrote of Stalin's beleaguered disciple, 'denounced and sneered at by youngsters who were toddlers when Harry set out on his thankless mission to create the British Communist Party.' His pugnacious response – 'if you've got a headache you should take an aspirin' was one memorable comment attributed to him – can have done little to ease the situation.[38]

The initial assumption of Evans and others, that Pollitt had by these pressures been compelled to relinquish the Party leadership, was a mistaken one. On the contrary, it was Pollitt himself who, in his son's words, forced his resignation down his colleagues' throats. The stated pretext was the further blow to his health when on 25 April he suffered a haemorrhage behind the eyes, depriving him temporarily of the ability to read. However, there was never any question of the old fighter succumbing meekly to his afflictions. 'They tell me it will clear up in six months if I do nowt', he wrote to Olive Arnot in May, 'but it's not going to take that long if I can help it.' Moreover, the Political Committee impressed upon him its willingness to allow him the period of rest that the doctors prescribed and to ensure that he undertook only much reduced duties thereafter. What did concern them was to avoid an untimely exit that would inevitably be construed in political terms. Even Pollitt's wife added her voice to those urging him to stay on, addressing him a long letter to this effect as he mulled things over at his sister's in Derbyshire. Her views had no more effect than when many years earlier she felt he should have stuck to his guns over the war. 'I stood alone in 1939', said Pollitt as he read her letter, 'and I'll stand alone now.'[39]

Only weeks earlier he had dismissed the very possibility of his resigning. He would moreover, as his health recovered, bitterly regret his decision to do so. It would be wrong, however, to see in his temporary weariness of office simply the tiredness and stubbornness of an ailing man. It had not escaped Pollitt that he

173

must in due course make way for a successor and for several years he had been grooming Gollan, who some accordingly dubbed the 'Crown Prince', for that very role. Possibly, in the uncertain aftermath of the Twentieth Congress, Pollitt calculated that by determining the timing of his own departure he also controlled the succession. Having bequeathed his post to Gollan, he no doubt counted on wielding the same influence over his protégé as he had in the past. He was, after all, to remain on the Political Committee as its chairman.

Underlying any such tactical considerations, however, was the profounder matter of a clash of loyalties to which only that of 1939 can be compared. Pollitt's agonising decision on that occasion, that loyalty to world Communism had ultimately to override all other allegiances, had held good ever since. Now, however, from the Soviet leadership itself there seeped rumours and allegations that seemed to mock the discipline and the sacrifices of an entire generation of Communists. To those like Pollitt sworn to follow the Soviet lead, there suddenly fell the obligation to belittle the hallowed figure who had, through so many years of struggle and achievement, personified their cause. This, as Evans rightly averred, Pollitt could not bring himself to do, and hence the feebleness of his pronouncements on the Stalin question. That Khrushchev speech, in fact, he regarded as 'bloody awful', and if he was not about to break ranks and denounce its apostasies in public, neither was he willing to bear the main responsibility for expounding the views he so deplored. Probably only by resigning could he see a way out of his dilemma and at the same time allow himself a last tacit gesture of solidarity with his forsaken hero.[40]

During the subsequent exchanges within the CP, the Party leadership maintained that it had, through all its apologetics for tyranny, at least acted in good faith. The precise extent of its complicity in Stalin's crimes was not, however, a question that would go away so easily. Already, in 1957, raised by Hyman Levy in emotional terms that Pollitt found distressing, the subject has caused controversy ever since. Did the leaders 'know', is what the question has usually boiled down to, and if so how much did they know? The macabre deceptions and self-deceptions of the Stalin period cannot in reality be reduced to any such formula. There was, alas, no clear dividing line between knowledge and ignorance, indicting some as it absolved others. Consider, for example, the story told by George

174

Matthews of how Pollitt reacted to the exposure as a Titoite agent of a Polish Communist known to him in the 1930s. 'You know, it's extraordinary', he said, 'I met this chap and I stayed in the same room as he did and he showed me his back with the scars on it which had been inflicted on him in Piludski's jails. Here's a man who's undergone these tortures for the Communists and he turns out to be a traitor.' Who could weigh up, and in what proportions, the credulous faith, the wilful suspension of judgement and the Bolshevik cult of toughness that lay behind such a response? 'You knew and you didn't know', one Communist recalled of the period, and it was true for Pollitt as for others; but how far one and how far the other is a much more imponderable matter.[41]

This is not to say that in one or two well publicised cases Pollitt's culpability, at least in so far as known injustices drew from him no audible protest, is not firmly established. One such case was that of Rose Cohen, a figure well known in London left-wing circles with whom Pollitt had had a warm friendship and even proposed marriage in the 1920s. Through her ill-fated preference for the hand of the Comintern representative Petrovsky instead, Cohen was sucked into the maelstrom of socialist construction and subsequently disappeared in Stalin's purges. Apparently it was over this case that in 1937 Pollitt made such vigorous representations to the Comintern leadership as to raise the question of his replacement as Party leader.[42] The intense concern he felt for a woman he had loved, however, could not move him even to admit her plight in public; and it goes without saying that the same was true of less emotionally charged cases. When alerted by Harold Laski to the imprisonment without trial of Freda Utley's Russian husband, the Party leadership refused to make even private representations to the authorities. 'Least of all', Dutt wrote to Laski, 'have we in other countries who have made a complete mess of our own Labour movement... any right to pose as superior critics and censors of those who have shown in practice that they are able to judge correctly the necessary measures to defeat the capitalist enemy.' The later imprisonment of Edith Bone, who in 1949 had entered Hungary with *Daily Worker* credentials, was not even made known to the *Worker*'s staff until her release, after seven years of solitary confinement, in 1956. Worse still, there is even evidence of the British Party collaborating in its own small way in the purges. At the

175

Political Bureau in April 1937 Pollitt reported that an individual he described as 'Stiff' had been arrested in connection with wrecking activities and asked 'all the leading comrades who had ever come in contact with him... to make a written statement of what they knew about him'. Who knows what dossier of murderous fabrications might have been drawn from this particular source?[43]

To specify one or two cases is however to adopt much too narrow a focus. What has to be understood is that in his dealings with Moscow a Communist of Pollitt's standing breathed an atmosphere of dissimulation, recrimination and subterfuge in which truth and the very instinct for truth withered. With his insider's knowledge, his breadth of contact at its highest levels and his native perspicuity, it is inconceivable that Pollitt should not have seen beyond the grosser distortions of reality to which he added his own voice. Even had he gleaned nothing in his sixty or so visits to the socialist countries, he had for one of his closest political associates the CP's representative in Moscow at the height of Stalin's terror, Johnny Campbell. There, as the purges cast their shadow over the Comintern's Hotel Lux, Campbell inhabited the Kafkaesque world evoked for us in Ernst Fischer's memoirs: the 'dense and clinging webb of paranoia, treachery, fear, cruelty, vengefulness, greed and folly'. 'It occurred to me later', recalled Phil Piratin, who in the mid-1950s prised from Campbell an account of his experiences in Moscow, 'that I suppose he must have told Pollitt, you've got to tell someone, and no-one else.' There is in Pollitt's papers a mutilated letter from Campbell on his return from Moscow in 1939 which suggests that the two did indeed confide on this as on other matters. Even had we no such evidence, however, to suggest that Pollitt knew nothing of Stalin's misdeeds would be to anticipate a much sharper revulsion on learning of them than ever Pollitt demonstrated. 'He's staying there as long as I'm alive', he said of the portrait of Stalin that hung in his living room; and stay there he did, his countless victims notwithstanding. A remark Pollitt made after the Soviet intervention in Hungary tells the same story. 'It's up to you youngsters', George Matthews recalls him saying. 'As far as I'm concerned they can't do anything wrong.' It is true that, from the vantage point of his Moscow apartment or his Black Sea sanatorium, Pollitt can have had no real conception of the scale of the atrocities committed. The real question confronting us, however, is that

which in her cruel and pointless bereavement troubled Freda Utley.
'To this day', she wrote, 'I find it difficult to understand how this
British working-class leader of nonconformist traditions [sic] came to
subordinate his conscience and sacrifice his personal integrity to
become a tool of Russian tyranny.' That, surely, is a more important
matter than how much exactly Pollitt 'knew'.[44]

Pollitt's devotion to the Soviet order had origins rather different
from those of the generation of intellectuals whose motivations
historians have so exhaustively explored. Essentially it was simply an
inversion of the ferocious hatred of capitalism he had learnt from the
cradle, for whatever else the workers' state did in Pollitt's lifetime
it did not again subject the working class to its historic exploiters.
How much this meant to him, he spelt out in a notable passage on
the Russian Revolution:

> The thing that mattered to me was that lads like me had whacked the
> bosses and the landlords, had taken their factories, their lands and their
> banks.... These were the lads and lasses I must support through thick
> and thin.... for me these same people could never do, nor ever can do,
> any wrong against the working class. I wasn't concerned as to whether
> or not the Russian Revolution had caused bloodshed, been violent, and
> all the rest of it.

Indeed, far from offering shame-faced excuses for the draconian
measures the Bolsheviks adopted, Pollitt celebrated every sign that
capitalism was to be extirpated once and for all. The impatience he
felt with liberal criticisms of Soviet methods he evinced in a review
of Stephen Spender's *Forward with Liberalism* in 1937. If only Spender
had experienced liberal capitalism as the workers had, Pollitt wrote,
he too would have been 'sufficiently embittered to understand why,
when a people have finally conquered power as in the Soviet Union,
they will never again take any risks that can lead to a restoration of
capitalism, why they will break with "rotten liberalism" in their
politics, and when Trotskyite traitors are found, will deal with them
as they deserve'. There was no notion here that socialism might
discover its own forms of oppression, but only an elementary
affirmation of class solidarity. 'Let us consider what sort of people
are responsible for baffling the spies and wreckers – outwitting the
Scotland Yards of so many Governments', he wrote, somewhat
ingenuously. 'It is the miners, engineers, peasants, textile workers –
men and women like you who read this article.' This infatuation

177

with the land where the workers were 'top dogs' bred an attitude that was, quite unabashedly, uncritical in every detail. 'The fundamental historic facts', he wrote, 'give rise to the simple truth that whatever the policy of the Soviet Union it is always in the interests of its people and the working people of every other country in the world.'[45]

While Pollitt never wavered in this public stance, his acceptance of the Kremlin's moral authority did have one significant qualification. In his memoir of working with Thorez and Togliatti, Giulio Ceretti insisted in this context that there existed in their minds an impenetrable barrier between the Communist International on the one hand and the Soviet Party and state on the other.[46] This was certainly putting it too strongly, but the distinction nevertheless had some force for Pollitt. His was not the historian's perception of the Comintern simply as an extension of the Soviet state, transmitting Moscow's directives to its pliant national sections. Having known the International in its earliest, more argumentative days, he never quite lost the habit of forming his own opinions, especially on questions directly affecting the British Party. If anything, in fact, his growing confidence as a revolutionary leader had brought with it a more robust independence of judgement. While during the CP's infancy he accepted the need for Moscow's guidance and material support, with its increasing maturity one of his chief concerns as Party leader was to secure for it a greater measure of independence and political responsibility. Hence perhaps his private boast in 1936 that the Party was 'a thorn in the side of the Comintern', as demonstrated by his conduct at its Seventh World Congress the previous year.[47] The occasion was the first fully to involve foreign Communists in the arcane rituals of the Stalin cult and there was therefore no mistaking Pollitt's meaning when his proposed address contained not a word as to the great leader's sagacity and omniscience. Hauled before the Comintern leadership to explain himself, he apparently challenged 'the method of deification and assumption of infallibility as contrary to the traditions and interests of the international communist movement'.[48] His concern more particularly for the interests of the British Party was shown when the CP's national organiser Dave Springhall was convicted of spying in 1942. So furious was Pollitt that he spent that night walking the streets and cursing the Russians in his sleepless rage. What, after all, did they care for his efforts to establish Communism in Britain if they could behave in so scandalous and irresponsible a fashion?[49] As his disillusionment with Soviet, actions in 1939 made so very clear, Pollitt retained until at least the time of the Comintern's dissolution in 1943 this vestigial sense that the Russians had obligations to the international movement as well as vice versa.

By the onset of the Cold War this lingering spirit of independence seems largely to have departed him. Paradoxically, the dissolution of the Comintern, correctly seen as an instrument of Soviet policy, removed the last of the formal mechanisms by which that policy could be queried, if nothing else. Henceforth there was nothing to camouflage or mitigate the CP's subordination to the Soviet authorities. More importantly, the wartime sacrifices by which the Soviet people justified the anxious hopes vested in them produced in Pollitt a still more fervent identification with their cause; and then the post-war achievements of socialism in power reinforced in Western Communists the sort of inferiority complex exemplified by Dutt's cringing remarks to Laski. Nor was the satisfaction which Pollitt drew from Soviet achievements entirely vicarious. His son recalls vividly a schizophrenic childhood spent mostly in North London, where schoolmates taunted the lad with the Bolshie father, but including trips abroad to be feted as the son of the British people's finest leader. 'In London, Pollitt was a man you were most likely to meet on a Number 11 bus or having a quiet pint in a tucked-away pub', Alan Winnington recalled. 'In China he had a special train and in between we stayed at the guest houses used by General Marshall.' The attentions and ovations he received cannot but have worked their subtle corruptions on Pollitt, for he had not by this time, if ever he had, the spirit of self-effacement and self-abnegation that could scorn such things. The material comforts were not unwelcome, perhaps, but it was the importance accorded the leader of a Communist Party in those countries on which his self-esteem came fatally to depend. As he wrote home in 1948, 'President Gottwald invited me to his palace to dine, Prime Minister Dimitrov invited me to his Palace to dine, so somebody thinks the Old Man is not so dusty.'[50]

Whatever the underlying explanation, no further displays of independence are known to us from the post-war period, even on questions acutely affecting the British Party and the whole

179

international movement. Pollitt's prompt condemnation of Tito, not even pretending to know the reasons why but insisting instead on the vast experience and proven infallibility of the Soviet comrades, was but the most blatantly Pavlovian of his reactions. Harry McShane recalled of this episode that 'it was the first time I had ever seen him completely at a loss; he couldn't reply to criticisms, and it was obvious that he knew no more than the rest of us'. Pollitt's vacuous and evasive printed statements fully bear this out. 'He just used all his authority', McShane went on, 'and his usual phrase when someone questioned party policy: "Comrade, you are attacking Comrade Stalin."'[51]

The Stalinist caricature to which Pollitt increasingly conformed was made by the events of 1956 to appear thoroughly anachronistic.[52] The debates set in motion by Khrushchev's revelations intensified when, in November, the same Khrushchev sent in Soviet tanks to quell the insurgent Hungarian masses. To its historic transgressions the CP leadership now added the recidivist folly of instantaneously backing this action; and by the time of the Party's special congress in April 1957 a fifth of its members had left in disgust, with more to follow. Pollitt himself, though Party chairman, made little direct contribution to that year's extraordinary discussions. Nevertheless, it was against the political culture that he above all personified that a younger generation formed in very different political circumstances now rebelled. Taking the issue far wider than the Party's identification with a flawed utopia, the livelier critics pondered the very meaning of Communism in a Britain as far as ever from revolution. Was a British Communist Party actually necessary, they asked, and if so what was its purpose and what the form of organisation appropriate to that purpose? What, indeed, was the socialism for which the Party claimed to stand, and how did it relate to the fundamental questions of justice, democracy and political morality to which it no longer seemed to provide a conclusive answer?[53]

For all that Pollitt understood of them, the questions might as well have been in Chinese; and it was, indeed, a frequent complaint of the Party rebels that, behind its ponderous bureaucratic defences, the leadership had 'not the faintest notion what we were talking about'.[54] For those even amongst his critics who remembered Pollitt in his prime, he remained a figure who commanded respect. 'To me

Harry is linked with Spain, anti-appeasement and the Hunger Marches', wrote John Saville to Edward Thompson, explaining his deletion of an attack on Pollitt from their samizdat journal *The Reasoner*. 'He's washed up now, but the affection for Harry is tremendous among my generation.' For younger Communists, however, these images of the past had little meaning. By some, Pollitt's own brand of revolutionary nostalgia was even treated with frank irreverence. In a *Daily Worker* series that August, the paper's youngest journalist, Llew Gardner, expressed his weariness in this 'age of television' of hearing of the movement's 'pioneers' at their 'street corners and market places'. 'By all means let us recharge our fighting spirit', he wrote. 'But let us understand that what was good enough for our grandfathers is not necessarily good enough for us.' At that, as at so much else in the Party press that year, one can only imagine Pollitt's ageing, spluttering indignation.[55]

The four years that remained to him might have been happier had he entered upon his retirement more willingly. Far from regarding himself as 'washed up', however, on overcoming his immediate health problems in 1956 Pollitt placed before his colleagues the impossible request that he be given his post back. For this last and cruellest self-deception, there were several possible reasons. One was his disappointment in Gollan, an aloof and colourless figure with a very different style of leadership from Pollitt's. He had, as the latter remarked, rather rueing his patronage, 'none of the humanities', and to the pliant efficiency becoming in an assistant he now added a quiet determination to lead the Party in his own right. No doubt Pollitt also felt dismay to see his disciplined Bolshevik party racked by such severe internal dissensions. However heavy-handed one might think the leadership's conduct that year, it certainly allowed its critics a latitude quite unknown in Pollitt's day and his 'party of great friends' seemed all of a sudden as much at war with itself as when he took over the leadership in 1929. Possibly also, by his conversations with Soviet leaders that summer Pollitt was reassured as to the very strict limits to Khrushchev's de-Stalinisation. Most of all, perhaps, after twenty-seven years almost uninterrupted as general secretary, he could not adjust easily to playing a supporting role. Can one wonder that as he viewed his Party's disarray, he felt in himself the urge to provide it once more with the special qualities of leadership that were his?

181

Presumably it was after his return from the USSR in August that he put forward his proposal. Only he, perhaps, could not see that it was politically unthinkable. According to one account, it was his old pal Johnny Campbell who made the first and decisive contribution at the Political Committee which rejected it. According to another, Pollitt was excluded from the proceedings at which his fate was decided. Possibly it was on this occasion that he rang downstairs for his friend Gladys Easton to come and cheer him up with her stories of South London slum life. She arrived to find him sitting dejected and alone, partitioned off from his Political Committee colleagues. 'You should be with the others, you're the Party chairman', she told him. 'Nonsense', he replied, 'I'm not the secretary any more, they don't need me any more.' He had done more than any of them to establish a Communist Party in Britain, and it is understandable that this proud and patriarchal figure should have been soured by the experience.[56]

It was indeed a bitter postscript to his career that followed. So closely were personal and political loyalties interwoven in his mind, and so fervently did he identify both with the unity of the Communist Party, that he could not help but experience the dissensions and defections of 1956 in terms of personal betrayal. Hence, for example, the angry and emotional scene in which, very much the worse for drink, he turned on the scientist J. D. Bernal on the weekend that Soviet troops intervened in Hungary. It was likewise with a feeling almost of personal rejection that he retired to the sidelines of Communist politics, there to complain to one comrade who remembered him that Christmas that 'so many people are forgetting that I ever existed'. Matters were exacerbated by the further, relentless deterioration of his health. At best this compulsive agitator was restricted to a couple of meetings a month. For prolonged periods, due to his spinal trouble and then a mild stroke, even this was impossible, and eventually his wife had to abandon going out to meetings herself because it so upset him. Just as his father before him had suffered in old age to have to live off his children, so now Pollitt himself had, again according to his wife, 'an absolute obsession about becoming "useless to the Party", a burden to the family, and financially dependent on the Party'.

For something to occupy him, his thoughts now turned to a book on trade union questions, almost as if to relive his first purposeful, exciting years with the CP and the Minority Movement. Only the synopsis, however, was completed. What fine moments remained to him were spent far from home, to be honoured in Moscow and Peking as one of world Communism's elder statesmen. The fortieth anniversary celebrations in Moscow he must have found particularly moving, as the nameless veterans of the Great Patriotic War marched before him, banners unfurled. 'Looking round, I saw that almost all of us had tears in our eyes', noted one Communist who stood with Pollitt above the enormous crowd. 'Forty years! What a long way mankind has come!' How much duller and more oppressive must his eventless life in a London suburb have been for Pollitt as he returned from such scenes. An increasingly strict and irascible old man, haunted by the fear of cancer, according to his wife Pollitt 'almost lost the will to live'.[57]

His last trip, to Australia and New Zealand in 1960, provided the happiest moments of his last years. Defying doctors' orders and basking in the attentions that he received, he addressed many more meetings than he should have and did not often refuse the lavish hospitality that was laid on for him. 'It was not that the Party worked him too hard, it was impossible to restrain him', recalled the Australian Communist who accompanied him on the tour. 'I gained the impression that he felt he had not much time left and wanted to put all he had into every minute.' Pollitt's wife confirmed that the tour did much to revive his spirits. His letters home, she recalled, 'breathed happiness and fulfilment in a good job well done, with full recognition for it and good comradeship'. Unknown to the audiences who so buoyed him up and restored to him some of his old fire and eloquence, the constant round of activity was more than his health could stand. Reluctant to rest and refusing hospital treatment for his worsening eyesight, he saw his tour through, and on 20 June set off on the long voyage back to England. Six days later he suffered the further stroke of which doctors had warned him, and at 2 a.m. the following morning, 27 June, Pollitt died from cerebral thrombosis.

The funeral, at Golders Green cemetery the following month, was the dignified revolutionary ceremony he would have wished. From ruling parties as well as those persecuted, but mainly just from ordinary comrades who had caught from Pollitt something of the 'gleam' or simply remembered a personal kindness, the tributes

183

poured in from far and wide. 'The Great Harry mainly influenced me to join the Party in 1924', wrote one of his own, a worker from Openshaw, '& I feel that I have lost my greatest Pal.'[58]

Notes

Abbreviations used in notes

CP	Communist Party archive
CR	*Communist Review*
DW	*Daily Worker*
HP	Harry Pollitt papers, CP archive
JK	James Klugmann's notes in CP archive
JS	John Strachey papers
LM	*Labour Monthly*
Mahon	J. Mahon, *Harry Pollitt*
M-O	Mass-Observation Archive, University of Sussex
MRC	Modern Records Centre, University of Warwick
RPA	R. Page Arnot papers, Hull University
RPD BL	Dutt papers, British Library
RPD CP	Dutt papers, CP archive
RPD WCML	Dutt papers, Working Class Movement Library
SMT	H. Pollitt, *Serving My Time*
TM	Tom Mann papers, Coventry Central Library
VG	Victor Gollancz papers, Modern Records Centre
WL	*Workers' Life*
WN(V)	*World News (and Views)*

For simplicity, I have described as minutes the stenograms and other records of the CP's leading bodies of which microfilms are now available in the CP archive.

Chapter 1

1 K. Marx and F. Engels, *On Britain* (Progress Publishers, Moscow, 1962 edn), pp. 74-5; A. Clarke, *The Effects of the Factory System* (George Kelsall, Littleborough, 1985 edn), p. 29.
2 The house, no. 14 Wharf Street, no longer stands.
3 Mahon, ch. 1; *SMT*, ch. 1.
4 Jessie Kennerley to John Mahon, Sept. 1969 (HP).
5 *SMT*, preface and ch. 1; letters on his mother's death in HP.
6 *DW*, 17.3.37. It is a pity that in his fine biography of Orwell (Penguin edn, 1982, p. 343) Bernard Crick so quotes from this review (e.g. the words 'a late

imperialist policeman' entirely removed from their sentence) as to reduce it to mere senseless abuse. Pollitt's accusations of ignorance, snobbery and an obsession with working-class smells were at least tenable, his tone was certainly no more offensive than Orwell's own, he admitted parts of Orwell's book were 'superb' and his criticisms of the parts he disliked had some substance to them. Orwell stands up well enough in his polemics with the Communists without the latter having always to be reduced to caricatures.

7 *SMT*, preface and ch. l; Mahon, ch. 1.

8 *SMT*, ch. l; Mahon, ch. l; Kennerley to Mahon, Sept. 1969; Margot Heinemann, interview; stenogram of CP PB discussion on the *Daily Worker*, 19.6.30 (WCML).

9 5*s* rising to 15*s*. For Pollitt's apprenticeship see *SMT*, pp. 30-2; Mahon, ch. 2.

10 R. Acland (ed.), *Why I am a Democrat* (Lawrence and Wishart, 1939), pp. 136-9.

11 *WN*, 1.10.55, pp. 767-8; *SMT*, p. 290.

12 This was the best result by far, compared to 148 votes in 1911 and 183 in 1913. The average Labour vote was around 1,500. See *SMT*, pp. 45-6, 52-3; Mahon, pp. 29, 32, 36, 42-3, which includes a reproduction of Pollitt's leaflet.

13 *SMT*, chs 2-3.

14 *SMT*, ch. 3; George Peet to *DW*, 14.7.60 (HP).

15 S. Macintyre, *A Proletarian Science* (Cambridge University Press, 1980).

16 R. C. K. Ensor, *England 1870-1914* (Oxford University Press, 1952 edn), pp. 334-5.

17 Pollitt, 'The Iron Heel', *Challenge*, 20.10.55.

18 *SMT*, p. 130; Pollitt's introduction to D. Torr, *Tom Mann* (Lawrence and Wishart, 1944 edn); Edmund Frow, interview and L. Cole to M. Pollitt, 28.6.60 (HP).

19 The passage is cited in C. Tsusuki's fine biography *Tom Mann* (Oxford University Press, 1991), p. 142.

20 Pollitt's introduction to Torr, *op. cit.*; Pollitt to Mann, 6.2.40 (TM); Pollitt to I. Mackay, 21.1.51 (MRC 74/6/2/86); Dutt to Pollitt, 4.1.35 and Pollitt to Dutt, 9.1.35 (RPD WCML); Pollitt, typescript memoir of Mann (CP). Mann joined the Central Committee in 1937.

21 *SMT*, ch. 5; William Brain to M. Pollitt, 28.6.60 (HP).

22 *SMT*, ch. 5; *Workers' Dreadnought*, 24.4.20; G. Askwith, *Industrial Problems and Disputes* (John Murray, 1920), pp. 396-7.

23 *SMT*, ch. 6, pp. 281-2; Mahon, ch. 7; J. Bush, *Behind the Lines. East London Labour 1914-1919* (Merlin, 1984), pp. 142-3, 197-9; *The Masses* no. 1, Feb. 1919 (HP). For Watson and the LWC see B. Pribicevic, *The Shop Stewards' Movement and Workers' Control 1910-1922* (Blackwell, 1959), chs 4-5.

24 *SMT*, ch. 6; 'Hands Off Russia' conference report, 18.1.19 (HP); W. P. and Z. Coates, *A History of Anglo-Soviet Relations* (Lawrence and Wishart/Pilot Press, 1943), pp. 135-52; J. Klugmann, *History of the Communist Party of Great Britain. Volume One. Foundation and Early Years 1919-1924* (Lawrence and Wishart, 1968), pp. 78-9; W. Kendall, *The Revolutionary Movement in Britain 1900-21* (Weidenfeld and Nicolson, 1969), p. 412.

25 *SMT*, ch. 6; Kendall, *op. cit.*, pp. 251-2; W. F. Watson, *Watson's Reply* (the author, 1920).

26 *SMT*, chs 6-7; Pollitt, *Looking Ahead* (CPGB, 1947), p. 42; Coates, *loc. cit.*; L. J. Macfarlane, 'Hands Off Russia. British Labour and the Russo-Polish War, 1920', *Past and Present* no. 38 (1967).

27 Lenin, speeches of October 1920 in *Lenin on Britain* (Martin Lawrence, 1934), pp. 202-5.

28 J. T. Walton Newbold, typescript memoirs (John Rylands University Library, Manchester).

29 *SMT*, pp. 122-6; J. E. Mortimer, *History of the Boilermakers' Society. Volume 2. 1906-1939* (George Allen and Unwin, 1982), pp. 120-2; *Workers' Dreadnought*, 13.9.19.

Chapter 2

1 John Strachey cited in M. Newman, *John Strachey* (Manchester University Press, 1989), p. 134.

2 *SMT*, pp. 122-4; *Communist*, 30.9.20, 28.10.20.

3 *SMT*, pp. 126-30 and material in HP; R. Martin, *Communism and the British Trade Unions 1924-1933* (Oxford University Press, 1969), pp. 5-12, 20-2; L. J. Macfarlane, *The British Communist Party. Its origin and development until 1929* (MacGibbon and Kee, 1966), p. 112.

4 CPGB EC *Report* to 4th Congress, 1922, p. 3; *SMT*, pp. 133-40; E. H. Carr, *The Bolshevik Revolution 1917-1923* vol. 3 (Penguin edn, 1966), p. 128; *Communist International* no. 19 (1921), p. 389.

5 *Report* to 4th Congress, p. 3; *SMT*, pp. 146-9; Macfarlane, *op. cit.*, pp. 75-7; Gallacher, submission to CP history commission, 23.10.57 (CP); Dutt, 'Memorandum on "The Communist"', Jan. 1922 (RPD BL).

6 *SMT* draft (HP); Dutt to Shaw, 8.2.49 (RPD BL).

7 Dutt, 'Theodore Rothstein as a champion of Marxist anti-imperialism' (1958) and 'On some experiences of the Communist International and the period of Stalin's leading role' (*c.* 1970) (CP); W. Gallacher, *Last Memoirs* (Lawrence and Wishart, 1966), p. 169; Dutt to Gallacher, 16.12.51 (RPD CP).

8 *Report on Organisation* presented to CP 5th Congress, Oct. 1922.

9 *Ibid.*, p. 5; Macfarlane, *op. cit.*, pp. 82-3; Dutt, 'On some experiences...'; T. Bell, *The British Communist Party* (Lawrence and Wishart, 1937), p. 84; *SMT*, p. 156; J. T. Murphy, *New Horizons* (Bodley Head, 1941), pp. 190-7.

10 Dutt, 'On some experiences...'

11 M. Woodhouse and B. Pearce, *Essays on the History of Communism in Britain* (New Park, 1975), pp. 77-8; CPGB extended Scottish Central Committee minutes, 15.8.22 (CP); Murphy, *op. cit.*, pp. 183, 186; Newbold, typescript memoirs; Dutt, *Times Literary Supplement*, 5.5.66, p. 387.

12 Losovsky cited in Martin, *op. cit.*, p. 28; Bell, *loc. cit.*

13 Pollitt to Salme Dutt, 1.7.23. All correspondence with Salme is with the Dutt material in the WCML.

14 The circulation was immediately increased to 35,000, rising to 65,000 by May

1924; see Dutt, *DW*, 1.3.48 and article for *Pravda*, June 1923 (RPD BL); *Report on Organisation*, pp. 29ff.; *SMT*, pp. 164-5.

15 Biographical information from Dutt's uncompleted memoirs (RPD CP) and R. P. Arnot's introduction to S. Dutt, *Lucifer and other poems* (Mitre Press, 1966).

16 R. P. Dutt to S. Dutt, 24.1.24; *SMT*, pp. 136-9.

17 R. P. Dutt to S. Dutt, 19.1.24, 2.2.24. The 'M' is for Mary, the 'P' presumably for Paris.

18 Pollitt to S. Dutt, 17.9.23 and Wintringham to S. Dutt, n.d. but June 1923.

19 Murphy, *op. cit.*, p. 196; R. P. Dutt to S. Dutt, 2.2.24; Pollitt to S. Dutt, 17.9.23.

20 Dutt, 'On some experiences...'; Dutt to Pollitt, 24.6.23, 8.7.23 (RPD WCML); Dutt to S. Dutt, 14.2.24; see also A. Kuusinen, *Before and After Stalin* (Michael Joseph, 1974), pp. 19-20, 144.

21 P. Spratt, *Blowing Up India* (Prachi Prakashan, Calcutta, 1955), p. 24. The only other published clue to her activities is in Arnot's introduction to Salme's posthumous collection *Lucifer and other poems*, Arnot having been closely attached to the nucleus. In Murphy's autobiography, published several years after his expulsion from the CP, and in Gallacher's frank unpublished memoir of these events, Salme is not even mentioned.

22 See e.g. Dutt to Pollitt, 23.12.30, 11.1.31, 26.2.31, 14.4.31 (HP); Dutt to J. Strachey, 5.4.33 (JS); Celia Strachey, draft memoirs (JS).

23 Pollitt to S. Dutt, 23.9.23.

24 As cited and endorsed by his wife Aino Kuusinen, *op. cit.*, pp. 34-44.

25 'The situation of the English working class movement', 2 drafts, May-June 1923; 'Propositions on the English question', June 1923 (RPD BL).

26 Wintringham to S. Dutt, n.d. but 30.6.23; Pollitt to S. Dutt, 1.7.23, 1.8.23.

27 Dutt to Pollitt, 8.7.23 (RPD WCML); *Communist Papers* (Cmd 2682, HMSO, 1926).

28 Gallacher, typescript submission to CP history commission, 23.10.57; *Workers' Weekly*, 16.6.23. The offending episode, the first in a second series, had no sequel. C. McKay, *A Long Way from Home* (Pluto, 1985 edn), pp. 197ff., tells of MacManus's drinking habits.

29 This according to Dutt, 'On some experiences...' Dutt attributed this behaviour to Gallacher's disagreement with the commission agenda, but Gallacher's own recollections suggest a different explanation.

30 Gallacher, typescript submission; Pollitt to S. Dutt, 25.7.23, 28.7.23.

31 *Times Literary Supplement*, 19.5.66.

32 The changes are summarised in Macfarlane, *op. cit.*, pp. 83-4.

33 Dutt, 'Statement on the proposal to form a trade union educational league in England', June 1923 (RPD BL); Bell, *op. cit.*, p. 85.

34 Dutt to Pollitt, 8.7.23, 21.7.23 (RPD WCML); Pollitt to S. Dutt, 1.8.23.

35 Pollitt to S. Dutt, 17.9.23.

36 Dutt to S. Dutt, 3.1.24; *SMT*, pp. 124-5; Murphy, *op. cit.*, pp. 196-7.

37 Pollitt to S. Dutt, 17.9.23.

38 Pollitt to S. Dutt, 16.7.23, 25.7.23, 28.7.23, n.d.

39 Pollitt to S. Dutt, 12.10.23; Pollitt to Wintringham, 30.8.23, cited by David

Fernbach in his unpublished biography of Wintringham.

40 Dutt to S. Dutt, n.d. and 30.12.23.

41 See his letters to Salme, 24.1.24, 28.1.24, 31.1.24.

42 'Memorandum on the situation and the immediate tasks of the British Communist Party', 26.3.24 (RPD WCML). Dutt's reply to the criticisms is in RPD BL.

43 Dutt to S. Dutt, 30.12.23, 3.1.24, 10.1.24.

44 Articles in CR, Jan.-April 1924.

45 Dutt to S. Dutt, 10.1.24.

46 Dutt to S. Dutt, n.d. but Feb. 1924, 28.3.24; CP EC Report to CPGB 6th Congress (1924); W. Gallacher, The Rolling of the Thunder (Lawrence and Wishart, 1947), pp. 46-8.

47 Dutt to S. Dutt, 31.3.24.

48 EC Report to 6th Congress; Pollitt and Dutt, 'Recommendation on election of the Central Committee', 17.5.24 (CP); Dutt to S. Dutt, 31.3.24.

49 Pollitt to E. Higgins, cited in J. N. Rawling's typescript history of the Australian CP, made available by Stuart Macintyre.

50 SMT draft (HP).

51 Martin, op. cit., provides a splendid account of the movement.

52 SMT, p. 144; Inprecorr, 15.10.25, pp. 1099-1100.

53 W. Citrine, Men and Work (Hutchinson, 1964), pp. 256-7; E. Wertheimer, Portrait of the Labour Party (Putnam's, 1929).

54 Pollitt to S. Dutt, 20.7.23.

55 Quotations from Pollitt's LM articles of Nov. 1923, Sept. 1924 and Oct. 1925 and from A. Hutt, British Trade Unionism (Lawrence and Wishart, 1941), p. 99.

56 LM, Oct. 1922, pp. 195-204, Jan. 1924, pp. 3-4.

57 Communist, 23.9.22; 'The Trades Union Congress', LM, Sept. 1924, pp. 525-34; TUC annual Report (1924), p. 287; Inprecorr, 16.10.24, pp. 807-8.

58 Pollitt to S. Chaplin, 1.8.25 (HP).

59 N. and J. Mackenzie (eds), The Diary of Beatrice Webb vol. 4 (Virago, 1985), pp. 77-8.

60 SMT, ch. 14; C. L. Mowat, Britain Between the Wars 1918-1940 (Methuen, 1968 edn), p. 297.

61 Mahon, pp. 133-4; 'The conference of executives', LM, Feb. 1927, p. 103; 'The Trade Unions Bill: a plan of action', LM, June 1927, pp. 354-5.

62 Mahon, pp. 147-50.

63 Dutt to Pollitt, 8.7.23, 21.7.23 (RPD WCML); his letters to Salme and an autobiographical note dated Aug. 1935 in RPD BL give some account of his Labour movement activities.

64 'A.S.' to Newsletter editor, 7.1.64 (CP); Salme's letters to Dutt and Dutt's to Pollitt in CP and WCML give some indication of their movements and ailments.

65 S. Dutt to Dutt, 2.10.29 (RPD CP); Dutt to Pollitt, 14.4.31 (HP).

66 Dutt to Pollitt, 11.9.29 (HP).

67 PRO FO 372/2476 for Clemens Dutt; Kuusinen, op. cit., pp. 143-4.

The 'Mary Peters' referred to is clearly Mary Moorhouse, confused perhaps with the May Peters who was in Moscow at that time.

68 CP CC minutes, 26-27.10.29 (JK); N. Branson, *History of the Communist Party of Great Britain 1927-1941* (Lawrence and Wishart, 1985), pp. 35-6.

69 Pollitt to the Dutts, 14.10.25 (RPD CP); Dutt to Pollitt, 13.8.26 (RPD BL) and 26.3.28 (HP).

70 Dutt, 'Some experiences...'; *DW*, 13.9.49.

Chapter 3

1 See e.g. T. Draper, *American Communism and Soviet Russia* (Vintage Books edn, 1986), ch. 17, and for personal accounts B. Gitlow, *I Confessed* (Dutton, 1940), pp. 516ff. and Pollitt, *DW*, 27.3.34.

2 Pelling, *The British Communist Party* (2nd edn, Black, 1975), p. 52.

3 Dutt to Pollitt, 11.11.29 (HP); see pp. 71-2 below.

4 Branson, *op. cit.*, ch. 2; CP CC minutes 7-9.1.28 (JK); Dutt to Pollitt, 6.1.28 (HP).

5 This and the majority thesis are in *Communist*, Mar. 1928; Pollitt's original statement, 24.1.28 is in JK.

6 Branson, *op. cit.*, chs 2-3; Dutt to Pollitt, 6.1.28, 27.2.28 (HP).

7 *WL*, 25.1.29, 1.2.29.

8 *SMT*, pp. 267-79 and unpublished drafts (HP).

9 *SMT*, pp. 284-5.

10 See Martin, *op. cit.*, ch. 6.

11 'The Edinburgh Congress', *LM*, Oct. 1927, p. 592.

12 *WL*, 11.1.29.

13 Branson, *op. cit.*, pp. 41-2; Mahon, p. 174; CP CC minutes 7-11.8.29 (JK); M. Ferguson, *WL*, 9.8.29.

14 Pollitt, 'The Party of the working class', typescript lecture, 10.2.37 (HP). There is a run of the *Boilermaker* in the WCML.

15 *WL*, 5.4.29, 12.4.29 and succeeding issues; M. Ferguson, 'Lessons of the Dawdon struggle', *CR*, Aug. 1929, pp. 454-5; CP Tyneside DC statement, *CR*, Oct. 1929, pp. 569-71.

16 'Letter from the CI to the Party Congress', *CR*, Feb. 1930.

17 Martin, *op. cit.*, pp. 117-18.

18 'Lessons of the Tenth Plenum', *CR*, Oct. 1929.

19 *WL*, 6.12.29; *DW*, 13.9.49; see also Wintringham to Dutt, 15.10.29, 8.11.29 (RPD WCML).

20 *Inprecorr*, 25.9.29, pp. 1139-41.

21 *Inprecorr*, 21.8.29, pp. 885-6.

22 CP CC minutes 7-11.8.29, 26-7.10.29 (JK); Idris Cox, typescript memoirs (CP).

23 Cant to CP CC, Jan. 1930; Inkpin to CP CC, 7.1.30 (RPD WCML); CP PB minutes 9.1.30, 23.1.30, 17.2.30, 26.2.30; CP CC minutes, 11-12.1.30; Pollitt, contribution to CP PB, 10.10.32 (RPD WCML).

24 CP CC minutes, 26-27.10.29 (JK); Dutt to Pollitt, 11.9.29, 7.11.29 (HP).

25 Dutt to Pollitt, 26.3.28 (HP).
26 See contributions of H. Burke and L. Jones, *WL*, 15.11.29.
27 CP CC minutes, 26-27.10.29 (JK).
28 Dutt to Pollitt, 1.8.30 (HP).
29 Dutt to Pollitt, 1.8.30; CP CC minutes 13.9.30 for British commission; Pollitt, *DW*, 1-5.9.30; Martin, *op. cit.*, pp. 157ff. for Workers' Charter.
30 CP CC minutes, 9.11.32.
31 See e.g. G. Allison, CP CC minutes, 13.9.30; R. P. Arnot, 'Position of the Party. October 1930', 5.11.30 (RPD WCML).
32 Dutt to Pollitt, 7.7.31, 14.7.31 (RPD BL), 13.7.31 (HP).
33 Pollitt at RILU Central Council, Nov. 1931, *RILU Magazine*, 1.2.32, pp. 68-70; CP CC minutes, 16.1.32; 'Building a Bolshevik Party in Britain', speech to CP CC plenum, Jan. 1932, *CR*, Mar. 1932, pp. 128-9.
34 E.g. 'Towards the National Charter Convention', *CR*, Mar. 1931.
35 *DW*, 20.8.32; CP CC minutes, 16-17.1.32, 14-15.3.32.
36 *RILU Magazine*, 1.2.32, pp. 68-70, 15.2.32, pp. 250-1.
37 'Building a Bolshevik Party in Britain', p. 127; see W. Allan, 'The Party and the Minority Movement', *CR*, Oct. 1932.
38 Dutt to Pollitt, 4.2.32 (HP); M. Ferguson, 'Have we liquidated the Minority Movement?', *CR*, Oct. 1932, pp. 480-2.
39 Dutt to Gallacher, 24.10.32 (RPD BL).
40 Pollitt, *DW*, 20.8.32, 26.9.32, 'The Newcastle Trades Union Congress', *LM*, Sept. 1932; Dutt, *DW*, 14.9.32, 19.9.32.
41 Dutt to Pollitt, 26.9.32, Rust to Pollitt, 11.9.32, 13.9.32 (HP); Dutt to Gallacher, 24.10.32 (RPD BL); Pollitt, contribution at CP PB, 10.10.32 (RPD WCML).
42 Dutt to Pollitt, 13.10.32 (HP); *DW*, 7.11.32.
43 Dutt to Rust, 8.2.33; Dutt to CP PB, 9.2.33; Dutt to CP CC, 14.2.33 (RPD BL).
44 CP CC minutes, 10.9.33.
45 Seaham election material in HP; CP CC minutes, 16-17.1.32; T. Wintringham, *DW*, 30.8.32.
46 Dutt to Pollitt, 14.4.32 (RPD BL) ; *Which Way for the Workers? Harry Pollitt versus Fenner Brockway* (CPGB, 1932).
47 CP CC minutes, 16.6.33.
48 CP CC minutes, 24.3.33.
49 Dutt to Pollitt, 8.2.35 (RPD WCML) . In the same collection is a letter to Pollitt dated 8.3.32 and containing proposals for anti-war campaigns which may well be a first communication from Fried.
50 CP CC minutes, 5.1.34, 6.4.34.
51 Ted Bramley, interview; Dutt to Pollitt, 20.7.34 (RPD BL); information from Nina Fishman and Brian Pollitt.
52 Pollitt, speech to ECCI Presidium, 11.10.34, in *Communist International*, 5.12.34, p. 915; Bramley, interview; Pollitt to Dutt, 7.2.35 (RPD WCML).
53 Dutt to Pollitt, 5.1.35, 14.1.35; Pollitt to Dutt, 9.1.35, 18.1.35 (RPD WCML).

54 CP CC minutes, 24.3.33.
55 Pollitt to Dutt, 3.4.35, 21.5.35; Dutt to CP Secretariat, 12.4.35 (RPD WCML). Campbell's speech was printed in the *Communist International*.
56 Dutt to Pollitt, 5.1.35, Pollitt to Dutt, 5.8.35 (RPD WCML). See E. H. Carr, *The Twilight of Comintern* (Macmillan, 1982), ch. 18 for one account of the congress.

Chapter 4

1 From 7,700 in July 1935 to about 18,000 at the outbreak of war.
2 Pollitt received 13,655 votes, his Labour opponent 22,088.
3 I. Cox, CP CC minutes 5.5.38.
4 'Critic' (Kingsley Martin), *New Statesman and Nation*, 13.4.40, p. 486.
5 A. L. Morton, *History and the Imagination* (Lawrence and Wishart, 1990).
6 See Pollitt to Dutt, 26.1.35, 15.2.35; Dutt to CP Secretariat, 17.10.35 (RPD WCML), Pollitt to V. Gollancz, Mar. 1936, cited in R. D. Edwards, *Victor Gollancz* (Gollancz, 1987), p. 234.
7 Report to CP CC, 24.9.39 (HP).
8 Dutt, *Times Literary Supplement*, 5.5.66. Apparently Pollitt had incurred Moscow's displeasure by 'raising questions concerning the conduct of the security organs'; see p. 175 below.
9 J. Paton, *Left Turn!* (Secker and Warburg, 1936), pp. 401-3, 426; F. Brockway, *Inside the Left* (George Allen and Unwin, 1942), pp. 248-9.
10 CP PB minutes, 13.11.36.
11 CP PB minutes, 13.11.36, 1.10.37; Brockway, *op. cit.*, pp. 264-9; Cripps to L. Elvin, 9.6.37 (Cripps papers, Nuffield College); for the Unity Campaign see B. Pimlott, *Labour and the Left in the 1930s* (Cambridge University Press, 1977), chs 9-10.
12 Brockway, *loc. cit.*; Mann, diary entry, 25.5.37 (TM).
13 A. J. Cummings, cited in Edwards, *op. cit.*, p. 243; Gollancz to Pollitt, 16.1.39 (VG); Pollitt, *WN*, 19.7.58, p. 463.
14 Dutt to Strachey, 2.6.33, Strachey to Dutt, 23.6.33, Strachey to Pollitt, 23.6.33 (JS); Gollancz to Strachey, 11.9.39, Laski to Gollancz, 12.9.39 (VG); see H. Thomas, *John Strachey* (Eyre Methuen, 1973); M. Newman, *John Strachey* (Manchester University Press, 1989).
15 Laski to Pollitt, 7.8.40, 13.8.40 (HP).
16 Laski's note of the meeting, which took place on 14.10.36, is published with an introduction by Colin Holmes in the *Bulletin* of the Society for the Study of Labour History no. 32 (1976).
17 'A working-class peace policy', *LM*, May 1936, pp. 302-3.
18 *The Path to Peace* (CPGB, 1936), p. 24.
19 K. Morgan, *Against Fascism and War* (Manchester University Press, 1989), pp. 79-81.
20 *DW*, 23.11.39; Sam Russell, interview; correspondence in HP.
21 Mahon, ch. 16; Pollitt, typescript reports of visits to Spain (HP); V. Gollancz (ed.), *The Betrayal of the Left* (Gollancz, 1941), p. 135.

22 H. Francis, *Miners Against Fascism* (Lawrence and Wishart, 1984), p. 230.

23 The anecdote first appears in H. Thomas, *The Spanish Civil War* (Penguin edn, 1965), p. 436. For Spender's recollections see his *World Within World* (Readers Union edn, 1953) and R. Crossman (ed.), *The God That Failed* (Right Book Club edn., n.d.).

24 S. Weintraub, *The Last Great Cause* (W. H. Allen, 1968), pp. 316-17; V. Cunningham, introduction to *The Penguin Book of Spanish Civil War Verse* (1980).

25 Pollitt in J. Lehmann, T. A. Jackson and C. Day Lewis (eds), *Ralph Fox. A Writer in Arms* (Lawrence and Wishart, 1937), p. 5; Mahon, p. 415.

26 The case that Copeman mentions, the onl̈y one known, is described as a case of treachery by Bill Alexander in his official account *British Volunteers for Liberty* (Lawrence and Wishart, 1986 edn), p. 82. The interview with Copeman preserved at the Imperial War Museum is both franker about alleged Communist misdemeanours and more generous to Pollitt than his *Reason in Revolt* (Blandford Press, 1948).

27 *Inprecorr*, 17.7.37, p. 668; *It Can Be Done* (CPGB, report of 14th Congress, 1937), pp. 28-30, 40-56.

28 See Morgan, *op. cit.*, pp. 70-3.

29 'The new situation and the next stage of the fight', Oct. 1938 (RPD BL).

30 CP CC minutes, 2.10.39, published in F. King and G. Matthews, *About Turn* (Lawrence and Wishart, 1990), pp. 199-200.

31 Pollitt to Mann, 1.12.38 (TM).

32 J. Gollan, *WN*, 19.6.54, p.496.

33 For Gollancz see Morgan, *op. cit.*, pp. 261-4; for the Cripps campaign see Pimlott, *op. cit.*, ch. 18 and Pollitt, *WN*, 9.8.58, pp. 503-4.

34 'First draft of proposed report to 16th Party Congress', c. Aug. 1939 (HP).

35 'The Communist Crusade', *LM*, Feb. 1939, pp. 68, 76.

36 Dutt to Pollitt, 13.1.39 (RPD BL).

37 CP CC minutes, 21.5.39, CP PB minutes, 27.4.39, 4.5.39, 1.6.39. Pollitt referred to this matter in the debate over the war; see King and Matthews, *op. cit.*, p. 197.

38 'First draft of proposed report...'; Campbell to Pollitt, c. July 1939 (HP).

39 'A working-class peace policy', p. 306; *Salute the Soviet Union* (CPGB, 1937); 'The Seventh Congress of the Communist International', *LM*, Oct. 1935, p. 617.

40 King and Matthews, *op. cit.*, p. 204.

41 *Ibid.*, p. 205.

42 *DW*, 26.8.39, 28.8.39.

43 See Morgan, *op. cit.*, ch. 5; M. Johnstone, introduction to King and Matthews, *op. cit.*

44 Unless otherwise stated, quotations in this and the succeeding paragraphs are from the CC meetings of 24-25.9.39 (HP) and 2-3.10.39 (published in full in King and Matthews, *op. cit.*) and Pollitt's points for his report to the earlier meeting (HP).

45 Preface to *SMT* (1950 edn), p. 7.

46 S. Dutt to Pollitt, 1.10.39 (HP).

47 Pollitt to CP PB, 18.10.39, 24.10.39 (HP).

48 Mahon, p. 253.

49 Pollitt to Dutt, 12.10.39, S. Dutt to Pollitt, n.d. (HP).

50 There was a brief initial statement in *DW*, 13.10.39, a joint statement with Campbell then signed individually but still rejected (HP) and a final recantation in *DW*, 23.11.39.

51 Both Raji and Salme wrote Pollitt letters of tact and sympathy on his mother's death (HP, 2.11.39) but Salme's ends significantly: 'My thoughts and feelings are all with her son although he does not care.'

52 M. Johnstone, introduction to King and Matthews, *op. cit.*, p. 40.

53 Wild to Pollitt, 9.10.39 (HP).

54 A. Winnington, *Breakfast with Mao* (Lawrence and Wishart, 1986), p. 48.

55 J. Attfield and S. Williams (eds), *1939. The Communist Party and the War* (Lawrence and Wishart, 1984), p. 88. For an account of this campaign, in which Pollitt polled less than a thousand votes, see Morgan, *op. cit.*, pp. 158-61.

56 *WNV*, 28.9.40, pp. 538-9.

57 See Morgan, *op. cit.*, pp. 240-1.

58 Pollitt to Mann, 26.1.38 (TM); Mahon, pp. 361-4.

59 See e.g. 'Where Mr Gollancz has gone', *LM*, June 1940, pp. 364-6; *WNV*, 22.3.41, pp. 189-90.

60 Pollitt to Mann, 31.1.40 (TM).

61 M. Jenkins, 'Prelude to better days', typescript autobiography, WCML, p. 190.

62 *DW*, 13.6.50, 11.9.40.

63 Foot, *Debts of Honour* (Davis Poynter, 1980), p. 106 and interview; Evans, *Daily Express*, 28.6.60; Winnington, *op. cit.*, p. 48.

64 Pollitt, 'Points on R.P.D. book' (RPD CP).

65 E. Scott in Attfield and Williams, *op. cit.*, p. 129.

66 *New Statesman and Nation*, 5.7.41.

67 See e.g. Pollitt's Political Letter for CP Secretariat printed in V. Gollancz, *Russia and Ourselves* (Gollancz, 1941), pp. 118-26; *Britain's Chance Has Come* (CPGB, 1941).

Chapter 5

1 The phrase is Louis Fischer's, describing Pollitt in his *Men and Politics* (Cape, 1941), p. 442.

2 Trevor Evans, *Daily Express*, 28.6.60.

3 M-O TC 25/8.

4 Foot, Joe O'Reilly, interviews; Pollitt to Dutt, 26.2.35 (RPD WCML); Mahon, p. 275; CP CC minutes, 4-5.6.32.

5 Pollitt to Dutt, 2.1.35 (RPD WCML).

6 Pollitt to H. Fagan, 10.7.44.

7 V. Shields to M. Pollitt, 12.7.60 (HP); M. Bowles to M. Pollitt, 7.7.60 (HP); J. N. Rawling, typescript history of Australian CP; Carritt, interview.

8 CP CC minutes, 2.7.38.
9 Dutt to S. Dutt, 10.1.24 (RPD WCML); Margot Heinemann, interview; Dutt to V. Gollancz, 30.6.38 (RPD CP); Pollitt, 'Points for CC report' (of 24.9.39) (HP).
10 Gollancz, *Reminiscences of Affection* (Gollancz, 1968), p. 41; Pollitt to Montagu, 21.7.40 (CP). For Spender see ch. 4 note 23 above.
11 Noreen Branson, interview, Imperial War Museum; Heinemann, interview; Pollitt, speech to CP professional workers, 20.1.46 (HP); Spender in R. Crossman (ed.), *The God That Failed*, p. 268.
12 Speech to professional workers; Brian Pollitt, Gladys Easton, Heinemann, interviews.
13 Speech to professional workers; M. Bowles to M. Pollitt, 7.7.60 (HP).
14 Pollitt to S. Dutt, 23.9.23 (RPD WCML); postcard re Cohen in CP archive; *SMT*, p. 208.
15 Pollitt to Mann, 7.12.40 (TM); *Harry Pollitt Speaks... a call to all workers* (CPGB, report of 13th Congress, 1935, p. 42); Pollitt to Dutt, 22.2.35 (RPD WCML).
16 Orwell in V. Gollancz (ed.), *The Betrayal of the Left*, p. 214; *The Road to Wigan Pier* (Gollancz, 1937), p. 195.

Chapter 6

1 Branson, *op.cit.*, p. 333.
2 Pollitt, *The World in Arms!* (CPGB, *c.* 1942), p. 1; *Britain's Chance Has Come* (CPGB, 1941); *The Communist Party and the Way to Win* (CPGB, report of national conference, 1942), pp. 38-9; political letter to CP membership, 8.7.41.
3 M. Johnstone, introduction to King and Matthews, *op. cit.*, p. 42.
4 Pollitt to Nehru, 29.7.42 (HP).
5 Speech to CP national literature conference in *Sharpening Our Weapons* (CPGB, 1943).
6 Mahon, p. 293.
7 M-O TC 8/5. Other notable speakers at Second Front rallies included Bevan, Foot, Owen, the *Sunday Express*'s editor John Gordon and the *Daily Mirror*'s 'Cassandra'. According to Michael Foot, Pollitt had no direct contact with Beaverbrook himself.
8 M. MacEwen, *The Greening of a Red* (Pluto, 1991), p. 96.
9 Pollitt, *WNV*, 26.7.41, p. 466; *The World in Arms*, p. 6.
10 Pollitt, *WNV*, 15.11.41, p. 734; *The World in Arms*, pp. 1-3; speech at Swansea, 14.3.42 in CP Midlands DC *Bulletin* (n.d.); *The Communist Party and the Way to Win*, pp. 59-60; *LM*, May 1942, p. 131; *DW*, 24.10.42, 21.11.42; *WNV*, 13.2.43, p. 51; *WNV*, 17.6.44, p. 194. Orwell's phrase is from *The Lion and the Unicorn*.
11 Pollitt, *Britain's Chance Has Come*; *LM*, Oct. 1941; speech at Swansea, 14.3.42; *DW*, 30.1.43, 6.11.43, 22.11.43.
12 Pollitt, *Coal* (CPGB, 1943), p. 7.

13 Gabriel Carritt and Margot Heinemann, interviews.
14 Heinemann, interview; Mahon, pp. 433-4; *DW*, 14.2.44; CPGB EC minutes, 20.2.44, 19.3.44 (CP); correspondence between CPGB South Wales DC Secretariat and Party centre, Feb. 1944, circulated to EC members (HP). For the Porter Award see H. Francis and D. Smith, *The Fed* (Lawrence and Wishart, 1980), pp. 410-13 and Pollitt's *Take Over the Mines* (CPGB, 1944).
15 Pollitt, *Coal*, p. 7; *Miners' Target* (CPGB, 1943), pp. 10-12; speech in South Wales, *DW*, 23.3.44; Margot Heinemann, interview.
16 *The Communist Party and the Way to Win*, pp. 34-5.
17 MacEwen, *op. cit.*, pp. 93-4. For this strike see R. Croucher, *Engineers at War* (Merlin, 1982), pp. 181-7.
18 For a few months before D-Day the CP did for a while take each contest on its merits, recommending in some cases abstention and even the rejection of a government candidate.
19 Pollitt, report to CP EC, Feb. 1945 (HP).
20 *The Communist Party and the Way to Win*, pp. 12-14, 18-19, 34-7.
21 *DW*, 18.12.44; Mahon, p. 299.
22 Report to EC, Feb. 1945; Pollitt, *How to Win the Peace* (CPGB, 1944), p. 3.
23 Report to CP, Feb. 1945; Pollitt, *The Crimea Conference: safeguard of the future* (CPGB, 1945), pp. 5-6; *How to Win the Peace*, ch. 10.
24 Pollitt to H. Fagan, 10.7.44 (HP); *Victory, Peace, Security* (CPGB, report of 17th Congress, 1944), pp. 12-16; *How to Win the Peace*, pp. 58-61.
25 *Answers to Questions* (CPGB, 1945).
26 *Ibid.*, pp. 38-42; *Victory, Peace, Security*, pp. 56, 60; *How to Win the Peace*, pp. 6-8.
27 *How to Win the Peace*, pp. 42-50, 56; *The Crimea Conference*, p. 16; *Victory, Peace, Security*, p. 8; *Answers to Questions*, pp. 30-7.
28 *Communist Policy for Britain* (CPGB, report of 18th Congress, 1945), pp. 7, 29.
29 See note 18 above. The leadership's conduct was however endorsed by the EC with only Cox dissenting.
30 CP PC political letter, 21.3.45; CP 18th Congress *Resolutions and Agenda* (1945), branch resolution 189; G. de N. Clark, *WNV*, 27.10.45, p. 335. Votes were registered on this and the question of reducing the number of CP candidates at meetings with a total attendance of 8,684 . What would be a thumping majority in most organisations obviously reads rather differently in the case of the CP.
31 Arnot to Pollitt, 12.3.45 (RPA).
32 'A letter to my comrades', 29.8.56 (Daly papers, MRC, 302/3/10); B. McIlhone, *WNV*, 3.11.45, p. 342; J. Sutherland, *WNV*, 10.11.45, p. 355; Betty Reid, Gladys Easton, Brian Pollitt, interviews.
33 'Report on the election campaign in Rhondda East', 2.8.45 (HP). Pollitt polled 15,761, his Labour opponent 16,733 and a Welsh nationalist 2,123.
34 Pollitt, points for EC and report to EC, Feb. 1945 (HP).
35 Malcolm MacEwen, letter to author.
36 Pollitt, report to EC, Feb. 1945.
37 CP 18th Congress *Resolutions and Agenda*, branch resolutions 27, 187-94,

202-3, 225, 227, 245, 293, 310; contributions in *WNV* from Marylebone CP (20.10.45), J. Smith and H. F. W. Taylor, and G. Clark (27.10.45), S . Beechey and J .R . Eastell (3.11.45), B. McIlhone (3.11.45, 10.11.45) and W. Zak (17.11.45).

38 *Communist Policy for Britain*, pp. 29-35; *DW*, 26.11.45.
39 Noreen Branson, Gabriel Carritt, James Friell, Betty Reid, interviews; H. McShane, *No Mean Fighter* (Pluto, 1978), pp. 224, 237; D. Hyde, *I Believed* (Heinemann, 1951), p. 154; C. Haldane, *Truth Will Out* (Right Book Club edn, 1949), pp. 132-3; F. Copeman, *Reason in Revolt*, pp. 166-7; C. Cockburn, *I Claud* (Penguin, 1967), pp. 220-1. The most favourable reminiscence is in MacEwen, *op. cit.*
40 CP EC minutes, 21.11.43; the issue was whether or not to support government candidates in particular by-elections.
41 Malcolm MacEwen, letter to author; Pollitt, undated note in Ivor Montagu's papers (CP) addressed to Montagu and Isabel Brown.
42 See e.g. 18th Congress branch resolutions 10-27. Malcolm MacEwen, a *Daily Worker* journalist who raised the question of Bevin's role at the congress itself, writes that he had no knowledge of 'any conscious Rust-led DW centre against Pollitt' (letter to author).
43 Pollitt, *WN*, 2.8.58, p. 492.
44 *Manchester Guardian, Daily Herald*, 26.11.45; *DW*, 26.11.45, 27.11.45; Ted Bramley for CP London DC to Pollitt, 14.12.45 (HP).
45 *DW*, 1.1.46.
46 Russell, interview; Hyde, *loc. cit.*
47 Pollitt for CP Secretariat, political letter to CP membership, 8.7.41; CP EC minutes, 15.8.43; *Communist Policy for Britain*, p. 32.
48 Pollitt, *Looking Ahead* (CPGB, Aug. 1947), pp. 103-11. Criticisms of this reluctance to support strikes had been a major issue at the 18th Congress.
49 *DW*, 26.5.47.
50 Pollitt, *Wages. What Should be Done* (CPGB, 1945); *Britain Will Make It* (CPGB, 1946); *Britain's Problems Can Be Solved* (speech to CP 19th Congress, Feb. 1947), pp. 8, 16-18; *Looking Ahead*, pp. 76, 112-13.
51 *Britain's Problems Can Be Solved*, pp. 10, 12; *DW*, 12.4.47; *Looking Ahead*, pp. 12, 66-7, 72-4.
52 *Looking Ahead*, p. 92.

Chapter 7

1 'Points for report to Executive Committee', 11.10.47 (HP); report to CP EC, 13.12.47, *WNV*, 20.12.47, pp. 577-87.
2 J. Little, *WN*, 18.2.56, p. 107; J. Lyons, *DW*, 26.3.56.
3 J. R. Campbell to M. Pollitt, 1.7.60 (HP).
4 Pollitt to Dutt, 24.4.23 (RPD CP); CP EC *Report* to 6th Congress (1924); CP CC minutes, 9.10.38.
5 See Mahon, pp. 329-33 based on a typescript account in HP.
6 Pollitt to Margot Heinemann, 12.5.50 (HP).

197

7 Pollitt to James Klugmann, 4.6.47 (HP); *DW*, 2.9.50, 7.4.51; *WN*, 17.12.55, p. 946, 20.12.58, p. 724.
8 *WN*, 1.10.55, p. 767.
9 Pollitt, *Looking Ahead*, p. 11; K. O. Morgan, *Labour in Power* (Oxford University Press, 1985 edn), p. 356; *DW*, 11.10.47.
10 'A policy for Labour', *LM*, Sept. 1952, p. 391; *DW*, 7.4.51.
11 *WN*, 17.12.55, p. 946; *The Challenge to Labour* (report to CP 23rd Congress, 1954), p. 36.
12 Pollitt to Arnot, 5.12.52 (RPA 1/45).
13 Pollitt, *Indian Diary* (CPGB, 1954); *The Challenge to Labour*, p. 8.
14 *WN*, 17.12.55, pp. 946-7; *The People Will Decide* (report to CP 24th Congress, 1956), p. 29; *DW*, 4.2.50; Michael Foot, interview.
15 Winnington, *op. cit.*, p. 178; *For Britain Free and Independent* (report to CP 20th Congress, 1948), p. 42; *DW*, 17.9.49; *Britain Arise* (report to CP 22nd Congress, 1952), pp. 48-52; *The Challenge to Labour*, pp. 45-8; 'A policy for Labour', p. 391.
16 James Friell, interview; Pelling, *op. cit.*, pp. 144-5.
17 McShane, letter to *Daily Herald*, 29.7.53; W. Gallacher, foreword to Pollitt's *Selected Articles and Speeches* vol. 1 (Lawrence and Wishart, 1953), p. 7.
18 *DW*, 22.11.50, 28.11.50; P. Kerrigan, 'Harry Pollitt', *CR*, Dec. 1950, pp. 355-61.
19 Letters and telegrams on Pollitt's twentieth anniversary as Party secretary (HP) from CP Hackney Borough Committee, 12.9.49, and Arthur Davies, n.d.
20 *WNV*, 23.11.50, p. 607.
21 Pollitt obtained 4,463 votes or 12.7 per cent of the total poll.
22 *DW*, 26.10.31, 18.2.50, 25.2.50, 6.3.50; 'Political Letter' to CP membership, 13.3.50; *Communist Policy to Meet the Crisis* (report to CPGB 21st Congress, 1949), p. 34.
23 See e.g. *The Challenge to Labour*, pp. 43-4.
24 *Peace Depends on the People* (report to CP EC, Oct. 1950), p. 36; *The Challenge to Labour*, pp. 43-4.
25 Pollitt, report to CP EC, 4.3.50, *CR*, Apr. 1950, p. 104; *The Fight for Peace and Working-Class Unity* (report to CP EC, 8.7.50); *WN*, 19.6.54; G. Matthews, 'Stalin's British Road', *Changes*, 14-27.9.91 provides further details of the programme's origins.
26 See *Looking Ahead*, pp. 90-2.
27 'If it is right and proper for the Slav peoples to talk of their indestructible unity', Pollitt told the first conference of Empire Communist Parties, 'it is nothing to be ashamed of if those of us who come from common stock and have a common language speak of our unity' (*DW*, 1.3.47).
28 K. Cornforth, 'British road to socialism, *CR*, Apr. 1947, especially p. 117.
29 E. P. Thompson, *The Reasoner*, no. 1, July 1956, p. 13.
30 Dutt to A. Hutt, 12.4.66 (RPD CP).
31 Pollitt, report to CP EC, *WNV*, 21.2.53, p. 88; *The People Will Decide*, pp. 21-3; *The Communist Party and the Labour Party* (CPGB, 1955), p. 7; R. Williams,

'Notes on Marxism in Britain since 1945', *New Left Review* no. 100 (1976), p. 83.

32 *Daily Express*, 14.5.56. While well informed about Pollitt's attitudes, Evans was wrong to infer that Pollitt had been forced to resign. For information about the events of 1956 and afterwards I am particularly indebted to Brian Pollitt.

33 V. Vidali, *Diary of the Twentieth Congress of the Communist Party of the Soviet Union* (Journeyman, 1984).

34 Winnington, *op. cit.*, p. 179; Sam Russell, interview; Pollitt was indeed taken to see a rubber factory.

35 *DW*, 24.1.56, 25.2.56, 2.3.56. Matthews also reported to the EC on the congress; see *WN*, 17.3.56.

36 The bland and evasive piece required of Russell was printed in the *DW*, 19.3.56; see also *DW*, 12.3.56 for Campbell's guillotine.

37 *DW*, 24.3.56; *WN*, 21.4.56, 5.5.56.

38 *Daily Express*, 14.5.56; James Friell, interview.

39 Brian Pollitt, interview; Pollitt to Oliver Arnot, 22.5.56 (RPA); M. Pollitt, *A Rebel Life* (Red Pen, 1989), p. 49.

40 *Daily Express*, 14.5.56, 28.3.56; Brian Pollitt, interview; report of television debate with Frank Owen, *DW*, 2.5.56; M. Johnstone, *Bulletin* of the Society for the Study of Labour History no. 33 (1976), p. 56; Winnington, *loc. cit.*

41 Levy's contribution to 1957 CP Congress, *DW*, 23.4.57; Levy to M. Pollitt, 16.7.60 and M. Pollitt to Dutt, 3.8.60 (HP); George Matthews, Gabriel Carritt, interviews.

42 See the letters of Dutt and B. Pearce, *Times Literary Supplement*, 5.5.66, p. 387, 19.5.66, p. 462.

43 Dutt to Laski, 26.10.37 (RPD CP); E. Bone, *Seven Years Solitary* (Hamish Hamilton, 1957); MacEwen, *op. cit.*, pp. 186-7; CP PB minutes, 15.4.37.

44 E. Fischer, *An Opposing Man* (Allen Lane, 1974), especially ch. 17; Phil Piratin, Brian Pollitt, George Matthews, interviews; F. Utley, *Lost Illusion* (Allen and Unwin, 1949), p. 35.

45 *Looking Ahead*, pp. 41-2; 'Liberalism and Communism', *LM*, Mar. 1937, pp. 188-9; *Inprecorr*, 19.3.38, pp. 309-10.

46 *A L'Ombre des Deux T* (Julliard, 1973), p. 372.

47 At his meeting with Laski and Morrison; see ch. 4 note 16 above.

48 Dutt, *Times Literary Supplement*, 5.5.66, p. 387 describes it as a collective and public demonstration of resistance. Noreen Branson (interview), to whom Pollitt related the matter at the time in Moscow, recalls that Pollitt's speech was the point at issue.

49 Betty Reid, George Matthews, interviews.

50 Winnington, *op. cit.*, p. 177; Pollitt to I. Montagu, 23.12.48 (CP).

51 McShane , *op. cit.*, pp. 244-5 ; see ' Points Yugoslavia, (HP) ; 'Yugoslavia', *CR*, Aug. 1948; speech in *WNV*, 17.7.48, pp. 295-302.

52 The articles by Saville, MacEwen and Heinemann on 1956 in the *Socialist Register* for 1976 (Merlin, 1976) provide the best account of these events.

53 See e.g. the editorial in the first issue of *The Reasoner* (1956).

54 Doris Lessing, *The Reasoner* no. 2 (1956), p. 11.
55 Llew Gardner, *DW*, 23.8.56; Saville to Thompson, 15.10.56, cited in Saville, 'The Twentieth Congress and the British Communist Party', *Socialist Register* 1976, p. 18.
56 Brian Pollitt, Bert Ramelson, Gladys Easton, interviews.
57 Margot Heinemann, Gladys Easton, interviews; Pollitt to Florrie (Mahon?), 20.12.56 (HP) ; M. Pollitt, *op. cit.*, pp. 103-4; M. Pollitt to Mahon, 24.12.71 (HP); *Manchester Guardian*, 23.4.57; Vidali, *op. cit.*, pp. 126-7; Brian Pollitt, interview.
58 Mahon, ch. 30; M. Pollitt, *loc. cit.*; G. F. Moore, letter on Pollitt's death (HP).

Bibliographical note

Primary sources

Pollitt's own papers, supplemented by material collected by John Mahon, are in the Communist Party archive. The collection comprises sporadic survivals of correspondence, notes for speeches and political reports, autobiographical drafts, memorabilia etc. The CP archive, now freely accessible to researchers, also has microfilms of Central Committee and Political Bureau proceedings from the 1930s received from Moscow, a minute book partly in Pollitt's hand of the Openshaw branch of the BSP, voluminous papers of Palme Dutt and much else that proved invaluable.

The second major primary source, particularly for the second and third chapters, was the Dutt material in the Working Class Movement Library.

Other manuscript collections containing Pollitt material include those of R. Page Arnot (Hull University), Tom Mann (Coventry Central Library) and John Strachey (in the possession of his family). The Cripps papers at Nuffield College had little of interest and Sir Maurice Shock assured me that there was nothing of relevance among those in his keeping.

Secondary sources

Pollitt's autobiography *Serving My Time* (Lawrence and Wishart, 1941 edn) is well worth reading, especially the early chapters, and Pollitt published some further such jottings in *World News* in 1958. Despite its bulk, *Harry Pollitt* by John Mahon (Lawrence and Wishart, 1976) does not provide a satisfactory account and its piety becomes wearing. Nevertheless, Mahon's was a real work of dedication and in writing this book it was impossible not to be grateful for his indefatigable researches and the materials he collected. Those who seek fuller details of the less controversial aspects of Pollitt's life will certainly find them there.

More generally, there have been few major contributions to CP history since I compiled the bibliography for my *Against Fascism and War* in 1989, although those who seek something of the flavour of internal Party debates should certainly read the verbatim Central Committee proceedings published in F. King and G. Matthews (eds), *About Turn* (Lawrence and Wishart, 1990). Willie Thompson's one-volume Party history *The Good Old Cause* (Pluto, 1992) appeared as this book was going to press. Otherwise, readers are referred for printed sources to the footnotes.

Index

Thaelmann, Ernst, 60, 85
Thompson, E. P., 181
Thorez, Maurice, 61, 84, 88, 171, 178
Thorne, Will, 158
Tillett, Ben, 12, 48
Tito and Titoism, 155, 180
Tochatti, James, 16
Togliatti, Palmiro, 172, 178
Trades Disputes Act (1927), 55
Trades Union Congress, 20, 48, 55: 1921, 26, 48; 1922, 49, 51; 1925, 50, 53; 1926, 58; 1927, 55
    General Council, CP's perception of, 49 ff.
trade unions and industrial affairs, HP's views and experiences, 6, 21, 42, 46 ff., 64, 66-8, 76-81, 125-6, 134-7, 152-3, 182-3
    see also boilermakers; strikes; Trades Union Congress
Tressell, Robert, 158
Tribune, 92

Ulbricht, Walter, 70
United Clothing Workers' Union, 67
united front policy: 1920s, 31; 1930s, 81, 82 ff., 90 ff.

United Mineworkers of Scotland, 67
United Nations Organisation, 140
United Peace Alliance, 101
Unity Campaign (1937), 91-2
Utley, Freda, 175-6

Vidali, Vittorio, 171

Walker, Melvina, 16
Watson, W. F., 16, 18, 19
Webb, Beatrice, 54
Wild, Sam, 113
Wilson, J. R., 71
Winnington, Alan, 116, 161, 179
Wintringham, Tom, 33, 35, 43, 69, 118
women, HP's views on, 126-7
Workers' Charter campaign, 74-7
Workers' Dreadnought, 16, 18, 21
Workers' Socialist Federation, 16, 20
Workers' Weekly, 33, 39-40, 42, 43-4, 56

Yalta (Crimea) agreement and HP's Yalta perspective, 138, 140 ff., 144, 146, 147
Young, Edgar, 162

Zinoviev, G., 39, 44, 51